# The Routledge Guidebook to the New Testament

As part of the Christian canon of scripture, the New Testament is one of the most influential works in history. Its impact can be seen in many different fields, but without an awareness of the historical, cultural, social, and intellectual context of early Christianity, it can be difficult for modern-day readers to fully understand what the first-century authors were trying to say and how the first readers of the New Testament would have understood these ideas.

*The Routledge Guidebook to the New Testament* offers an academic introduction to the New Testament examining:

- The social and historical context in which the New Testament was written
- The primary text, supporting students in close analysis from a range of consensus positions
- The contemporary reception and ongoing influence of the New Testament

With further reading suggestions, this guidebook is essential reading for all students of religion and philosophy, and all those wishing to engage with this important work.

**Patrick Gray** is Associate Professor of Religious Studies at Rhodes College.

D0145773

# THE ROUTLEDGE GUIDES TO THE GREAT BOOKS
## Series Editor: Anthony Gottlieb

The Routledge Guides to the Great Books provide ideal introductions to the texts which have shaped Western Civilization. The Guidebooks explore the arguments and ideas contained in the most influential works from some of the most brilliant thinkers who have ever lived, from Aristotle to Marx and Newton to Wollstonecraft. Each Guidebook opens with a short introduction to the author of the great book and the context within which they were working and concludes with an examination of the lasting significance of the book. The Routledge Guides to the Great Books will therefore provide students everywhere with complete introductions to the most significant books of all time.

## AVAILABLE:

Routledge Guides to the Great Books

# The Routledge Guidebook to the New Testament

Patrick Gray

 Routledge
Taylor & Francis Group

LONDON AND NEW YORK

First published 2017
by Routledge
2 Park Square, Milton Park, Abingdon, Oxon OX14 4RN

and by Routledge
711 Third Avenue, New York, NY 10017

*Routledge is an imprint of the Taylor & Francis Group, an informa business*

© 2017 Patrick Gray

*British Library Cataloguing-in-Publication Data*
A catalogue record for this book is available from the British Library

*Library of Congress Cataloging-in-Publication Data*
Names: Gray, Patrick, 1970- author.
Title: The Routledge guidebook to the New Testament / Patrick Gray.
Description: 1 [edition]. | New York : Routledge, 2017. | Series: Routledge philosophy guidebooks | Series: Routledge guides to the great books | Includes bibliographical references and index.
Identifiers: LCCN 2016045351| ISBN 9780415729031 (hardback) | ISBN 9780415729048 (pbk.) | ISBN 9781315208695 (ebook)
Subjects: LCSH: Bible. New Testament—Introductions.
Classification: LCC BS2330.3 .G73 2017 | DDC 225.6/1—dc23
LC record available at https://lccn.loc.gov/2016045351

ISBN: 978-0-415-72903-1 (hbk)
ISBN: 978-0-415-72904-8 (pbk)
ISBN: 978-1-315-20869-5 (ebk)

Typeset in Times New Roman
by Swales & Willis Ltd, Exeter, Devon, UK

# Contents

# SERIES EDITOR PREFACE

"The past is a foreign country," wrote a British novelist, L. P. Hartley: "they do things differently there." The greatest books in the canon of the humanities and sciences can be foreign territory, too. This series is a set of excursions written by expert guides who know how to make such places become more familiar.

All the books covered in this series, however long ago they were written, have much to say to us now, or help to explain the ways in which we have come to think about the world. Each volume is designed not only to describe a set of ideas and how they developed, but also to evaluate them. This requires what one might call a bifocal approach. To engage fully with an author, one has to pretend that he or she is speaking to us; but to understand a text's meaning, it is often necessary to remember its original audience, too. It is all too easy to mistake the intentions of an old argument by treating it as a contemporary one.

*The Routledge Guides to the Great Books* are aimed at students in the broadest sense, not only those engaged in formal study. The intended audience of the series is all those who want to understand the books that have had the largest effects.

Anthony Gottlieb

Series editor **Anthony Gottlieb** is the author of *The Dream of Reason: A History of Philosophy from the Greeks to the Renaissance.*

# ABBREVIATIONS

## GENERAL

| | |
|---|---|
| BCE | before the Common Era |
| ca. | *circa* |
| CE | Common Era |
| d. | died |
| e.g. | for example |
| ESV | English Standard Version |
| KJV | King James Version |
| LXX | Septuagint (Greek translation of the Old Testament) |
| NIV | New International Version |
| NRSV | New Revised Standard Version |
| RSV | Revised Standard Version |
| RV | Revised Version |

## OLD TESTAMENT/HEBREW BIBLE AND DEUTEROCANONICAL BOOKS

| | |
|---|---|
| Gen. | Genesis |
| Exod. | Exodus |
| Lev. | Leviticus |
| Num. | Numbers |

| | |
|---|---|
| Deut. | Deuteronomy |
| 1–2 Sam. | 1–2 Samuel |
| 1–2 Kgs. | 1–2 Kings |
| 1–2 Chron. | 1–2 Chronicles |
| Ps(s). | Psalm(s) |
| Prov. | Proverbs |
| Eccles. | Ecclesiastes |
| Isa. | Isaiah |
| Jer. | Jeremiah |
| Ezek. | Ezekiel |
| Dan. | Daniel |
| Hosea | Hosea |
| Joel | Joel |
| Amos | Amos |
| Mic. | Micah |
| Hab. | Habakkuk |
| Zech. | Zechariah |
| Mal. | Malachi |
| 1–4 Macc. | 1–4 Maccabees |
| Wis. | Wisdom of Solomon |
| Sir. | Sirach |

## NEW TESTAMENT

| | |
|---|---|
| Matt. | Matthew |
| Mark | Mark |
| Luke | Luke |
| John | John |
| Acts | Acts |
| Rom. | Romans |
| 1–2 Cor. | 1–2 Corinthians |
| Gal. | Galatians |
| Eph. | Ephesians |
| Phil. | Philippians |
| Col. | Colossians |
| 1–2 Thess. | 1–2 Thessalonians |
| 1–2 Tim. | 1–2 Timothy |
| Titus | Titus |

| Philem. | Philemon |
| Heb. | Hebrews |
| Jas. | James |
| 1–2 Pet. | 1–2 Peter |
| 1–3 John | 1–3 John |
| Jude | Jude |
| Rev. | Revelation |

## OTHER ANCIENT SOURCES

| *1 Apol.* | Justin Martyr, *First Apology* |
| *2 Bar.* | *2 Baruch* |
| 1QpHab | *Pesher Habakkuk* (Dead Sea Scrolls) |
| 11QMelch | *Melchizedek* (Dead Sea Scrolls) |
| 1QS | *Community Rule* (Dead Sea Scrolls) |
| 1QSa | *Rule of the Congregation* (Dead Sea Scrolls) |
| *Agr.* | Tacitus, *Agricola* |
| *Ann.* | Tacitus, *Annales* |
| *Ant.* | Josephus, *Antiquities* |
| *b.* | Babylonian Talmud |
| *b. Ned.* | *Nedarim* |
| *b. Sanh.* | *Sanhedrin* |
| *C. Ap.* | Josephus, *Contra Apionem* |
| *Claud.* | Suetonius, *Claudius* |
| *Clem.* | Seneca the Younger, *De Clementia* |
| *Controv.* | Seneca the Elder, *Controversiae* |
| *Dial.* | Justin Martyr, *Dialogue with Trypho* |
| *Ench.* | Epictetus, *Enchiridion* |
| *Ep.* | Pliny the Younger, *Epistles* |
| *Haer.* | Irenaeus, *Adversus haereses* |
| *Hist. eccl.* | Eusebius, *Historia ecclesiastica* |
| *J. W.* | Josephus, *The Jewish War* |
| *Legat.* | Athenagoras, *Legatio pro Christianis* |
| *Legat.* | Philo, *Embassy to Gaius* |
| LXX | Septuagint |
| *m. 'Abot.* | *'Abot* (Mishnah) |
| *Metam.* | Ovid, *Metamorphoses* |
| *Nat.* | Pliny the Elder, *Natural History* |

| | |
|---|---|
| *Oct.* | Minucius Felix, *Octavius* |
| *P.Oxy.* | Oxyrhynchus Papyri |
| *Pan.* | Epiphanus, *Panarion* |
| *Phil.* | Polycarp, *To the Philippians* |
| *Poet.* | Aristotle, *Poetics* |
| Pss. Sol. | *Psalms of Solomon* |
| *Superst.* | Plutarch, *De Superstitione* |

# INTRODUCTION

Few books have been read, studied, meditated on, or fought about as frequently or with as much energy as the New Testament. To appreciate its literary, theological, and historical richness, however, it is necessary to read closely and carefully. Reading the New Testament closely and carefully involves asking questions in order to make sense of the text. In order to make sense of any text, all readers are—consciously or unconsciously—constantly asking and immediately answering such questions: Who is the author of this text? When was it written? What is its genre? What is the main idea or purpose? Is it reliable? The New Testament is really no different from any other book in this respect. Of all the possible questions one could pose—about the life and teaching of Jesus, his impact on his followers, and the meaning of his death and resurrection for the conduct and convictions of those who hailed him as the Messiah and worshipped him as Lord—some are more germane than others. Some are necessary for understanding the texts that are eventually included in the Christian Scriptures, while others, however interesting, focus on peripheral matters. Certain basic questions will apply to any and every text, but each text also elicits its own particular questions.

*The Routledge Guidebook to the New Testament* is intended to serve as an aid in asking the right questions. Since the rise of modern biblical criticism in the seventeenth century, scholars have tended to regard as "the right questions" those that seek to clarify what is often referred to as "the world behind the text." This phrase refers to the real-world circumstances that contributed to the composition of the texts. Books that belong to the genre of "New Testament introduction" (*Einleitung* in the German of its earliest practitioners) traditionally seek to bring this "world" to life by providing answers to questions about the cultural, social, political, literary, and religious context of the flesh-and-blood author and the first flesh-and-blood readers: Do the gospels provide an accurate depiction of Jesus' ministry? What was Luke trying to communicate to his readers about the significance of the resurrection in his telling of the story of Jesus? What concrete conditions in Rome influenced the way Paul expressed himself in his letter to the faithful who lived there? How did the destruction of the temple in Jerusalem alter messianic expectations among the early Christians and their relations with the Jewish groups from which they had begun to emerge? Who comprised the original audience for Matthew's gospel? Is Paul the author of all the letters that are ascribed to him? How did the author of Hebrews think that texts from the Pentateuch related to the persecution experienced by his readers? Broadly speaking, these introductory questions are historical in nature, and it would not be inaccurate to characterize "modern" study of the Bible as thoroughly attentive to its historical dimensions. This focus is often announced on the cover, as one sees, for example in Robert M. Grant's *A Historical Introduction to the New Testament* (1963) and Helmut Koester's *History and Literature of Early Christianity* (1982), among many others that may not reflect it in their titles.

While it is impossible to describe the world "behind the text" in an exhaustive manner, a primary objective of this guidebook is to enable readers to make sense of what its authors were trying to say and do in their original settings as well as how their first readers would have understood them. But one may also approach the New Testament with questions that focus on the world "of the text" that are less historical than literary in nature. This approach is often favored by interpreters who worry that, at such a distance and with so many gaps in the record, it may not be possible to find adequate answers to many of the most pressing historical questions, or that the text itself is in danger of being swallowed up in "background." David L. Barr's *New Testament Story* (1994) and Kyle Keefer's *The New Testament as Literature* (2008) lean in this direction. "The world of the text" refers to the literary, aesthetic, or structural characteristics of the author's work, with minimal concern for "the world behind the text." This approach usually applies to narrative works such as the gospels, with analysis of plot and character, but it also applies to writings with rhetorical features such as the speeches in the Acts of the Apostles or the letters of Peter and John. How does the brevity of the temptation scene shape the portrait of Jesus in Mark? How do the "signs" performed by Jesus in John's gospel compare with the way in which the miracles function in the other gospels? What sort of logic governs Paul's argument for the bodily resurrection in 1 Corinthians? Based on its structure, should Revelation be read as a single, continuous story or as a series of vignettes recapitulating a common set of themes? The boundaries separating the worlds "behind" and "of" the text can be quite blurry, and interpreters display varying degrees of scrupulosity in making sure they remain intact.

Finally, inquiry may focus on what takes place between the words on the page and the readers who engage them. This vast space is occupied by "the world in front of the text," borrowing the language of Paul Ricoeur, from whom the "behind/of/in front of" taxonomy derives (1981: 141–4). How has the gospel of John influenced attitudes about and treatment of Jews? Why did Martin Luther want to leave the Letter of James out of the canon? What factors account for the obsessive attention paid by some communities to the Book of Revelation? How have Paul's letters shaped church doctrine and practice in the time since they were first sent to various groups scattered around the Mediterranean? How have they inspired or perplexed the faithful? How have they comforted the afflicted and afflicted the comfortable? How have artists, poets, and politicians interpreted or misinterpreted its contents? These are historical questions of a different sort in that they attend to the countless ways in which the New Testament has had an impact on subsequent centuries of culture and society rather than on the ways in which first-century culture and society shaped the form and content of the earliest Christian writings.

Introductions to the New Testament typically give this "world" much shorter shrift than the other two worlds, notwithstanding the undisputable fact that its enormous cultural footprint is a primary motivation for the tireless efforts of generations of scholars at solving its historical and literary riddles. Other books in the Western tradition have been the subject of enduring scrutiny, though none has generated so massive a body of scholarship or supplied the source of so many allusions found in the arts and popular culture. In no small part, this is a function of the fact that the overwhelming majority of its readers have until quite recently regarded it as holy writ and thus worthy of sustained investigation. To neglect this vast and multifarious body of material—known collectively as the New Testament's reception history—is to ignore valuable evidence that it is worth so much trouble. Even eccentric examples offer a benefit to those concerned with historical or literary matters in that they force the reader to consider the factors that make one interpretation more persuasive than another. Taking note of the wide range of responses to the New Testament also serves as a salutary reminder that texts do not interpret themselves. Different readers have posed the particular questions they have deemed the most pertinent. Thus one finds guidebooks written self-consciously from a particular perspective or attuned to a special dimension of the text. Examples include Elizabeth Cady Stanton's *The Women's Bible* (1895), Samuel Sandmel's *A Jewish Understanding of the New Testament* (1957), Brevard S. Childs's *The New Testament as Canon* (1984), Eduard Schweizer's *Theological Introduction to the New Testament* (1991), and Brian K. Blount's *True to Our Native Land: An African American New Testament Commentary* (2007).

Of the many fine guidebooks available, many tend to provide such comprehensive surveys of each document that students have little reason left to read the primary text for themselves. This guidebook, written with both first-time readers and those already familiar with the Christian Scriptures in mind, provides the requisite background for readers of the New Testament while stopping short of actually reading the text for them. In the pages that follow, sections devoted to individual books will discuss standard introductory matters—for example, the author and intended audience, dating, the circumstances that occasioned its composition, its purpose, and its literary or rhetorical structure. In place of exhaustive summaries, there are close readings of select passages that illustrate salient themes, abiding concerns, and any special interpretive challenges presented by the text.

Supplementing this analysis will be frequent references to highlights from the reception history—noteworthy instances of appropriation, application, speculation, literary inspiration, artistic representation, and theological disputation, as well as familiar phrases that have entered the English language (usually by way of the King James Version). Each major chapter includes a brief annotated bibliography directing readers to scholarly resources for those who wish to continue their study in greater detail.

\* \* \*

This guidebook is divided into seven chapters. It is not necessary to read them in any particular order, though it will perhaps be most help-ful to beginning students to start at the beginning. Chapter 1 surveys the relevant historical, cultural, social, and political settings of Greece, Rome, and Palestine, and highlights the religious, philosophical, and literary movements and concepts with which Jews and non-Jews were engaged. The emergence of Christianity in the first century is in part a result of this engagement. Following this "scene-setting" is a book-by-book treatment of the New Testament's contents, appearing roughly though not precisely in their canonical ordering. Chapter 2 introduces the narratives that comprise the largest portion of the New Testament, the Gospels and the Acts of the Apostles. After consid-eration of the interpretive questions raised by these books (e.g., their literary genre; their relationship to the historical Jesus; the "Synoptic problem"), the distinctive aspects of each one will receive attention with the aim of enabling the reader to experience them on their own terms rather than prematurely merging Matthew, Mark, Luke, and John into a composite narrative that may inadvertently distort the objectives of their individual authors. Chapter 3 considers the let-ter as a literary genre in Greco-Roman antiquity. Its importance in the rise of Christianity can be seen in the fact that all but six of the New Testament writings take the form of letters. The focus is on the arguments and ideas they contain and on the rhetorical strategies pur-sued by Paul and other authors to shape the beliefs and behaviors of their audiences. Chapter 4 attempts to orient the reader to the context, structure, symbolism, and frequently bizarre reception history of the Book of Revelation, the only full-scale example of the apocalyptic genre in the canon. Chapter 5 explains the meaning and significance of sixty terms, names, and concepts frequently encountered in the New Testament and in the secondary literature devoted to it. Chapter 6 provides answers to a baker's dozen of "frequently asked questions" that arise when reading the New Testament and attempting to make sense of the myriad interpretations of its contents, such as "What do we know about the life of Jesus?" "Why does the New Testament contain (only) twenty-seven books?" "How should one read the non-canonical writings?" and "What special methods do scholars use to interpret the New Testament?" Chapter 7 contains discussion questions for each New Testament book that facilitate close reading and engagement with major exegetical, theological, philosophical, historical, and ethical issues the various texts raise.

# 1

## THE CONTEXT OF EARLY CHRISTIANITY AND THE NEW TESTAMENT

If reading the New Testament entails the framing of appropriate questions to pose to a text and then figuring out how to answer them, it is surely significant that the authors are no longer available to confirm or deny the results yielded by any such question-and-answer process. According to one school of thought, however, the inaccessibility of the author matters little. When asked what he meant by an odd simile in the opening lines of one of his poems in which he compares an evening to "a patient etherised upon a table," T. S. Eliot curtly replied, "I meant, 'like a patient etherised upon a table'." As a practitioner of the New Criticism that would gain sway among mid-century literary critics, Eliot believed that a poem is an autonomous, self-contained text that should be interpreted without recourse to the author's stated or unstated intentions. Ultimately, it is impossible to understand a poem or a comic strip or a novel or any other text without importing prior assumptions about the world or imposing some frame of reference, however minimal, even if it is one's objective to carry out an ahistorical reading after the fashion of the New Critics. In the same way that one can, for example, enjoy George Orwell's *Animal Farm* unaware that it is a fable dealing with Soviet communism and its discontents, or watch *Apocalypse Now* without realizing that it is a post-Vietnam War adaptation of Joseph Conrad's *Heart of Darkness*, one can read the New Testament without a broad familiarity with the Greek, Roman, and Jewish contexts in which it was written. Whether one's appreciation is anything at all like what its authors had in mind is another question.

This chapter proceeds on the assumption that it is essential to know something about the wider world in which the New Testament authors lived in order to understand what they were trying to accomplish. Their writings presuppose, evoke, and hint at an array of social, cultural, historical, and religious concerns on every page. The Jews, Greeks, and Romans who people the pages of the New Testament do not move about in separate spheres but, variously, cooperate in ordinary affairs and collide in ways that disturb the peace for all parties involved. Sometimes the encounter between the Jews who were Jesus' first followers and this world "behind the text" is impossible to overlook, as in Acts 17:16–34 when Paul quotes the Greek poet Aratus when preaching before Epicurean and Stoic philosophers on the Areopagus in Athens, or in John 19:17–20 when the Roman prefect Pontius Pilate has the sign declaring Jesus "King of the Jews" written in Greek, Latin, and Hebrew. Elsewhere it may be more subtle yet no less significant, as when other titles reserved for the emperor ("savior," "son of God") are applied to Jesus or when the admonition to extend hospitality to strangers (Heb. 13:2) recalls not only stories from the Hebrew Bible about angelic visitors (Gen. 18–19) but also the myth of Baucis and Philemon (Ovid, *Metam*. 8.626–724).

Jesus Christ may be "the same yesterday and today and forever" (Heb. 13:8), yet he appears on the scene at a culturally specific moment in human history. In their narratives about Jesus' life, death, and resurrection and in their letters probing his significance for matters as weighty as the fate of the body and soul after death or as mundane as whether one should eat pork, the early Christian writers are attempting to articulate a new faith. It is not a process that occurs in a vacuum.

## POLITICAL SETTINGS

Christianity begins as a sect within Judaism which, in turn, had begun centuries earlier as the form of Hebrew religion practiced in Judah, a region that will later be called Judea. During the tenth century BCE, according to biblical accounts, the tribes of Israel are united under the monarchies of David and Solomon. Upon the death of Solomon, a split between the northern and southern tribes results in the formation of two separate kingdoms, Israel in the north with its capital at Samaria, and Judah in the south with its capital at Jerusalem. The northern kingdom falls to the Assyrians in 722 BCE and its inhabitants, the so-called "ten lost tribes of Israel," are assimilated by other peoples. The southern kingdom, Judah, along with the smaller tribe of Benjamin, survives the Assyrian conquest for another century or so, albeit in a weakened state, until the arrival of the Babylonians under Nebuchadnezzar. The siege of Jerusalem in 597 BCE marks the beginning of the Babylonian Exile, when the leading families of Judah are deported to Babylon and much of the remaining population is dispersed when the temple is destroyed in 586 BCE.

A generation later, the exiled Judeans witness a reversal that strikes them as nothing short of a miracle. Cyrus the Great leads the Persians in their defeat of the Neo-Babylonian Empire and in 538 BCE issues an edict permitting the exiles to return to their land and rebuild the temple. (The reference to Cyrus as "the Lord's anointed" in Isa. 45:1 nicely expresses their admiration.) Persian rule over Palestine lasts until 332 BCE, when it becomes part of Alexander the Great's vast Hellenistic empire stretching from Greece to north Africa and east to the edge of the Indian subcontinent. Without a male heir when he dies a decade later, Alexander divides his kingdom between his top generals, leaving Judea and Palestine caught in between and subject to the rival military aspirations of the Antigonid, Ptolemaic, and Seleucid dynasties that succeed him.

The author of 1 Maccabees (1:5–9) describes the deathbed scene in which Alexander divides his empire because he realizes its cultural as well as its political consequences for the Jews. Antiochus IV takes advantage of a situation in which the Jews of Jerusalem are divided in their responses to Hellenistic culture and attempts to undermine Jewish resistance by proscribing Jewish religious rites, such as circumcision and observance of the Sabbath. This exacerbates internal dissension but also sparks a rebellion in 167 BCE against Seleucid Greek rule led by the family of Mattathias, whose sons become known as the Maccabees. After three and a half years of the "abomination of desolation" (1 Macc. 1:54; cf. Matt. 24:15–16), the Maccabees succeed in recovering the temple, the rededication of which is commemorated in the festival of Hanukkah. By 142 BCE, the Maccabees establish independent rule over Judea in the form of the Hasmonean dynasty. This period of independence would last for less than a century, and a sovereign Jewish state would not be declared again until 1948.

Roman involvement in Judea begins as a response to overtures from Hyrcanus II and Aristobulus, brothers who were engaged in a civil war for control of the Hasmonean throne. Pompey, the Roman general who was already in the neighborhood annexing Syria, was all too happy to intervene when Hyrcanus invites him to choose sides. The followers of Hyrcanus and of Aristobulus fought among themselves as Pompey laid siege to the city for three months. Judea thus becomes a vassal state in 63 BCE. Hyrcanus is allowed to retain the high priesthood, though politically he is relegated to the role of collecting the tribute demanded by Rome, a task that does little to endear him to his fellow Jews.

Herodian influence waxes as Hasmonean power wanes. With the support of Antony and Octavian, Herod the Great reigns as king of the Jews from 37 to 4 BCE. During his brutal reign, he greatly expands the temple (cf. John 2:20) but strips the high priesthood of any independent power it previously possessed. While there is no independent attestation of Herod's order to slaughter the infants of Bethlehem at the time of Jesus' birth (Matt. 2:16), such brutality would not be at all out of character if other ancient sources are to be trusted in their descriptions of his way of dealing with rivals. His kingdom is divided among his three sons, who rule as clients beholden to Rome upon his death. Judea is administered directly as a Roman province beginning in 6 CE. The northern region of Galilee is governed until 39 CE by Herod's son Herod Antipas, the "Herod" who has John the Baptist beheaded and appears later as a player in the trial of Jesus (Mark 6:1–28; Luke 23:6–12).

Rome is itself embroiled in a century of intermittent civil war when it inserts itself into Jewish affairs. After defeating Carthage in the third and final Punic War (149–146 BCE), Rome effectively dominates the Mediterranean even if the Roman Republic does not "officially" give way to the Roman Empire until 27 BCE. Social, political, and military upheaval accelerates in 133 BCE with the populist tribuneships (and subsequent violent deaths) of Tiberius and Gaius Gracchus. The decades that follow witness a series of slave revolts, civic unrest, and bloody showdowns between generals seeking to enhance their own power at the expense of the Senate. Julius Caesar vanquishes Pompey in the largest of these civil wars before fearful defenders of the dying Republic assassinate him a few years later in 44 BCE. Caesar's nephew Octavian (later given the title "Augustus") defeats Mark Antony and Cleopatra at Actium in 31 BCE, leaving him as emperor in all but name.

Readers who have trouble understanding how writers, like Virgil in his *Aeneid*, could celebrate the accession of a dictator should keep in mind the grim alternative played out in the preceding century. To be sure, many Romans saw the end of the Republic as a bittersweet reality. Neighboring tribes and nations as well fail to see empire as a blessing and continue to resist as Rome expands its borders, reaching its greatest territorial extent under Trajan (98–117 CE). Tacitus has the Caledonian chieftain Calgacus deliver a blistering critique of the propaganda that casts grievous exploitation as enlightened despotism: "To robbery, butchery, and pillaging, they give the lying name of 'government' (*imperium*); they create a desert and call it 'peace'" (*Agr.* 30). Order was maintained through an extensive apparatus, including the administration of censuses like the one that takes Joseph and the very pregnant Mary on an arduous, eighty-mile journey from Nazareth to Bethlehem in Luke 2:1–5. Ruling authorities in the ancient world do not undertake censuses for the purpose of ensuring fair and equitable participation in legislative assemblies; it is about taxation, not representation. Resentment at such times could thus erupt into outright rebellion as in the case of Judas the Galilean (Acts 5:37).

Yet the advantages of the *Pax Romana* were hard to discount. A scene from the 1979 comedy *Life of Brian* nicely captures the ambivalence of Rome's subjects. Plotting rebellion, the leader of a band of Jewish insurgents asks, rhetorically, "What have the Romans ever done for us?" His co-conspirators, as it turns out, can think of several things: roads, aqueducts, sanitation, wine, medicine, education, irrigation, and public order. Whatever drawbacks came with life as part of a subject people—and there were many, including heavy taxation, loss of political self-determination, slavery, and military occupation—it could also yield many benefits, and many Jews and Christians considered the imperfect peace of Rome to be a perfectly acceptable trade-off. Paul and other Christian missionaries take advantage of the extensive system of roads in order to spread their message far and wide. Without the safe travel made possible by the ever-present legions, Jesus might have been born somewhere other than the city of his ancestor David. In this way, according to the gospel writers, even the imperial authorities who will eventually execute Jesus during the reign of Augustus' successor, unwittingly further the divine plan. Looking back from the eighth century, the Venerable Bede remarks on the happy coincidence of the prince of peace being born in such a time of relative tranquility (*Homilies on the Gospels* 1.6)

At the very least, many first-century Jews and Christians sensed that the Roman Empire showed no signs of crumbling any time in the near future and, instead of quixotically resisting this political reality, got along as best they could. Except, that is, when they decided they could not. Provincial rule in Judea becomes increasingly unbearable in the 50s and 60s. While Caligula (37–41 CE) may have been insane when he issued a (thwarted) command to set up a statue of himself in the temple, the men who govern Judea in this period are corrupt and incompetent. Even "moderate" Jews conclude that Rome cannot hold up its end of the tacit bargain whereby acquiescence to the occupation was to be exchanged for stability and religious tolerance. Palestine erupts in 66 CE. While the revolt in Galilee is quickly subdued, Jerusalem holds out through the tumultuous "Year of Four Emperors," when Nero is overthrown and three other generals seize power in succession before Vespasian emerges as the victor. Infighting again plagues the Jewish resistance, and in 70 CE the temple is burned down. Another unsuccessful rebellion breaks out half a century later (132–135 CE) when Rabbi Akiba acclaims Bar Kokhba as the Messiah. With the establishment of Jerusalem as the Roman colony Aelia Capitolina and the construction of a temple to Jupiter on the former site of the destroyed temple, militant Jewish nationalism goes dormant. Although it continues over a longer period, the gradual "parting of the ways" between Judaism and Christianity accelerates in the interval between these two revolts and involves the relevant political and ethnic forces at play as well as the theological disputes that are more evident when one reads the New Testament (Becker and Reed 2003).

## RELIGION AND PHILOSOPHY

### JUDAISM IN THE HELLENISTIC PERIOD

When the early Christians profess that "all scripture is inspired by God and is useful for teaching, for reproof, and for training in right-eousness" (2 Tim. 3:16), they have in mind the Hebrew Bible—what Christians call the Old Testament—and not the New Testament. This fact is certain because, first of all, the New Testament did not yet exist. The texts that comprise the New Testament were still in the process of being written over the course of several decades and are accorded scriptural status only at a later stage. And second, "Scripture" meant the Hebrew Bible because Jesus and all of his ear-liest disciples were Jews (notwithstanding bizarre nineteenth-century theories to the effect that, based on post-exilic immigration patterns, the residents of Galilee must have been of Aryan extraction). All students of the New Testament are thus in agreement that a thorough grounding in the Jewish Scriptures is necessary for understanding the Christian Scriptures.

An appreciation of the literary milieu requires familiarity with more than those works included in the canon. It has been suggested that the boundaries of the Jewish canon were fixed by the end of the first century CE, around the same time that the latest of the New Testament books were nearing completion. But ancient Jewish writers produced many other works that were not canonized: pseudepigrapha such as the *Testaments of the Twelve Patriarchs*, the *Apocalypse of Zephaniah*, and the *Prayer of Manasseh*; works contained the Catholic canon but labelled "apocrypha" by Protestants, such as Tobit, 1–2 Maccabees, and Judith; the Dead Sea Scrolls; the philo-sophical musings of Philo of Alexandria and the historical surveys of Flavius Josephus, the two most prolific Jewish writers of the first century CE; Aramaic paraphrases and interpretations of biblical writ-ings known as Targums; and the rabbinical discussions later codified in the Mishnah. Whatever one thinks of *sola scriptura* as a guiding principle for adjudicating doctrine, however, it is clear that "Scripture alone" is insufficient for reconstructing either the social, cultural, and political realities of ancient Jews or their worldviews, if only because individuals have a habit of believing things they are not supposed to believe and engaging in activities that are nowhere described or prescribed in "official" sources. These and many other examples attest to the rich diversity of Jewish literature in the centuries leading up to and contemporaneous with the birth of Christianity.

However much they shed light on Jewish life during the so-called intertestamental period between the last of the biblical prophets (ca. 400 BCE) and the birth of Jesus, these works only scratch the surface. Just as there is much more to Islamic history than the Qur'an and the hadith, understanding Judaism in the first century involves much more than reading its literature. This is true for the ancestral homeland of Palestine and Judea as well as in the Diaspora, a term used for the Jewish community located outside the land of Israel, where the majority of Jews made their homes ever since the Babylonian conquest of Jerusalem in 586 BCE. Whereas institutions and ideas such as the land, the covenant, the law, and the temple are integral to all forms of Judaism, different groups emphasize different aspects and offer competing interpretations of their meaning.

The variegated nature of ancient Judaism is in evidence even when one focuses on the relatively restricted territory of Palestine. Josephus mentions four main sects that dominate Palestinian Judaism in his day: the Pharisees, the Sadducees, the Essenes, and the Zealots (*Ant.* 18.11–25). To this list one might add the Samaritans, with their priesthood and sanctuary at Mount Gerizim in the north as opposed to Jerusalem in the south. Their mutual animosity is palpable. Judeans denigrated Samaritans as "half-breeds," while Samaritans considered themselves the true keepers of Israelite faith traditions. While the questions about which they argue affect the lives of ordinary Jews, the majority of the population were not members in a formal sense of any sect. The situation is somewhat comparable to the denominationalism that characterizes modern Christianity and Judaism, though one also finds in each case traits more commonly found among philosophical schools of thought and political parties.

New Testament authors mention the Pharisees far more than the other three groups. Their origins are usually traced to the Hasmonean era, but earlier scribes like Ezra in the emerging synagogues of the post-exilic period are equally important in understanding the Pharisees in that they were above all concerned with interpretation and application of the Mosaic law, following the dictum of the first-century BCE rabbi Shammai to make the study of Torah "a fixed habit" (*Avot* 1.15). They held that Moses had received the Oral Torah at Sinai along with the Written Torah, and that the former was an authoritative guide in parsing the intricate stipulations of the 613 commands contained in the latter. Shammai's younger and more famous rival, Hillel, has in mind this vast body of oral law passed down from sage to sage in his oft-quoted reply to the Gentile who comes to him promising to convert to Judaism if he could teach him the law while standing on one foot: "Whatever is hateful to you, do not do it to your neighbor. That is the whole of Torah; the rest is commentary" (*b. Shabbath* 30b). It would thus be a mistake to equate the Pharisaic approach with legalistic obscurantism. Their conviction that the law was of concern to all Jews of all times and places and not just to the elites has been described as a democratization of Judaism. This view resonates with the Talmudic story about Moses being transported from his seat in heaven to the second-century academy of Rabbi Akiba and understanding nothing the rabbi says (*Menachot* 29b). When a student asks about his reasoning, Akiba replies that it came from the law received by Moses at Sinai. Shocked but then pleased, Moses returns to heaven with the assurance that the eternal Torah remains alive in the world even as it bears little obvious resemblance to its original form. According to Acts and to his own letters, Paul was a Pharisee (Acts 26:5; Phil. 3:5). The attention in the gospels devoted to Jesus' clashes with the Pharisees may in part reflect the heightened tensions between the early church and this sect that gains ascendancy after the destruction of the temple in 70 CE.

The Sadducees were members of a conservative aristocracy associated with the high priesthood that oversaw the sacrificial cult centered at the temple in Jerusalem. Their name is usually derived from the name of a priest, Zadok, who served in the time of David. They rejected the Oral Law prized in Pharisaic tradition as well as doctrines they believed were not found in the Written Law, such as the immortality of the soul and the bodily resurrection on which they attempt to confound Jesus with their questions (Matt. 22:23–33; Paul later plays the Sadducees off against the Pharisees by raising the question at his own trial in Acts 23:6). In part because they held sway in the Sanhedrin, the great council that issued decisions on matters of religious and political import, many Jews viewed the Sadducees as collaborators with their Roman overlords. They lose all influence in Jewish affairs after the destruction of the temple.

Living in semi-isolation at Qumran, a settlement near the Dead Sea, the Essenes were an ascetic sect that regarded both Pharisees and Sadducees as inadequately faithful to the covenant. By means of a distinctive scheme of interpretation (*pesher*), they read the ancient prophets as containing coded messages about their own leader, the Teacher of Righteousness, and about the circumstances confronting their community. Habakkuk 1:5, for example, is quoted in 1QpHab, but instead of reading it as a reference to the Babylonians as instruments of divine justice, the author of the *pesher* explains it as a reference to apostates from the Qumran community. It is widely thought that the Dead Sea Scrolls, discovered in 1947, comprised their library. Archaeological evidence indicates that the Essene compound was destroyed during the Jewish revolt in the late 60s, after which they disappear from the historical record. The messianic and apocalyptic speculation found in these writings, as well as practices such as baptism by immersion, celibacy, and communal sharing of goods, have parallels with some strands of early Christian thought, though the degree to which Essene ideas directly influence Jesus, John the Baptist, or the New Testament writers is disputed.

"Zealot" is a commonly used term for a loose coalition of Jews who were not content to endure the increasingly corrupt and oppressive Roman occupation. Josephus sees a rebel movement from decades earlier he calls "the Fourth Philosophy" as a forerunner of this coalition that plays a major role in the revolt beginning in 66 CE. Various bandits, such as the *Sicarii* ("dagger men"), sought to assassinate Jews they believed to be collaborating with the Romans. They thought of themselves as freedom fighters whom God would aid once the rebellion was under way, though Rome—who, according to Acts 21:38, may have suspected that Paul belonged to their number—saw them as terrorists with whom no compromise was possible. Their decision to commit mass suicide at Masada in 73 CE rather than surrender was taken as confirmation of this assessment. That Jesus, whose followers included Simon Zēlotes (Luke 6:15), was executed as "king of the

Jews" may also reflect Roman fears that he was the leader of a group of militant nationalists.

Uprisings were more practicable in Palestine if only because it was the only place where Jews constituted a majority of the population. Yet large populations of Jews in cities like Rome and Alexandria had put down roots for centuries before the birth of Christianity, at which time Jews in the Diaspora actually outnumbered those in Palestine perhaps by a factor of two to one. All together, it has been estimated that Jews made up ten percent of the Roman Empire's population. When this number is spread out across the entire Diaspora, however, it means that Jews are in the minority everywhere even when one adopts the broadest possible conception of what makes a person "Jewish." Is it a matter of geography, in which case there is little distinction between being Jewish and being Judean? Is it biological, following a traditional formula whereby the identity of the mother determines that of her children? Is it more religious in nature, whereby adherence to the Torah is what counts most? Or can it even indicate political loyalties, as one sees reflected in the uneasiness of Roman authorities at solidarity between Jerusalem and Jewish communities in cities across the Mediterranean?

Despite, or in some cases on account of, their minority status, Jews captured the imagination of the Gentiles among whom they made their home. The venerable antiquity of their polity could not be denied even by their adversaries. Moses was regularly lauded by non-Jewish writers as a great leader like Aeneas or Alexander, whose accomplishments included victories in glorious battles and the founding of great cities. As lawgiver, Moses was also responsible for the reputation enjoyed by the Jews as adhering to the highest ethical standards, embodied in the Torah. Their practice of the cardinal virtues of wisdom, courage, justice, and self-control, according to Greek writers like Megasthenes, gave evidence that they were a race of philosophers by birth (Feldman 1993: 201–32). Along with the strong communal ties, these moral and intellectual qualities attracted numerous converts. While the number of such converts is impossible to determine, they were on occasion so numerous as to make local authorities take notice. And many who were not quite willing to fully identify with the Jewish community were nevertheless active as "God-fearers," admiring their religious teachings and adopting various customs without undergoing the ritual of circumcision (cf. Acts 10:2; 13:26, 43).

At the same time, Jews were frequently the object of ridicule, prejudice, and harassment. They were called to be a "peculiar people" (Deut. 14:2), set apart from the rest of the nations, and were constantly reminded of just how peculiar they could appear in the eyes of their non-Jewish neighbors. Communal solidarity could be seen as clannish insularity if not outright misanthropic disgust for non-Jews. While their strict monotheism commanded the respect of many intellectuals, others saw it as a manifestation of a stiff-necked exclusiveness that implicitly denigrated the pantheon of Greek and Roman deities worshipped by everyone else. Their readiness to accept the pronouncements of priests as the word of God also marked them out as overly credulous. Sabbath observance could be construed as an excuse for laziness in a world lacking the concept of a "weekend." Circumcision was widely regarded as a deformity disqualifying one from participating in the Olympics, where athletes competed in the nude, and its infliction on male infants was seen as barbaric. Dietary restrictions such as abstention from pork made no sense to pagans who considered its flesh one of nature's most delectable blessings. It seemed arbitrary when the Jews were willing to sacrifice so many other animals, a point Antiochus IV takes sadistic joy in emphasizing when he has a pig sacrificed in the Holy of Holies and forces the high priest to eat it (Josephus, *Contra Apionem* 2.137; Diodorus Siculus, *Bibliotheca historica* 34/35.1.4). The growth of the Jewish population in Rome and their perceived influence in political affairs made many in the aristocracy nervous about their perceived loyalty to foreign interests, periodically leading to imperial edicts (e.g., in 19 and 49 CE) expelling the Jews from the capital. The relative wealth of the Jews, accumulated through successful business ventures in addition to tax collection and money-lending, could also become a source of tension, especially when the masses witnessed their community thriving even in times of economic turmoil. These and many other themes were mainstays of anti-Jewish prejudice and can still be heard up to the present day.

Whether due to logistical pressures or out of genuine attraction, in various ways Diaspora Jews came to terms with Hellenism, the term for the fusion between the cultures of Greece and of the lands conquered by Alexander. This process had linguistic, religious, social, and literary dimensions. Were it not for Alexander's heirs establishing Greek as the common language of the Mediterranean basin, the stories in the New Testament about the early Jewish followers of the Jewish Messiah would have been written in Aramaic or Hebrew. In these narratives as well as in the letters they exchanged among themselves, they usually quote the Jewish Scriptures in their Greek form. Beginning in the third century BCE, Jews had begun rendering the Hebrew Bible into Greek for the benefit of those who could not read it in the original language. This version, the Septuagint (and often designated by the abbreviation LXX), takes its name from a legend about its miraculous production by a team of seventy Alexandrian translators and likely represents an attempt to address Diaspora concerns that its sacredness had somehow become diluted in the process. These worries are reflected in the translator's preface to the Book of Sirach, itself included in the Septuagint, where the author's grandson concedes that "what was originally expressed in Hebrew does not have exactly the same sense when translated into another language" and that even the Law and the Prophets "differ not a little when read in the original." An Italian proverb puts it more unequivocally: *traduttori traditori*, "translators are traitors." Jesus does not dwell on it when he proclaims that "until heaven and earth pass away, not one letter, not one stroke of a letter, will pass from the law until all is accomplished" (Matt. 5:18), but one can easily imagine the thought occurring to the rabbis who rejected the Septuagint as authoritative. Ambivalence about the LXX is reflected in the rabbinic tradition (*Megillat Ta'anit*) which calls for fasting on the anniversary of its completion, saying that with it "darkness descended on the world for three days" and likening it to the day when the Golden Calf was made.

Other writers have few qualms about accommodating their Jewish heritage to the Greek culture in which they were immersed. Philo of Alexandria synthesizes Israelite religion with Pythagorean and Platonic philosophy, speculating that Moses was the true source of Plato's signature doctrines. The author of 4 Maccabees is nearly indistinguishable from a Stoic philosopher when he says that a key tenet of the Mosaic Law can be summed up in the phrase "reason is sovereign over the emotions" (1:1). Theodotus retells the story of the rape of Dinah in Genesis 34 in dactylic hexameter as if he were an epic poet. Ezekiel the Tragedian presents the story of the Exodus in the form of a Greek drama. Artapanus "goes native" to a degree perhaps unmatched by any of his fellow Jews in his portrait of Moses as culture-bringer.

According to Artapanus, Moses not only invented ships, irrigation, and philosophy, he also introduced Egyptians to the worship of cats, dogs, and ibises! If that were not enough, Moses was the teacher of Orpheus and was called Hermes because of his skill in interpreting the sacred texts of the Egyptians. Not everyone in the Diaspora exhibited the same syncretistic tendencies, but it is clear that many Jews felt very comfortable living alongside their Gentile neighbors.

Had Jesus' followers returned to the countryside in Judea or Galilee after his death, it is possible that Christianity would have been swept into the proverbial dustbin of history or, at best, remained a tiny sect within the fold of Judaism. Its spread to urban areas in the Diaspora was a major factor in the early community's survival, gaining traction among populations for whom the Hebrew or Aramaic language or sundry Jewish customs might well have proven insuperable barriers to entry. It would nonetheless be a mistake to conclude that the adoption of the Greek language by the New Testament authors was nothing more than a savvy marketing strategy aimed at reaching a broader audience. The related notion that Christianity abandoned its Jewish roots the more it strayed geographically from the ancestral homeland and adapted to Greco-Roman culture likewise overlooks an important fact, namely, that Judaism even in Palestine had been already subject to Hellenistic influence (Hengel 1974). Although it does not necessarily mean that Jesus attended performances of Plautus's comedies or Ennius's tragedies, a large Roman theatre has been excavated in Sepphoris, an hour's walk from Nazareth. Tombs at the necropolis at Beth She'arim, where Judah ha-Nasi established the seat of the Sanhedrin, bear epitaphs written mostly in Greek and even include the occasional epigram in Homeric style or mythological motif on recycled sarcophagi. To be sure, some groups were so strict in their religious observance that they elected not to fight on the Sabbath even when it meant certain destruction in the war with Antiochus IV, and the Maccabees succeeded in driving the pagans from Jerusalem. But it was a pyrrhic victory insofar as the inspiring story of their fight against the encroachment of Greek culture has survived not in Hebrew but only in Greek. The burgeoning Christian faith one encounters in the New Testament, then, springs from a geographically, politically, ethnically, linguistically, religiously, and philosophically diverse Judaism that had continued to evolve in the years since the last books of the Hebrew Scriptures had been written.

## GREEK AND ROMAN PHILOSOPHY

Any distinction in this milieu between "religion"—whether Jewish, pagan, or a syncretistic hybrid—and "philosophy" is not so sharp as one might expect based on the modern usage of these terms. When Jesus asks the crowds what they expected to find when they went out to hear John the Baptist, with his garment of camel's hair and diet of locusts and wild honey, they could have answered "philosopher" as easily as "prophet" (Matt. 3:4; 11:7–10). While some scholars have exaggerated the similarities in sartorial and rhetorical style as well as in the substance of their respective messages, John's manner of dress and his anti-establishment message, like that of Jesus and his disciples (Mark 6:8–9), invite comparison with the itinerant Cynic philosophers. So-called for the dog-like (*kynikos*) disregard for social convention of their founder, Diogenes of Sinope (d. 325 BCE), the Cynics' popular appeal was limited by the extreme austerity they advocated. They remain noteworthy for their influence on the two principal philosophical schools in the Hellenistic world, Stoicism and Epicureanism.

Founded by Zeno of Citium (d. 263 BCE), Stoicism sees the universe as providentially ordered in accordance with rational principles (*logos*). Accordingly, it is best to live "according to nature" and adjust one's expectations to match the way things are rather than striving to reshape the world to fit one's hopes and desires, which will only lead to disappointment. Emotions like fear and anger are the greatest threats to human flourishing and must therefore be purged. Stoics thus promise to help their followers reach a state of *apatheia*, or "freedom from passion," by focusing their attention on those things that are in the control of the individual. The goal of life—attaining virtue—is within one's control. Everything besides virtue and vice is indifferent (*adiaphora*) and should be of no serious concern to the Stoic. Misfortune should be seen as an opportunity to grow in virtue. "Remember that you are an actor in a play of such a kind that the author chooses," Epictetus tells his students (*Ench.* 17). One's role may be major or minor, long or short, happy or sad. The point, he says, is to play one's part well and to realize that it is someone else's role to assign the parts. With its emphasis on duty, Stoic teaching resonated with Roman writers such as Cicero, Seneca, and Marcus Aurelius.

Epicureanism emerges in the same era and is named for its founder, Epicurus (d. 270 BCE), whose followers lived in community, memorized his aphorisms, and celebrated his birthday as a holiday. Its aim is to help the individual attain *ataraxia*, or "freedom from disturbance." Their reputation as hedonists is not entirely deserved inasmuch as they regarded the avoidance of pain as a path to tranquility no less viable than the pursuit of pleasure. The Roman Epicurean Lucretius and others mercilessly attack popular religion because they see it as allowing baseless anxieties, especially fear of the gods and fear of death, to spoil the enjoyment to be had in this life by causing worries about things that will never materialize. The gods are blissfully unconcerned about humans, and as for death, the individual, body and soul composed entirely of physical "atoms," will no longer exist to suffer any alleged ills the gods might wish to inflict on them. In further contrast to the Stoics, the Epicureans recommended a retiring life far from the madding crowd so as to avoid the violent convulsions that often come with involvement in political affairs.

Whatever their differences, the Stoics and Epicureans shared three dispositions. First, they want their philosophies to be eminently useful. The modern stereotype of the navel-gazing philosopher absorbed in abstract questions and out of touch with the everyday concerns of ordinary people was familiar to ancient audiences. Galen says that Romans considered Greek philosophy as no more useful than drilling holes in millet seeds (*De praecognitione* 1). During the Hellenistic period, philosophers increasingly spurn the highly theoretical systems associated with Plato and Aristotle or adapt them to answer more practical questions. This concern for how to live a happy, fulfilled life can be seen in the titles of essays written by Epictetus, Seneca, and Philodemus, such as "On Friendship," "On Old Age," "On Frank Criticism," "On Anger," "On Travel," "On Cleanliness," "On Exercise," and "On Personal Adornment." Critics of the Stoics and Epicureans like Plutarch likewise strive to address topics relevant to the proverbial man on the street in such essays as "How to Tell a Flatterer from a Friend," "On Talkativeness," and "Against Borrowing Money."

Philosophers of all stripes also criticize superstition, and many of the phenomena given this label strike philosophical observers in antiquity as no less bizarre than they do today. It was thought, for example, that dreams about turnips and rutabagas augured an impending surgery, that spirits did not do the bidding of people with freckles, that salamanders could put out fires, and that whispering in a donkey's ear transfers a scorpion sting from the person stung to the donkey (Artemidorus, *On the Interpretation of Dreams* 1.26; Pliny, *Nat.* 28–30). Such notions were mocked by members of the *Kakodaimonistai*, a "Bad Luck Club" in Athens that met for meals on ill-omened days when feasting was prohibited (Burkert 1985: 313). Superstition (Grk. *deisidaimonia*) is also the standard term in the ancient Mediterranean for defective religiosity, consistently applied to Christianity in the earliest surviving references to the new faith made by non-Christian writers. Tacitus, in describing the fire at Rome during Nero's reign, speaks of a "pernicious superstition" breaking out after being temporarily checked by the death of Jesus (*Annales* 15.44; cf. Suetonius, *Nero* 16.2; Pliny the Younger, *Ep.* 10.96). Had the Epicureans come across the remark by the author of the Letter to the Hebrews that "it is a fearful thing to fall into the hands of the living God" (10:31), they might have applied the label to Christianity even sooner, as it would seem to them a telling expression of the anxiety that all religion engenders. For this reason, in addition to the political suspicions associated with foreign cults and philosophies as well, many writers put Jews and Christians alike in this category (Plutarch, *Superst.* 169C).

Finally, however much Stoics and Epicureans mercilessly castigate each other in addition to the many aspects of popular religion they deem foolish, wrong, or dangerous, they have in common a firm belief, shared also with Jews and Christians, that what one thinks is indelibly tied to how one lives. Over against the popular syncretism promoted by Alexander in which elements from disparate religions and philosophies are freely mixed and matched, they insist on rigorously examining systems of belief and behavior for coherence and consistency. Stoics and Epicureans make exclusive claims on the loyalties of their members. Not the least of their affinities with Jesus and John the Baptist, then, is their call for a conscious, deliberate "turning" (*metanoia*) upon recognizing the error of one's ways of thinking and acting (Mark 1:15; 6:12; Luke 3:3, 8; Epictetus, *Ench.* 34; cf. Nock 1933).

## SOCIAL CONTEXTS

Among the most important social settings in which Christianity took shape are (1) the household, (2) voluntary associations, and (3) the patron–client system.

The household was the basic unit of Greek and Roman society. Girls usually married in their teenage years and it was normally assumed that motherhood was their primary vocation. Despite high birth rates, population growth remained modest due to high infant mortality rates and the widespread practice of abortion and infanticide, especially of female offspring. In one surviving papyrus letter, an Egyptian father away on business tells his pregnant wife to take care of the child if it is a boy and to abandon it if it is a girl (*P. Oxy.* 744). From the Augustan period onward, legislation was passed with the intent of encouraging childbirth, though Tacitus (*Ann.* 3.25) notes that such legal measures did not achieve the desired effect. By law and by custom, the oldest male in Roman households had almost absolute power over all his descendants, including the families of grown sons (Crook 1967). Only death, formal emancipation, adoption into another family, or the father being declared *non compos mentis* suspended this power, knows as *patria potestas*. Children could not technically own their own property or make legally valid wills. The male-dominated nature of the Roman family can be seen in the brutal punishment meted out for patricide: father killers were subjected to the *poena cullae*—tied into a large sack with a monkey, a dog, a snake, and a rooster and then thrown into the river.

Remarriage was unexceptional—due in part to the relative ease of obtaining a divorce under Roman law—and so many children were combined into families with stepbrothers and stepsisters. The result all too frequently was even greater friction than already existed between biological siblings. Tensions mounted at the parent's death when the time came to divide the estate, a perennial sore spot reflected in New Testament texts (Luke 12:13; 15:11–32). Seneca the Elder refers to a law that many parents still observe: "let the elder brother divide the patrimony, and let the younger one choose" (*Controv.* 6.3). Sibling relations could become even more acrimonious than normal when complicated by adoptions. It was not uncommon in ancient Greece and Rome to adopt adult males, usually for political or financial purposes rather than for the benefit of orphaned children. Paul's letters reflect some of the relevant legal and social conventions even as he uses the ideas of adoption and inheritance as metaphors (Gal. 4:1–7). Despite the fraught nature of the fraternal relationship, early Christian communities employ the metaphor of brotherhood rather than friendship in describing their fellowship. (Nowhere in Paul's letters does he call his followers friends. Jesus uses friendship language in a few instances but indicates that his understanding of the relationship is not exactly what ancient or modern readers mean by the term "friend" when he states in John 15:14, "You are my friends if you do what I command you.")

Many households also included slaves. War, kidnappings, and unpaid debts are among the circumstances that increased the supply of slaves, with many more born into slavery due to their parents' status. Unlike its American counterpart in the antebellum period, race played little role in determining who might be a slave, many slaves had the opportunity to purchase their freedom, and education was highly prized, with many Greek slaves serving their noble Roman masters as tutors for their children. It is estimated that slaves made up over ten percent of the Roman Empire's population and as many as one in three on the Italian peninsula. Seneca (*Clem.* 1.24) reports that a law was once proposed in the Senate that slaves should be distinguished from the free population by their dress. When it occurred to some prudent politician that the slaves would then see just how vast their numbers were, the legislation quickly died. The degree to which Roman society depended on slavery is illustrated by the decisive response to the revolt led by Spartacus that was finally quashed in 70 BCE. Six thousand slaves were crucified along both sides of the 200-kilometer or so Appian Way between Rome and Capua. That means a traveler—and any slaves along for the ride—would have passed by two men dying a gruesome death every thirty-five meters for the entire journey (Appian, *Civil Wars* 1.14.116–121). Paul's habit of referring to himself as the "slave [*doulos*] of Christ" (Rom. 1:1; Gal. 1:10) takes on a new perspective in light of these bleak realities.

Outside the household, an individual might join one of the many clubs and voluntary associations that, depending on their size, could gather in public meeting spaces or private homes. These groups, or *collegia*, which had their own patron deities, bylaws, officeholders, and membership fees, could fall into one of three categories. The most common *collegia* were akin to trade guilds, devoted to practitioners of a specific profession, such as doctors, leatherworkers, or metalsmiths. The activities of the *sodalitates* (Grk. *thiasoi*) were more purely religious in nature. In addition to sacrifices or other worship rituals, members would often partake of a communal meal. With its attention to religious instruction and charitable outreach, non-Jews might have thought of the synagogue as one of these groups. A third group was the funerary society, which provided a form of insurance for those ordinarily unable to afford a proper burial. Due to the preponderance of foreigners in their ranks and their tendency to engage in political discussion, the Roman government was suspicious of the *collegia* and regulated their activities (Wilken 1984: 31–47). Based on information gleaned from Paul's letters, from surviving inscriptions, and from ongoing archaeological excavations, many scholars believe that the early Christian assemblies in many locales resembled these voluntary associations in composition and structure.

The operational expenses of the *collegia* were often subsidized by a wealthy patron. Patronage is the formal name for the network of hierarchical relationships that define social life in the first century. Much of the epistolary activity in the Greco-Roman world is carried out in the context of the patronage system. A patron is an individual in a position of superiority vis-à-vis another individual. Those in a subordinate position are clients. Everyone was someone's patron (except for the lowest slave) and also someone's client (except for the emperor). To their patrons, clients owed honor and respect, which entailed greeting the patron in the morning, joining his entourage, and offering assistance in his political or economic endeavors. Patrons, in turn, used their position to protect the client's interests, for example, by giving them food, aiding them in securing employment, and other benefactions. In a world lacking a social safety net on the scale of the modern welfare state, this unofficial infrastructure was crucial in meeting the basic needs of individuals that might otherwise go unmet. Insofar as patron–client relationships can be described as "friendships," they are alliances or partnerships, as when Pilate is accused of not being "Caesar's friend" in John 19:12. Reciprocity in the form of gift-giving and promised loyalty is often characterized in language (e.g., *pistis*, "faith," and *charis*, "grace") that takes on a slightly different nuance in the New Testament.

## CONCLUSION

At every turn, the modern reader is met by references, assumptions, and allusions that come into clearer focus when they are considered within the cultural milieu of the authors and the original audiences. Many of Jesus' parables presuppose a working knowledge of common business practices and subsistence farming. In his instructions to the Romans to obey the governing authorities, Paul counts on his readers to know what he means when he urges them to "pay to all what is due them," be it taxes, respect, or honor (Rom. 13:7). Ancient theories about embryology may inform remarks about Sarah's role in the conception of Isaac in Heb. 11:11. John's account of Jesus' first miracle culminates with an exchange about wedding customs, including the rate at which the guests get drunk. Conjecture about the timing of the Second Coming in 2 Peter 3:8 ("one day is like a thousand years, and a thousand years are like one day") shares concerns with popular Greek religious speculation such as one sees in Plutarch's essay "On the Delays of Divine Vengeance." For the reader who enjoys discovering unexpected connections across the boundaries that conventionally separate various traditions, the New Testament supplies an abundance of riches, even if their precise "fit" within this wider background remains less than obvious.

Those who view early Christianity as utterly unique and those who see it as no different from the many other Hellenistic mystery cults or Jewish sects both miss the mark. On many points, the Christian message closely resembles other religious and philosophical systems in place in the first century. At the same time, the distinctive way in which it brought together various ideological ingredients—not the least of which were the claims its adherents made about the centrality of particular historical events and personages—produced results that were genuinely novel. Where the assumptions shared with their contemporaries remain unstated, it is possible to get the impression that early Christian teachings are even more original than they actually were. Jesus' running arguments with the Pharisees provide a case in point. They fight tooth and nail in the gospels, with the Pharisees continually attempting to trip Jesus up and Jesus excoriating the Pharisees as hypocrites and lovers of glory who ignore the spiritual heart of Torah. This conflict makes it easy to overlook the fact that Jesus saw himself as a devout Jew who came "not to abolish but to fulfill" the law (Matt. 5:17). On the many occasions when they share a meal, he rarely reviews the many matters on which they agree. Rather, he spends his time on the points where they disagree.

One finds this narrow focus on the differences in Paul's letters as well, which inadvertently produce a skewed picture by making the conflict seem to be more comprehensive than is probably the case. This sometimes gives rise to the anachronistic charge that Paul is anti-Semitic. Much of what Jesus and the New Testament authors say is well within the normal bounds of intra-Jewish theological debates in the first century. It is nevertheless possible to overcorrect for the problem of ignoring context. On the basis of assumptions about what "no first-century Jew" could or would have believed, for example, it is sometimes argued that Paul was certainly a Jew but not a Christian and by implication that Christianity as it has developed over many centuries is at its root a perversion of the teachings of the historical Paul and the historical Jesus. But in reality, authors sometimes say things they should not say or that no one would expect them to say. That Paul might in fact say such things is precisely what makes him—depending on one's confessional stance—inspired or heretical or mad.

It is also possible to read too much into the points of contact between the New Testament writings and other ancient texts. James Frazer popularized the practice of compiling long lists of parallels between Jesus and various Greek and Egyptian deities and charismatic healers, such as Osiris and Horus or Apollonius of Tyana, in his 1890 magnum opus *The Golden Bough.* Many of the parallels are truly astonishing until one notices how selective and superficial they frequently are, ignoring key differences, glossing over matters of chronology, and investing too much significance in ambiguous details (J. Z. Smith 1987). Contrary to the claims of proponents of the "Christ myth" theory, by no means do the similarities between Jesus and such "dying and rising gods" prove that he never existed, even if it remains exceedingly difficult to reconstruct his biography with any degree of certainty.

Noting the similarities between two figures or movements as if their meaning is self-evident is not the same thing as explaining their relative significance. The habit of confusing the two is sometimes referred to as "parallelomania." Whether the New Testament authors should be read with or against the grain of their Mediterranean context is not always clear. Many features of the early Christian message undeniably echo those of other religions. But differences can reveal equally important clues about the relationship between various texts and traditions. Yes, Jesus and others use the same Greek word (*parousia*) as Hellenistic authors in describing the visit of a dignitary (Matt 24:3; 1 Thess. 3:13; Jas. 5:7), but they differ in the emphasis they put on it, in the importance they attach to it, and in the responses deemed appropriate when it is applied to the return of Jesus to judge the living and the dead. Yes, Luke's physical descriptions of the short man Zacchaeus (19:1–10), the bent woman (13:11–13), and the Ethiopian eunuch (Acts 8) may draw on conventions from the ancient "science" of physiognomy, but they may subvert them as well. And while ongoing research fills in the gaps in our knowledge about the first century, answers to many questions continue to elude interpreters. Why does John specify that, with the help of the risen Jesus, the disciples haul in a catch of exactly 153 fish? Whose identity is concealed by 666, "the number of the beast" (Rev. 13:18)? What was the precise nature of Paul's "thorn in the flesh" (2 Cor. 12:7)? Who in Corinth was practicing the otherwise unattested ritual of baptism for the dead (1 Cor. 15:29)? Surviving texts on numerology, medicine, and the mystery cults may contain hints, but their authors were not thinking of what a reader might need to know 2,000 years after the fact. A close and careful reading of the New Testament will always entail determining which allusions and associations are more and less relevant in the complicated matrix of Mediterranean society and what to do when clear answers to the most pressing questions are not forthcoming.

## SUGGESTIONS FOR FURTHER READING

For concise description of nearly any topic a general reader will come across in reading ancient texts, two one-volume dictionaries are indispensable: S. Hornblower and A. Spawforth, eds., *The Oxford Classical Dictionary* (3rd ed.; Oxford, UK: Oxford University Press, 1996), covers the Greco-Roman world from several centuries before the time of Jesus up to late antiquity. F. L. Cross and E. A. Livingstone, eds., *The Oxford Dictionary of the Christian Church* (3rd ed.; Oxford, UK: Oxford University Press, 2005), covers virtually every aspect of the Christian tradition from its beginnings up to the present day.

The most comprehensive resources for studying the texts and topics related to the study of the New Testament are two multi-volume "dictionaries" which are encyclopedic in scope: D. N. Freedman, ed., *The Anchor Bible Dictionary* (6 vols.; New York: Doubleday, 1992); and K. D. Sakenfeld, ed., *The New Interpreter's Dictionary of the Bible* (5 vols.; Nashville, TN: Abingdon, 2006–2009). Both contain entries for every name appearing in the Bible as well as entries for countless subjects that may or may not appear in the Bible in any explicit form (e.g., art and architecture, trade and commerce, magic), often accompanied by maps, charts, photographs, and illustrations. Those wishing to pursue more advanced study of a subject will benefit from the bibliographies that appear with most entries.

For narrative treatments of the historical and cultural milieu of the New Testament, one may consult H. Koester, *Introduction to the New Testament, Volume 1: History Culture, and Religion of the Hellenistic Age* (2nd ed.; Berlin: de Gruyter, 1995); E. Ferguson, *Backgrounds of Early Christianity* (3rd ed; Grand Rapids, MI: Eerdmans, 2003); and J. B. Green and L. M. McDonald, eds., *The World of the New Testament: Cultural, Social, and Historical Contexts* (Grand Rapids, MI: Baker Academic, 2013). For attention to the Jewish setting, see J. M. G. Barclay, *Jews in the Mediterranean Diaspora: From Alexander to Trajan (323 BCE–117 CE)* (Edinburgh, UK: T & T Clark, 1996); and S. J. D. Cohen, *From the Maccabees to the Mishnah* (2nd ed.; Louisville, KY: Westminster John Knox, 2006). Annotated excerpts from primary texts are found in L. H. Feldman and M. Reinhold, eds., *Jewish Life and Thought Among Greeks and Romans: Primary Readings* (Philadelphia, PA: Fortress, 1996); and L. H. Schiffman, ed., *Texts and Traditions: A Source Reader for the Study of Second Temple and Rabbinic Judaism* (Hoboken, NJ: Ktav, 1997).

The social world of early Christianity is the subject of a number of more specialized surveys: J. A. Glancey, *Slavery in Early Christianity* (Oxford, UK: Oxford University Press, 2002); J. E. Stambaugh and D. L. Balch, *The New Testament in Its Social Environment* (Philadelphia, PA: Westminster, 1986); C. Osiek and D. L. Balch, *Families in the New Testament World: Households and House Churches* (Louisville, KY: Westminster John Knox, 1997); Philip A. Harland, *Associations, Synagogues, and Congregations: Claiming a*

*Place in Ancient Mediterranean Society* (Minneapolis, MN: Fortress, 2003); M. R. Lefkowitz and M. B. Fant, eds., *Women's Life in Ancient Greece & Rome* (3rd ed.; Baltimore, MD: Johns Hopkins University Press, 2005).

Collections of Jewish and Christian non-canonical texts are found in J. H. Charlesworth, ed., *The Old Testament Pseudepigrapha* (2 vols.; Garden City, NY: Doubleday, 1983–1985); and J. K. Elliott, ed., *The Apocryphal New Testament* (Oxford, UK: Clarendon, 1993). These volumes provide English translations and detailed introductions that explore literary and thematic connections to the books of the Old and New Testaments. C. A. Evans, *Ancient Texts for New Testament Studies: A Guide to the Background Literature* (Peabody, MA: Hendrickson, 2005), surveys a wider range of ancient literature and focuses more closely on their relevance for understanding the New Testament.

---

## THE CONTEXT OF EARLY CHRISTIANITY: KEY EVENTS

| | |
|---|---|
| 586 BCE | Destruction of the Jerusalem Temple by the Babylonians |
| 538 BCE | Exiled Judeans permitted to return and rebuild the temple after the Persians, under Cyrus, defeat the Babylonians |
| 333 BCE | Alexander the Great establishes Greco-Macedonian rule over Palestine |
| 167–164 BCE | Maccabean revolt against Antiochus IV's program of forced Hellenization |
| 73–71 BCE | Slave revolt led by Spartacus |
| 63 BCE | Roman occupation of Palestine begins |
| 44 BCE | Julius Caesar assassinated |
| 31 BCE | Octavian defeats Antony and Cleopatra at Actium; declared "Augustus" by Senate four years later |

*(continued)*

*(continued)*

| | |
|---|---|
| 4 BCE (?) | Birth of Jesus |
| 29 CE (?) | Death of Jesus |
| 49 CE | Expulsion of Jews from Rome under Claudius |
| 64 CE | Great Fire of Rome; death of Peter and Paul (?) |
| 68–69 CE | "Year of the Four Emperors" after death of Nero |
| 66–73/74 CE | Jewish revolt against Rome; Second Temple destroyed in 70 |
| 79 CE | Eruption of Vesuvius, destruction of Pompeii and Herculaneum |
| 115–117 CE | Jewish uprisings in Egypt, Cyrenaica, Cyprus, and Mesopotamia |
| 132–135 CE | Bar Kokhba revolt |
| 325 CE | Council of Nicaea |
| 367 CE | Festal Letter of Athanasius containing list of twenty-seven New Testament writings |

# 2

## THE LITERATURE OF THE NEW TESTAMENT

### The Gospels and the Acts of the Apostles

The narratives about Jesus compiled in the New Testament are among the best known in world literature and the most significant in the impact they have made on culture, especially but by no means exclusively in the West. As early as the second century, they were referred to as "gospels." The Greek word usually rendered "gospel" or "good news"—*euangelion*—was not a Christian neologism. It has a pre-Christian history. *Euangelion* denotes an especially auspicious announcement, frequently associated with the arrival of a dignitary or the victorious outcome of a military campaign. It undergoes a terminological shift before its application to Matthew, Mark, Luke, and John, as well as to later works attributed to such figures as Peter, Thomas, Philip, and Mary. During his earthly ministry, Jesus preaches "the gospel of the kingdom," which had as its referent the transcendent reality that God would bring into existence and, indeed, had already dawned with the healing of the sick, the forgiveness of sins, and other wondrous deeds (Matt. 11:5; Mark 1:14–15; Luke 4:18).

In the preaching of his earliest followers in the period after his death, the proclaimer becomes the proclaimed as "gospel" comes to denote not only a message about God but about Jesus as well, indicating that the God of Israel had decisively intervened in human history through his son (Rom. 1:16; 15:19–20; 1 Cor. 1:17; Gal. 1:6–9; 2 Tim. 2:8). The degree to which Jesus was himself already a part of his good news about God is a matter of some dispute.

Not until several decades after his death does "gospel" refer to a literary composition about Jesus, when Justin Martyr (*1 Apol.* 66.3) uses it in discussing "memoirs of the apostles," though it may have taken on this sense much earlier. The fluidity it maintains is perhaps evident in the sentence fragment that begins the Gospel according to Mark (1:1): "The beginning of the good news of Jesus Christ, the Son of God." Grammatically and semantically, the text allows any of the three Christian senses of *euangelion*/"gospel," that is, news announced by Jesus, news about Jesus, and literary genre focusing on Jesus. Any written narratives that may have existed before Mark—thought to be the earliest, written ca. 70 CE—have not survived for posterity. Why does no one put the story down on papyrus until then? Perhaps, in light of Jesus' apparent promise of an imminent return to usher in the end of the ages, no one expected there to be any "posterity" of which to speak. More likely, by that time most of the individuals with a living memory of Jesus would have already died, leaving the community of believers with few "quality control" mechanisms in the vital process of preserving and transmitting the historical bases of the faith. Setting the story down in a relatively fixed form would be all the more critical with the scattering of the earliest community following Rome's conquest of Jerusalem in 70 CE.

The role of this community in the formation of the gospels cannot be overestimated. Historians interested in recording traditions associated with an itinerant preacher from the backwaters of the empire without any compelling personal reason for doing so were rare in the ancient world. Josephus, a Jewish historian who had participated in the Jewish revolt, is the only surviving first-century author who so much as mentions Jesus, and even then it is only a few casual sentences buried in several hundred pages of text that many scholars believe were in part inserted by later Christian editors. Had the early Christians not been intentional about preserving the story of

Jesus, it might well have been lost forever. It is a truth neatly captured in the opening frames of the 1965 biblical epic *The Greatest Story Ever Told*. The film begins with a shot of the interior of an Orthodox Church that fades into a shot of the Galilean countryside, and it ends inside a church as well. While no part of the story takes place inside a church, there is something fitting about it in light of the church's role in shaping and handing on the gospels as they have come down through history.

Matthew, Mark, Luke, and John were not alone in their belief that Jesus was a central figure in the greatest story ever told. Neither were they the first to relate various chapters of that grand narrative. The first few decades after Jesus' death were the setting for a lively oral tradition circulating individual vignettes and sayings within the context of worship, teaching, missionary preaching, and theological and ethical disputes with one another and with Jews who did not share their beliefs about Jesus. Much of this activity is present in the letters contained in the New Testament, many of which were written before the gospels. Written collections of Jesus' sayings may have been made during this period, but no such manuscripts have survived.

On the basis of the attention it receives and the shape it takes in each of the canonical gospels, the account of Jesus' death, traditionally referred to as the Passion, was probably the first extended part of the story to be put into writing. Each of the four gospels trace roughly parallel arcs: John the Baptist appears announcing the coming of Jesus, who gathers disciples and provokes opposition as he works wonders and teaches the people about God, dies on the cross, and rises on the third day. Prior to the final week before his crucifixion, however, they exhibit several marked differences in content, emphasis, and even sequence. These differences are more pronounced between John and the other three gospels. Once Jesus enters Jerusalem on Palm Sunday, the respective accounts align much more closely in terms of content, chronology, and the level of detail in which events are described. These qualities point to the creation of a written account which, compared with the earlier portions of the narrative, stands in closer proximity to the events it chronicles. Moreover, each of the authors devotes a disproportionate amount of space to the days leading up to the cross. Such is the imbalance that the gospels have been characterized as "passion narratives with extended introductions" (Kähler 1964: 80).

It is this inordinate attention to his death that, for all the similarities with the writings of Plutarch, Philostratus, and Diogenes Laertius, makes it difficult to classify the gospels as simply four more examples of Greco-Roman biography.

Literary considerations thus suggest that the gospels came together in reverse order, so to speak. More crucially, theological and psychological factors point in the same direction. Jesus attracted a following before his execution ca. 30 CE. Whatever they thought of him at the time, it is clear that shortly afterwards his disciples began to apply a number of exalted titles to him: Lord, Savior, Son of God, and above all, Messiah. So central is the category of "messiah" for their understanding of Jesus that the Greek translation of this Hebrew term meaning "the anointed one"—*Christos*—that it practically functions as his second name in their writings. Whether they ought to have identified him as the Messiah is for theologians to ponder. Historians in their capacity as historians are not equipped to determine whether these claims are true in any ultimate sense but may ascertain that this development occurred and can attempt various explanations for its origin (Dahl 1974).

And the contours of early Christian teaching certainly call out for an explanation insofar as they are not what one might have expected. They are not, at any rate, what the early Christians themselves appear to have expected when they first became followers of Jesus. An abiding conviction that Jesus had risen from the grave and was no longer among the dead is closely connected to their identification of him as the Messiah. While the gospels portray Jesus foretelling his death and resurrection (Matt. 17:22–23; 20:17–19; Mark 9:9, 30–32; 10:33–34; Luke 18:31–34), the dismay and, later, elation of the disciples on Good Friday and Easter Sunday suggest that they either misunderstood or did not take any such predictions seriously.

Their confusion and, at times, outright disbelief at the news of his resurrection is understandable, especially in light of the diversity of messianic expectation among Jews in the first century. Several documents from the Second Temple period speak of the Messiah (*Pss. Sol.* 17:21–34; *4 Ezra* 7:26–35; *2 Bar.* 72.2–73.4; 1 QS 9.9–11; 1 QSa 2.11–21; CD 12.23–13.1). Was the Messiah to be a military conqueror? A priestly figure? How many messiahs would God send? What events would accompany his advent? On these and other questions, Jews gave a wide range of answers. On one point, there seems to have been tacit agreement: it went without saying that the Messiah would not experience the ignominy of a death cursed by God after condemnation by a Jewish court for blasphemy and law-breaking (Deut. 21:23; Gal. 3:13–14; cf. Hooker 1994: 7–12). For this reason, it is clear that the early Christians were hardly appropriating an image of the Messiah that would have been recognized by many (if any) of their fellow Jews, who may have been impressed by miracles and enlightened by parables but did not demand these qualities of the Lord's anointed.

Why, then, did they conclude that Jesus was the Messiah and that he was a singular figure on whose fate all of God's plans for Israel and the rest of the world hinged? Answers that will satisfy anyone who may ask this question remain elusive. This clash of expectation and experience was palpable, and the tension it produced could not for long go unresolved. They could not blithely repeat his teachings and exchange tales of his exploits if he were simply another false prophet or foiled revolutionary like Judas the Galilean before him (Acts 5:37) or Simon bar Kokhba after him. Coming to terms with his humiliating death was absolutely necessary for any semblance of his movement to continue. Something happened to convince them that the end of Jesus' life did not end in defeat but, rather, constituted a victory over death and prefigured the resurrection that many Jews expected all the faithful would experience on the Day of Judgment.

This process unfolds in the Passion narratives, as it does earlier in the oral tradition preserving other memories of Jesus' life and in the letters of Paul, who summarizes his message as "Christ crucified" and in the same letter declares that "if Christ has not been raised, then . . . your faith has been in vain" (1 Cor. 1:23; 15:14). Modern readers sometimes regard as essential certain traits, such as the power to work miracles or rising from the dead, that ancient readers saw as incidental to any claims of messiahship. It is a mistake to assume that there was a single, standardized "job description," found in the Hebrew Scriptures, and that the birth of Christianity was simply a matter of consulting this checklist when candidates presented their messianic credentials. On the one hand, it is undeniable that the early Christians saw in Jesus the fulfillment of biblical prophecies. Matthew is especially fond of connecting the dots for his readers (e.g., 1:22–23; 2:17–18; 4:13–16; 12:15–21). On the other hand, it is noteworthy that many of the texts they highlight as having found their fulfillment in Jesus were not previously deemed messianic prophecies by other Jews. One such text is the Song of the Suffering Servant in Isaiah, telling of one who "was wounded for our transgressions . . . yet did not open his mouth" when "like a lamb that is led to the slaughter . . . he poured out himself to death" (52:13–53:12; cf. Matt. 8:17; Acts 8:32–33; 1 Pet. 2:22–25). Whether he does it on his own or his disciples do it for him, Jesus essentially redefines the role of the Messiah.

The early believers in Jesus often work in the opposite direction of what one might have expected, not from Scripture to their experience but from experience to Scripture (Johnson 1999: 107–20). So affected are they by their experience of Jesus having conquered death that they re-read the Hebrew Scriptures using this experience as the controlling hermeneutical key. In other words, their experience influences their reading of the texts much more so than their reading of the texts guides them in processing their experience. The process is not entirely unlike what happens in watching a movie with a surprising twist at the end. The immediate impulse is to watch it again to see how the director set up the ending: Were there clues that were easy to miss but stand out on a second viewing? Or did the ending come out of the blue, without any real connection to the story preceding it? The movie itself has not changed. Now privy to the surprise ending, it is the viewer that has changed. To use a slightly different metaphor, knowledge of the ending provides a set of spectacles allowing the viewer to notice details that were present all along but invisible for all practical purposes. Thus were the early Christians able to maintain their trust in the fidelity of the God of Israel and simultaneously proclaim that Jesus, despite any appearances and expectations to the contrary, represented the fulfillment of divine promises contained in the Scriptures (Hays 2014).

As his death and vindication on Easter made the life leading up to them worth remembering, they provided the decisive impulse for the writing of the first gospels. This is not to say that he was not a source of profound ethical insight or did not set an unimpeachable moral example, only that in these respects he was not terribly unique when compared with other Jewish teachers in antiquity. The end of his life supplied the authors with a criterion for deciding which of his words and deeds going back to the beginning were worthy of remembrance and relevant to the needs of their readers. Although they were subordinate to the Passion in terms of their existential import for the author, the record of Jesus' teachings and actions constitute a major part of the gospels' cultural legacy.

## THE SYNOPTIC PROBLEM

The greatest story ever told must be told in the right way, and each of the authors has particular ideas about how it should be told and what it should include. They share a common subject, but one need not be a scholar to see that the first three share more with one another than any of them does with the fourth. Patristic writers comment on the distinctive character of the Fourth Gospel, as does John Calvin, who is perfectly comfortable leaving John out of his harmony of the gospels. Beginning with the publication in the eighteenth century of gospel synopses—volumes in which the first three gospels are printed in parallel columns—scholars converge on a consensus that there must be some sort of organic literary relationship to account for the similarities as well as the differences among Matthew, Mark, and Luke, known collectively as the Synoptic Gospels.

One or more of these authors is dependent on the work of one or more of the others, and the task of sorting out their relations is known as the Synoptic Problem. Consider these statistics: Matthew (1,068 verses) contains approximately four-fifths of the 661 verses contained in Mark. Luke (1,149 verses, but shorter than Matthew) contains approximately two-thirds of this Markan material. In both cases, moreover, the vast majority of the common material appears in the same sequence, with much of it appearing in all three gospels. The exact correspondence in wording used in multiple texts at several points is striking. For example, in his last discourse, Jesus warns the disciples of the "desolating sacrilege" that will occur as one of the signs of the end-times. When this begins, he says, "those in Judea must flee to the mountains" (Matt. 24:16; Mark 13:14). Curiously, in both Matthew and Mark this directive is immediately preceded by the exact same parenthetical comment "let the reader understand." Jesus, of course, did not utter, "let the reader understand," and it is highly improbable that both authors inserted it independently, at the same point, and in the same words.

Since antiquity, when the issue was broached at all it had been assumed that the canonical order coincided with the order of composition. Later theories retained Matthew as the earliest gospel which was used by Luke, before Mark, with access to both Matthew and Luke, produced an abbreviated gospel. For over a century now, the most widely accepted solution to the Synoptic Problem posits Mark as the first gospel written, followed by Matthew and Luke using his text independently of one another. (Luke 1:1 implies that the author has read "many" other accounts, though he unfortunately does not name his sources.) Whereas there are aspects of the interrelationships among the three that are difficult to explain on the assumption of Markan priority, alternative theories raise as many questions as they answer. The analysis in the following sections presupposes the consensus view.

On the hypothesis that Mark provides the textual basis from which Matthew and Luke begin, it becomes possible to draw interpretive conclusions upon observing their editorial activity. What stories, sayings, or details have they added? What have they omitted? What have they retained but altered in subtle or not-so-subtle ways? Redaction criticism is the technical term for the study of an author's editorial decisions as a means of discerning the ideas and attitudes that inform them. What was the purpose of Jesus' ministry? What was his relationship with God? What did he teach about the law? Did Jesus think of himself as divine or as a normal human being? Did his followers accurately understand his teachings? Did Jesus intend to provoke Jewish and Roman authorities in such a way that his death would result, or did he let things "get out of hand," as Judas puts it in the opening number of the 1973 rock opera *Jesus Christ Superstar*? What, precisely, did it mean to call him the Christ? The Synoptic writers give various answers to these and other fundamental questions, which may be inferred through careful examination of the accumulated similarities and differences and the patterns that emerge from them.

Where one can be reasonably certain of the sources employed, redaction criticism can yield valuable information about the theological perspectives of the authors. Where such certainty cannot be had, the interpreter must proceed with more caution. This is the case when it comes to another aspect of the relations between the Synoptic Gospels. In addition to the material shared by all three, Matthew and Luke also share over 200 verses that are not found in Mark, almost exclusively in the form of dialogue spoken by Jesus. In the temptation scene, for example, whereas Mark simply remarks that Jesus was "in the wilderness forty days, tempted by Satan" (1:13), Matthew (4:1–11) and Luke (4:1–13) both supply the familiar disputation in nearly identical language, albeit in a different order. The verbal parallels throughout Matthew and Luke are so detailed and extensive that scholars believe they are both drawing from a written source consisting of Jesus' sayings. No such source has survived or is even mentioned by ancient writers, but this hypothetical source is conventionally referred to as Q (from the German *Quelle*, "source"). Alongside Mark, Q is the second major source that helps to account for the similarities and differences found among the Synoptic Gospels. This "Two-Source Hypothesis" is usually illustrated by means of a diagram:

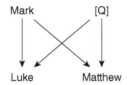

Because it no longer exists, Q must be reconstructed on the basis of its extant form(s) in Matthew and Luke. Sayings from Q constitute additional material that Matthew and Luke have added to the basic narrative inherited from Mark and thus give some indication of their interests in portraying Jesus. But because it is impossible to know with any certainty what Q looked like, how much of it they have borrowed, what they may have left aside, or how one or both authors may have altered the sayings they incorporate, redactional analyses based on Q must remain tentative in their conclusions.

As a compendium of sayings, Q is thought to lack narratives about Jesus' birth, miracle-working, death, or resurrection. The discovery in 1945 of the Coptic *Gospel of Thomas*, a collection of sayings attributed to Jesus but lacking a narrative frame, shows that Q would not have been unique in taking this form. Their purported absence from Q leads many scholars to conclude that it attached little significance to these aspects of the Jesus tradition. To deduce from the reconstructed form of this hypothetical document that there were first-century Christian

communities for whom Jesus' death and resurrection made no difference, however, is highly suspect. Such a conclusion seems to assume
not only that Q comprehensively reflects the convictions of specific
communities, but also that members of these communities never read
any other writings about Jesus or believed anything they may have
contained beyond what was already included in Q.

In addition to their use of Mark and a source of Jesus' sayings,
Matthew and Luke have also incorporated distinctive material that
appears in their respective gospels and nowhere else. Sayings and stories found only in Matthew are conventionally labelled "M" material,
while material found only in Luke is labelled "L." Thus the Two-Source
Hypothesis is commonly expanded into the Four-Source Hypothesis:

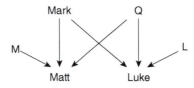

It is not necessary to determine the actual sources from which
Matthew and Luke have drawn this material in order to appreciate
how it fits with and furthers their overarching authorial aims and
inclinations.

## THE GOSPEL AND THE GOSPELS

In the subsequent sections devoted to the gospels—including John—
the aim will be to cultivate an appreciation of each author's accom-
plishment by highlighting the distinctive character of the stories
they tell. Popular presentations of the story of Jesus more often take
a different tack, combining diverse elements from the rich store of
tradition into a single, inclusive narrative with little regard for their
literary origin. The temptation was present in antiquity and has proven
hard to resist ever since. Tatian's *Diatessaron*, a second-century har-
monization of the four gospels, was enormously popular in Syria,
where it remained the standard text used in the liturgy well into the
fourth century, around the time Augustine produced his own version

(*De consensu evangeliorum*). Christmas often provides the occasion for merging the nativity accounts of Matthew and Luke, as one sees in the poetry of John Donne and Ben Jonson, crèche scenes, and school pageants. Holy Week, the period immediately preceding Easter, likewise witnesses the harmonizing impulse at work in dramatic and musical settings, with the staging of Passion plays and composers such as Haydn, Beethoven, and Gounod setting the "Seven Last Words" from the cross to orchestral accompaniment. Apart from the works of Pier Paolo Pasolini (*The Gospel according to St. Matthew*, 1966) and Philip Saville (*The Gospel of John*, 2003), the interpretive choices made by filmmakers almost always include attempts at fusing all four gospels into a cohesive script. Even *Godspell* (1973), which bills itself as "a musical based on the Gospel according to St. Matthew," includes numbers based on parables that appear only in Luke.

Churches have always had theological reasons for resisting the call to simplify matters and collapse the four gospels into a single narrative. While the rationale offered by Irenaeus—just as there are four points on a compass, there should be four gospels (*Haer.* 3.11.8)— may not strike every reader as self-evident, that he would make such a peculiar argument is a testament to the value he and other patristic writers saw in having a multiform witness to the founding of the faith. They were well aware of the inconsistencies that come to light when reading one version alongside another but also, perhaps, sensed that the story of Jesus was too rich to be reduced to a single telling. John says that all the libraries in the world would not do justice to the subject matter (21:25). The traditional titles—which were likely added after the fact and may or may not represent claims of authorship— perhaps acknowledge the point, not presenting themselves as "*The Gospel*, by ____," but as the gospel "according to" Matthew, Mark, Luke, and John respectively.

Apart from any theological value to be gained by focusing on each gospel on its own terms, there are compelling literary and historical reasons for reading them one at a time. One need not read the gospels as holy writ to recognize them as classics of world literature. Overlooking the individual character of the texts violates their literary integrity. And one need not be a historian to wish that "the world behind the text" was more readily accessible to the reader. To be sure, there are many disagreements about the accuracy of the gospel accounts. By focusing on them one at a time, it is possible to operate inductively, gleaning information about the authors, their particular purposes for writing a gospel, their cultural contexts, and the audiences they intend their works to reach. The general consensus among scholars is that the gospels were written primarily or exclusively for specific communities and that an awareness of these social settings is the most important hermeneutical key for interpreting them. It may well be that this consensus view overcorrects for anachronistic notions about the "publication" of the gospels for a general readership (Bauckham 1998). Given the shifting positions of scholars, moreover, there is always the risk that taking a specific historical reconstruction of the early Christian movement as an interpretive point of departure and only then approaching the text will put the reader one step further removed from history than closer to it.

Aristotle famously defines tragedy as an imitation of an action of a certain magnitude that is complete with a beginning, a middle, and an end (*Poet.* 50b). No one believes the evangelists were consulting Aristotle as they went about writing their gospels, yet his definition provides a useful heuristic device and organizing principle for analyzing their narratives. Rather than rehearse their plots in exhaustive detail, the following sections will summarize the basic interpretive issues and then highlight aspects of the beginning, the middle, and the end that illustrate each author's understanding of Jesus' significance. Each gospel has a distinctive beginning which previews specific questions and concerns that will emerge later in the narrative. Likewise, each text ends with an empty tomb but describes the resurrection in its own way. How a story ends has quite a lot to do with what the story means, even if the bulk of that story appears in "the middle." There is considerable overlap among the four plot lines, but each author also includes episodes that the others do not. An awareness of these differences will at the same time throw their shared convictions into sharper relief.

## SUGGESTIONS FOR FURTHER READING

Because they tell the seminal story of the beginning of Christianity, scholars have naturally explored the literary, historical, and theological dimensions of the gospels and Acts in great detail. Valuable resources for understanding Jesus and the earliest texts devoted to his life in their original context include J. B. Green, J. K. Brown, and N. Perrin, eds., *Dictionary of Jesus and the Gospels* (2nd ed.; Downers Grove, IL: InterVarsity, 2013); and D. L. Dungan and D. R. Cartlidge, eds., *Documents for the Study of the Gospels* (2nd ed.; Minneapolis, MN: Fortress, 1994). The cultural legacy of Jesus, in the West and beyond, is the subject of several fine works, including J. Pelikan, *Jesus Through the Centuries: His Place in the History of Culture* (New Haven, CT: Yale University Press, 1985); R. Wightman Fox, *Jesus in America: Personal Savior, Cultural Hero, National Obsession* (San Francisco, CA: HarperSanFrancisco, 2004); L. Houlden, ed., *Jesus: The Complete Guide* (London: Continuum, 2005); and G. A. Barker and S. E. Gregg, eds., *Jesus Beyond Christianity* (Oxford, UK: Oxford University Press, 2010).

Attempts at fleshing out the life of the historical Jesus have become more modest since the heyday of the nineteenth century, but a number of scholars have made the effort by applying new methods and models to the meagre biographical data the gospels contain. The most detailed and judicious is the five-volume work of J. P. Meier, *A Marginal Jew: Rethinking the Historical Jesus* (New Haven, CT: Yale University Press, 1991–2016). Arriving at more skeptical conclusions about the reliability of the gospels, J. D. Crossan, *The Historical Jesus: The Life of a Mediterranean Jewish Peasant* (New York: HarperCollins, 1991) provides the most comprehensive study employing the social sciences as an analytical tool for understanding the historical Jesus. Shorter but responsible in the conclusions they draw are E. P. Sanders, *The Historical Figure of Jesus* (London: Penguin, 1993); and P. Fredriksen, *Jesus of Nazareth, King of the Jews: A Jewish Life and the Emergence of Christianity* (New York: Knopf, 1999). The competing assumptions at work in these different portraits are explored in J. K. Beilby and P. R. Eddy, eds., *The Historical Jesus: Five Views* (Downers Grove, IL: InterVarsity, 2009). On the historical issues involved in understanding the beginning and end of Jesus' life, one should consult the enormous works of R. E. Brown, *The Birth of the Messiah* (Garden City, NY: Doubleday, 1977) and *The Death of the Messiah* (2 vols.; New York: Doubleday, 1994); as well as N. T. Wright, *The Resurrection of the Son of God* (Minneapolis, MN: Fortress, 2003). Particular attention is paid to Jesus' Jewishness by Geza Vermes, *Jesus in His Jewish*

*Context* (London: SCM, 2003); and B. H. Young, *Jesus the Jewish Theologian* (Peabody, MA: Hendrickson, 1995). For an overview of the methodological issues, see M. A. Powell, *Jesus as a Figure in History* (Louisville, KY: Westminster John Knox, 1998).

The question of the gospels' literary genre is discussed by W. S. Vorster, "Gospel Genre" *Anchor Bible Dictionary* 2:1077–1079. The dimensions of the Synoptic Problem are surveyed by D. L. Dungan, *A History of the Synoptic Problem: The Canon, the Text, the Composition, and the Interpretation of the Gospels* (New Haven, CT: Yale University Press, 1999); and K. F. Nickle, *The Synoptic Gospels* (rev. ed.; Louisville, KY: Westminster John Knox, 2001). Study of the Synoptic Gospels requires a volume that lays them out in parallel columns, such as those of B. H. Throckmorton, *Gospel Parallels* (Nashville, TN: Thomas Nelson, 1993); and Z. A. Crook, *Parallel Gospels: A Synopsis of Early Christian Writing* (Oxford, UK: Oxford University Press, 2012), which also includes John and the *Gospel of Thomas*. The hypothetical sayings source "Q" is reconstructed by J. S. Kloppenborg, *Q, the Earliest Gospel: An Introduction to the Original Stories and Sayings of Jesus* (Louisville, KY: Westminster John Knox, 2008). Essays by the vocal minority who are unconvinced of Q's existence are collected in M. Goodacre and N. Perrin, eds., *Questioning Q: A Multidimensional Critique* (Downers Grove, IL: InterVarsity, 2004). On the parables, see R. Zimmerman, *Puzzling the Parables of Jesus: Methods and Interpretation* (Minneapolis, MN: Fortress, 2015).

Noncanonical gospel literature is collected and translated in B. D. Ehrman and Z. Pleše, eds., *The Other Gospels: Accounts of Jesus from Outside the New Testament* (Oxford, UK: Oxford University Press, 2014); and M. Meyer, ed., *The Nag Hammadi Scriptures* (San Francisco, CA: HarperOne, 2007).

# Mark

| 1:1–15 | Preparing the Way of the Lord |
|---|---|
| 1:16–8:26 | Jesus' public ministry: preaching, parables, and miracle-working |
| 8:27–10:52 | The suffering Son of Man: Passion predictions |
| 11:1–12:44 | Heightening conflict with Jewish leadership |
| 13:1–37 | Jesus' final discourse |
| 14:1–15:47 | The Passion narrative |
| 14:1–72 | Last Supper, betrayal, arrest, trial, denial |
| 15:1–47 | The Crucifixion |
| 16:1–20 | The empty tomb and the Risen Lord |

While it was likely the first gospel to be written, the Gospel of Mark has in many ways flown below the radar for much of Christian history. The other gospels supply a greater store of distinctive images, stories, and sayings to artists, poets, and composers who look to the Bible for inspiration. Theologians likewise need not rely on Mark, it was often assumed, since nearly all of his account can be found elsewhere in Matthew or Luke. And since John was thought to be an apostle and eyewitness, it was deemed a better guide to the life of Jesus.

The reception of Mark begins to change in the nineteenth century. Interest in solving the Synoptic Problem shifted the scholarly consensus. No longer was Matthew believed to be the earliest gospel. Source critics demonstrated that it was easier to explain the literary relations among the Synoptic Gospels by assuming that Mark had been written first and then used by the other two. Notwithstanding the unique perspectives found in Matthew and Luke, then, Mark deserves much of the credit for introducing the narrative of Jesus that over time has become an archetype assumed and explored in both sacred and secular contexts. In relation to the "Quest for the Historical Jesus," moreover, Mark's stock rose dramatically. If it was the earliest gospel, it was argued, then its unvarnished account was closer to the events of Jesus' life and of more historical value than those of Matthew and Luke. This expectation that Mark might offer an unfiltered, "just the facts" report was soon shown to be naïve, as the early community of believers had already engaged in intense theological reflection on the significance of Jesus' life, death, and resurrection well before the appearance of a full-scale gospel.

The author of the Gospel of Mark nowhere names himself or makes any claim to authorship. Justin Martyr (*Dial.* 106.3) in the mid-second century is the first writer to reflect the tradition of Markan authorship in discussing the "memoirs" of Peter. Eusebius (*Hist. eccl.* 2.15; 3.39.15) cites a contemporary of Justin, Papias, as describing Mark as the "interpreter" of Peter who recorded—however, "not in order"—stories and sayings of Jesus. Most scholars identify this Mark with the Mark mentioned elsewhere as a companion of Paul, Peter, and Barnabas (Acts 12:12, 25; 15:36–39; Col. 4:10; 2 Tim. 4:11; Philem. 24; 1 Pet. 5:13). Church tradition (Eusebius, *Hist. eccl.* 2.16) holds that Mark introduced Christianity to Egypt and was the first bishop of Alexandria. With so little information about this or any other Mark, and without any other writings to serve as a standard of comparison, there is no firm basis for confirming or rejecting claims of Markan authorship. Similarly, it is difficult to determine the place of composition or the location of the audience for whom the author was writing. Rome is the leading candidate for both author and audience, though Syria and Galilee have also been put forward as possibilities. The author is writing for Greek-speakers, and his work shows few signs of having been translated from Aramaic. That Gentiles are included in this audience is indicated by the author's occasional explanations of Jewish customs (e.g., 7:3–4).

When and why the author is writing are more crucial for understanding Mark than the precise identity of the author or audience or where they may reside. There is an unusually broad and specific consensus when it comes to the date of composition. Proponents of Markan authorship as well as skeptics agree that the gospel was written in the late 60s or early 70s. The independent use of Mark by Matthew and Luke, usually dated ca. 85 CE, rules out a later date. Jesus' final discourse in Mark 13 appears to reflect the milieu of Jerusalem during the Jewish revolt that begins in 66 CE. Jesus' prediction of the temple's destruction in Mark 13:2 may indicate that Mark is writing shortly after 70 CE, though Josephus (*J. W.* 6.300–309) mentions other prophets who made the same prophecy during the revolt.

Had Mark followed Luke's example and stated his purpose in writing, it would not be necessary to draw as many inferences from the text he has left behind. His emphasis on the necessity for Jesus to suffer and die may be motivated in part to correct the notion that he belonged to a Jewish genus of the "divine man" (*theios anēr*) species, a type of charismatic wonder-worker in the Hellenistic world. Yes, Jesus possessed power from on high, but this was not his most important attribute according to Mark. Whatever one may have thought of his brief but spectacular career, his shameful death required an explanation. Mark goes to great lengths to demonstrate that Jesus' death was indeed essential to his mission and not merely incidental or accidental. He has Jesus tell his disciples that it is God's will that he pour out his life as "a ransom for many" (10:45; 14:24). His Sonship entails embracing this daunting mission.

Perhaps members of the audience were unaware or preferred to forget that suffering might await them as followers of the crucified Messiah. The light of the glorious resurrection might have banished the dark shadow of Golgotha, yet this must not lead believers to conclude that they are exempt from the call to take up their cross. The cruciform shape of the narrative reminds readers that "those who want to save their life will lose it, and those who lose their life for . . . the sake of the gospel, will save it" (8:35). Other audience members may have already experienced abuse, perhaps in the Neronian persecutions of the mid-60s (13:9–13; Winn 2008: 139–50). For these readers, the portrait of the disciples functions as a form of encouragement: if they could fail in times of trial and then recover, then all is not lost for others who may succumb to weakness or lack of faith.

## THE BEGINNING OF THE GOOD NEWS

The author is in such a hurry to tell the story of Jesus that he forgets to finish his first sentence: "The beginning of the good news of Jesus Christ, the Son of God" (1:1). Is this a title? Is it a summary of the ensuing narrative? Or, as has been hypothesized, has the original beginning of Mark been lost due to defective transmission of the manuscript? Instead of stating his purposes or setting the scene, he allows Scripture to introduce the *dramatis personae*:

> See, I am sending my messenger ahead of you, who will prepare your way; the voice of one crying in the wilderness: "Prepare the way of the Lord, make his paths straight."

The beginning of the gospel thus begins before the beginning, as it were, in the pages of the Hebrew Bible. Mark attributes to Isaiah the "quotation" that is an amalgam of multiple texts replete with Exodus imagery (Exod. 23:20; Isa. 40:3; Mal. 3:1). This motif will recur in the Passover meal on the night before the crucifixion.

Instead of Jesus, the reader is first introduced to John the Baptist, who is dressed in garb that recalls prophets like Elijah. He tells the Judeans who come to him at the River Jordan, "The one who is more powerful than I is coming after me; I am not worthy to stoop down and untie the thong of his sandals. I have baptized you with water; but he will baptize you with the Holy Spirit" (1:7–8). His insight that Jesus was the chief protagonist in Israel's story becomes central to the new faith. His subsequent execution when he becomes a nuisance to Herod and his unlawfully wedded wife Herodias foreshadows Jesus' own fate (6:17–29).

John recognizes Jesus as a pivotal figure even before the Spirit descends on him at the baptism—the sky is "torn apart," described with the same verb used in reference to the tearing of the temple curtain at the moment of Jesus' death (15:38)—and the voice from heaven declares, "You are my Son" (1:11). Does anyone besides Jesus hear the voice? Does it only confirm something Jesus already knows? Does the author expect the reader to recognize it as an allusion to a messianic psalm (Ps. 2:7)? Before any answers to such questions are offered, the same Spirit that descends on him drives him into the wilderness for forty days of testing by Satan. By the time of his return, John has been arrested, clearing the way for Jesus to take center stage.

## FROM GALILEE TO GOLGOTHA

Jesus begins his public ministry with a flurry of activity that causes his fame to spread throughout Galilee. He performs exorcisms, heals all manner of disease and infirmity, and displays other forms of preternatural power (1:21–2:12; 3:1–6; 5:1–43; 6:30–44; 7:24–8:26; 9:14–29; 10:46–52). The narrator struggles to keep up with the frenetic pace, using the word *euthys* ("immediately") over forty times. When the friends of a paralytic bring him to the house in Capernaum where Jesus is teaching, lowering him through the roof on account of the crowd, Jesus offers commentary on his work (2:1–12). Rather than heal him right away, Jesus instead tells the man, "Son, your sins are forgiven." The scribes in attendance see this as tantamount to blasphemy. After all, "Who can forgive sins but God alone?" Jesus takes the initiative in provoking a confrontation. In order to make the point that his wonder-working has a larger purpose, he makes it explicit: it is "so that you may know that the Son of Man has authority on earth to forgive sins." Subsequent actions, such as unabashedly eating with sinners and tax collectors, further illustrate that Jesus is one who teaches "with authority" (1:27; 2:15–17). As he tells the Pharisees who criticize him for allowing his disciples to pluck grain on the Sabbath, "The Sabbath was made for man, and not man for the Sabbath; therefore the Son of man is Lord also of the Sabbath" (2:27–28 KJV).

The most puzzling aspect of Mark's depiction of Jesus' ministry is his habit of ordering those who have benefitted from his miraculous power to remain silent about it (1:34, 44; 3:12; 5:43; 7:36; 8:30; 9:9). He even commands the demons he has cast out to keep quiet. Are not such events part and parcel of the good news Jesus proclaims? Scholars refer to this tendency as the Messianic Secret (Tuckett 1983). It is far more pronounced in Mark than in the other gospels. It is a poorly kept secret since those who are healed routinely ignore his command, so joyful are they at their good fortune. Did Jesus in fact tell his followers not to spread word of his exploits or disclose his messianic identity? Many historians believe that this motif was invented by the early church to account for the awkward fact that very few people believed he was the Messiah. This view presupposes that Jesus made no such claims on his own behalf and was conscious only of a prophetic calling to proclaim the kingdom of God. Other historians conjecture that his concern was for privacy, a desire to conduct his affairs without undue interference, and to prevent the people from concluding that he was one of many "divine men" like Honi the Circle Drawer or Apollonius of Tyana and that demonstrations of power (to be wielded, perhaps, against the imperial overlords oppressing the Jews) were at the heart of his mission. On these grounds, they argue, there is no need to suppose that the depiction is unhistorical.

Whatever one makes of Jesus' aversion to publicity, it cannot be denied that, apart from John the Baptist and the unclean spirits he casts out (1:23–24, 34; 3:11; 5:7), few characters in Mark understand who he is. Even members of his own family seem embarrassed by him (3:21). His proclivity to speak of the "Son of Man" instead of in the first person also makes it difficult to discern the contours of his self-consciousness (e.g., 2:10; 8:38; 9:9, 12; 10:33; 14:21, 41). "Son of Man" can function as a circumlocution for "I" in the Aramaic Jesus probably spoke as his first language, but it can also refer to a mysterious figure mentioned in the Hebrew Scriptures and other Jewish literature who will "come in clouds with great power and glory" to gather God's chosen people and judge the nations (Dan. 7:13, quoted in Mark 13:26; 14:62; *1 Enoch* 71; cf. Chilton 1999).

The silence to which Jesus enjoins his disciples and his enigmatic mode of self-reference may contribute to widespread misunderstandings of his person and mission. His manner of teaching in parables may exacerbate the situation. Of Jesus' many teachings in the gospels, the parables often count as the most memorable. Parables have been called "earthly stories with heavenly meanings," but Jesus' commentary on his own parables in Mark 4:10–12 demonstrates that the matter may be more complicated than that (Ambrozic 1967). After he tells the Parable of the Sower, the Twelve ask Jesus privately about his parables. He responds:

> To you has been given the secret of the kingdom of God, but for those outside, everything comes in parables, in order that "they may indeed look, but not perceive, and may indeed listen, but not understand; so that they may not turn again and be forgiven."

This explanation, which Jesus articulates by quoting Isa. 6:9–10, gives most readers pause. Jesus appears to be saying that his express purpose for speaking in parables is to confound outsiders and that their imperceptiveness is in some sense foreordained.

Has something been lost in translation? This is one of many theories put forward to make sense of Jesus' counterintuitive rationale: that the purpose clause ("in order that") in v. 12 should be rendered "with the [unavoidable?] result that" (a result clause), or "because," implying that "outsiders" can understand if and only if they are addressed in parables. But one may ask, if confusion is so obviously the result of teaching in parables, why does Jesus continue to teach in this way unless that is precisely his purpose? It seems that parables simultaneously reveal and conceal, albeit to different audiences. They prove nothing by themselves but, rather, confirm truths already accepted as a mystery. At the same time, they perplex those who do not have ears to hear, such that they induce a form of invincible ignorance. At the very least, Jesus' explanation is a reminder that the obscurity of many of the parables is not solely a function of cultural distance.

Approaches to the interpretation of the parables have varied over the centuries (Kissinger 1999). The Alexandrian school represented by Origen treated the parables as allegories from which the interpreter might excavate hidden spiritual meanings. The Antiochene school, by contrast, focused on the literal sense which, when properly understood, would teach valuable moral lessons. Reformation-era interpreters mined the parables for the theological ore they contained, with special attention to their doctrinal implications with respect to faith, grace, law, and justification. Modern interpreters are divided as to the most appropriate way to make sense of the parables on a number of questions. What are the defining elements of a parable? How many are there in the New Testament? Are they *sui generis*, or do they have parallels among contemporary Jewish or Greco-Roman teachers? Do they have a single point? Are they ambiguous by design? Are they self-explanatory or do they demand certain qualities from the reader before they yield their message? Are they meant to illustrate how the world works now? Or how it ought to or will work in the future, when the kingdom of God arrives? Do they require familiarity with the social world inhabited by Jesus? Or are they more reflective of the *Sitz im Leben* ("setting in life") of the early church and its apologetic concerns later in the first century? Are they best approached as works of art that may in turn be interpreted via the medium of art, as in Ian Pollock's series of forty surrealist paintings based on the parables?

Depending on one's definition of the form, Mark contains approximately ten parables, nearly all of which reappear in Matthew and Luke in the same or slightly altered forms:

- New and Old Wineskins (2:21–22). Marcion in the second century takes this parable as confirming his view that the Old Testament and the teachings of Jesus and Paul are incompatible.
- The Strong Man's House (3:23–27). Jesus delivers this parable in response to the charge that he is casting out demons by the power of Satan.
- The Sower (4:3–8). This is one of the very few parables for which Jesus offers an interpretive key. It is, so to speak, a parable about parables.
- The Light under a Bushel (4:21–22). This parable is the basis for "This Little Light of Mine," a popular children's song that later becomes a Civil Rights anthem associated with Fannie Lou Hamer.
- The Seed Growing Secretly (4:26–29). The second in a series of three seed parables, many scholars believe it functioned to reassure the early church in the face of the perceived delay of the Parousia.
- The Mustard Seed (4:30–32). The proverbial smallness of the mustard seed is echoed in Jesus' rebuke of the faithless who, if only they had "faith the size of a mustard seed," would be able to move mountains (Matt. 17:20; Luke 17:6). Citing ancient writers who describe it as an annoying weed that is difficult to eradicate, some scholars emphasize the subversive humor of Jesus' telling.
- What Defiles a Man (7:14–23). Guidelines about ritual purity described in Torah and "the traditions of the elders" (7:3) were hotly debated in the early church and caused tensions between Jewish and Gentile Christians (Gal. 2:1–14). This parable is also a reminder of the centrality of table fellowship in Second Temple social relations.
- Salt and its Savor (9:50). The fact that salt cannot lose its saltiness presents a special exegetical challenge, leading scholars to wonder if "salt" here is something other than sodium chloride.
- The Wicked Tenants (12:1–11). More transparently than do other parables, in alluding to Isa. 5:1–7 and Ps. 118:22–23 this text presents Jesus as someone even greater than the long line of God's prophets rejected by Israel. The Jewish authorities perceive that it is directed at them and, in their desire to arrest Jesus, unwittingly participate in the Scripture's fulfillment (12:12; cf. 3:1–6).
- The Fig Tree (13:28–29). Earlier in Mark (11:12–14, 20–21), Jesus curses a fig tree in a symbolic gesture that likewise makes a statement about Israel's eschatological fate.

Some interpreters would add a few others to this list (e.g., Mark 2:19–20; 13:34–37). Taken out of their narrative framework, the parables can admit wildly divergent interpretations, as their fascinating reception history amply attests.

Despite having privileged access to Jesus' explanations of the parables and receiving power to heal the sick and cast out demons (4:33–34; 6:7–13), even the disciples who have been with him from the beginning fail to grasp his message or comprehend his true identity. Jesus reproves their lack of faith when a storm rocks the boat they have boarded (4:35–41). On a subsequent boat trip, when they fail to recognize him as he walks toward them on the water, Mark states that "they were utterly astounded, for they did not understand about the loaves" (6:52), implying that the power Jesus had just demonstrated in the feeding of the five thousand should have taught them a lesson about Jesus' dominion over nature (6:30–44, 52). Even with a lower degree of difficulty—a crowd of merely 4,000—they are uncertain of Jesus' ability to feed the people (8:4). Afterwards, when Jesus uses figurative language to warn them to "beware the yeast of the Pharisees," they misconstrue his meaning, taking it as a rebuke for forgetting to bring bread for the trip (8:14–21). Jesus is indeed exasperated, but not about their poor planning: "Do you still not perceive or understand?"

Peter has a momentary epiphany at Caesarea Philippi, where Jesus withdraws from the crowds and asks the disciples a pivotal question (8:27–33): "Who do people say that I am?" John the Baptist, Elijah, and other prophets are mentioned. When Jesus puts the question directly to the Twelve, Peter replies, "You are the Messiah." As he does so often in Mark at revelatory moments, Jesus orders them to keep quiet and then tells them that the Son of Man must suffer and die before rising on the third day. Peter protests, indicating that his grasp of Jesus' messianic identity is not so firm as his initial confession had suggested. "Get behind me, Satan!" is Jesus' stinging rebuke. (A medieval formula used by exorcists—*vade retro Satana*—is an adaptation of the Vulgate rendering of this verse.)

From this point forward, Jesus impresses on the disciples that suffering will be integral to his mission, as it will be also for anyone aspiring to follow him. They must be prepared to deny themselves and "take up their cross" (8:34–9:1). More often than not, however, the disciples continue to overlook this aspect of their calling. Upon hearing his second Passion prediction, they fail to understand and instead argue with one another about who is the greatest (9:30–37). Still more obtuse is their response to the third Passion prediction (10:32–45). No sooner does he describe the appalling fate that awaits him than James and John want to know which of them will sit at his right hand in his glory! They have clearly not been paying attention. "You do not know what you are asking," Jesus says, or else they would know that "whoever wishes to be first . . . must be slave of all," just as "the Son of Man came not to be served but to serve, and to give his life a ransom for many." One disciple betrays him, another denies him three times, and the rest eventually desert him (14:10–11, 50, 66–72). The cumulative effect is a portrait of the disciples that is anything but flattering. This serves as a sobering reminder to any of Mark's readers who may identify with the disciples and share their faith but forget that they will be called on to suffer for the good news they deliver and may not be immune to weakness and doubt.

The entry into Jerusalem on what comes to be called Palm Sunday (11:1–11) represents a gesture that is more explicitly messianic in its overtones than one sees earlier in Mark. It is followed by the cleansing of the temple, the first in a final series of confrontations with the Jewish authorities that will result in his death (11:15–19, 27–12:44). Pharisees and Sadducees engage him in debates about paying taxes, the afterlife, and the identity of the Messiah as foretold in Scripture. His replies strengthen their resolve to have him arrested. They hesitate because they fear the crowds gathered there for Passover, the festival commemorating the Exodus of Israel from the land of Egypt (12:12).

Jesus' demonstration against the temple and the authority it represents escalates into a prophecy of its destruction at the outset of the "Apocalyptic Discourse" delivered from the Mount of Olives in Mark 13:1–37. Its destruction will serve as just one of many signs that will appear: "wars and rumors of wars," earthquakes, persecution on account of their allegiance to Jesus, "the abomination of desolation," false messiahs, cosmic upheaval, and "the Son of Man coming on clouds." To remark that this speech is difficult to interpret is an understatement. Assessing Jesus' claim that "this generation will not pass away until all these things have taken place" is a challenge when the cryptic nature of his references, couched in thoroughly apocalyptic language, makes it hard to know exactly what "all these things" are

(13:30). Is he speaking of events that will accompany the temple's destruction or of the end-times, if these should be distinguished at all? Or are they veiled, after-the-fact allusions to the martyrdoms of Peter and other Christians in the persecutions that break out in Rome after the fire of 64 CE? Is this a prediction that, after nearly 2,000 years, has been disconfirmed? Libraries could be filled with books wrestling with the historical and theological dimensions of these questions (Collins 1996). In the midst of this fantastic imagery, Jesus' refrain emphasizes the need to remain "alert" or "awake" (13:3, 5, 9, 23, 33, 35, 37). The disciples are not to allow these events to lead them astray or distract them from proclaiming the good news to all nations, as whoever "endures to the end will be saved" (13:10, 13).

The plot against Jesus has resumed when he meets with followers at the house of Simon the leper (14:1–9). An argument erupts when an unnamed woman pours precious ointment on his head. Some disciples (including Judas, according to John 12:4) scold her and say it ought to have been sold and the proceeds given to the poor. But Jesus approves her action on account of its prophetic symbolism. She is anointing his body for burial. Left unstated is the additional resonance of her action: "messiah" means "anointed one," and insofar as it was the custom to anoint the kings of ancient Israel, it is furthermore fitting that Jesus submits to it in advance of his crucifixion as "King of the Jews."

When preparations are made, Jesus meets with the Twelve for the Last Supper (14:12–25). He transforms the Passover meal in such a way that it not only points backward to the story of the Exodus but also becomes yet another occasion for pointing forward and explaining the significance of his impending death. Over the course of the meal, Jesus equates his body with the unleavened bread the Israelites were commanded to eat and his blood with the sacrifice that sealed the covenant with Yahweh at the foot of Mount Sinai (Exod. 12:14–20; 24:4–8). He thus intimates that the liberation of the Israelites from Egyptian bondage prefigured the deliverance from sin, sickness, and the power of Satan brought about by his life and death. In speaking as ambiguously as he does when uttering the "words of institution" later used to celebrate the Lord's Supper (also called Eucharist or Communion), Jesus also leaves enough room to wonder whether he is speaking literally or only metaphorically of his body and blood.

Protestants and Catholics agree that the question is of fundamental importance but have disagreed on the answer for half a millennium.

The singing of the hymn that concludes the Passover ritual brings only a temporary respite from the somber mood that had settled on their gathering when Jesus told the Twelve that one of them would betray him. All the rest will desert him, he says, and Peter will deny him three times before the cock crows twice (14:26–31). Some scholars believe that this provides the key for understanding the true nature of the Passion narrative. Mark's gospel is laced throughout with scriptural allusions. It is impossible to deny that the density of these allusions increases dramatically in his narration of the last day of Jesus' life. At times, it almost seems as if Jesus and his enemies are acting out a script written by the Psalmist and other biblical authors long ago. But if the disciples deserted Jesus, how can the early Christians possibly know any of the details of what transpired? They cannot have known anything beyond the bare fact that he died. To fill out the story, they search the Scriptures, and thus the Passion narratives are better understood as "prophecy historicized" than "history remembered" (Crossan 1995: 1–13). It is an intriguing thesis that would be more persuasive were not the motif of the disciples' abandonment of Jesus itself cast as a fulfillment of Scripture (Mark 14:27; 49–50; Zech. 13:7; cf. Goodacre 2006). Claims that the evangelists had no choice but to fabricate the whole story in the absence of witnesses or other individuals with information about the sequence of events also downplays Mark's mention of Mary Magdalene, another Mary, and "many other women" who had followed Jesus from Galilee to Jerusalem (15:40–41).

Mark's Christology, with its emphasis on the suffering required of the Son of Man, comes into clearer focus in Gethsemane (14:3–50). Peter, James, and John fall asleep while Jesus, "deeply grieved," prays for a reprieve. Having warned his disciples that they must suffer if they are to follow him (10:39), he now prays that God might "remove this cup" as the hour approaches. Jesus' reproof of the disciples for their inability to stay awake—"the spirit indeed is willing, but the flesh is weak"—might also apply to himself, but he overcomes any reluctance when he sees Judas arrives with a cohort from the Jewish authorities.

The disciples scatter after a brief skirmish, but Mark adds an enigmatic note about "a certain young man . . . wearing nothing but a linen cloth" who runs off naked when they try to catch him (15:51–52). Is this the "rich young ruler" who keeps the commandments but is unwilling to give his goods to the poor (10:17–27)? Is it the "young man" who will appear at the empty tomb (16:5–7)? Does he simply stand for all of the followers who have deserted their master? It has been claimed that this vignette is an abbreviated form of a story taken from a different version of Mark that actually predates the canonical version, in which Jesus spends the night with a nearly naked young man who "looked at him intently and loved him, . . . teaching him the mystery of the Kingdom of God." This text, usually referred to as the *Secret Gospel of Mark*, is now considered a forgery produced centuries later, perhaps by the very scholar who "discovered" it in monastery near Jerusalem in 1958.

Historians would like to know more about the procedures followed by the first-century Sanhedrin in order to determine the plausibility of the trial Mark describes (14:53–65). As it unfolds, it is by turns a travesty of justice and yet another fulfillment of Scripture with Jesus remaining mostly silent before his false accusers (Ps. 35:11; 38:13–14; Isa. 53:7). When the high priest asks, "Are you the Messiah?" Jesus finally answers ("I am") and implies that he is the Son of Man who will come in judgment of those now judging him. This is enough to convince the Sanhedrin that he is guilty of blasphemy and deserving of death. Because the right to inflict capital punishment was reserved for the Roman authorities, the Sanhedrin hands Jesus over to Pontius Pilate. Mark portrays Pilate as disinclined to execute Jesus and only agrees when it becomes clear that the crowds, stirred up by the chief priests, will only be appeased if he instead releases Barabbas in accordance with an otherwise unattested Passover custom.

In the absence of other contemporary accounts, it is often wondered whether this portrayal is faithful to history. Especially in light of the heinous manner in which the gospel accounts have been misappropriated to paint all Jews as "Christ-killers" uniquely responsible for Jesus' death, there is a temptation to dismiss any suggestion that any Jewish figures had anything to do with it and to place all the responsibility on the Romans. The truth is probably more complicated. Rome had little interest in arbitrating sectarian disputes. Crucifixion was reserved not for theological offenses like blasphemy but for serious crimes—above all, for anything that had the whiff of revolution. Since Jesus was crucified as "King of the Jews," one might ask: did the punishment fit the crime? In other words, was Jesus in fact a rebel, a political threat of the sort that would elicit a decisive Roman response in the form of the cross? Or was he not? Most scholars reject the notion that Jesus was part of a movement that sought to overthrow Rome. If he did not seek to establish himself as a political or military ruler but was executed as if he were, the most likely explanation may be that the sentence was handed down on trumped up charges. The Romans would not likely fabricate such charges since they were mainly concerned with real threats and not imaginary ones. If certain Jewish groups in Jerusalem ca. 30 CE had wanted to undermine a rival or defuse a movement that might disturb the peace to the detriment of all the Jews, it would not be the first time for them to draw Rome into their internecine disputes.

Once Pilate decides to mollify the crowd, Jesus' fate is sealed (15:16–39). Earlier predictions that the Son of Man will suffer now come to fulfillment at a quickening pace. Already weakened, he is flogged, spat upon, mocked by the soldiers, and jeered at even by those who are crucified with him. His powerlessness is underscored by the taunt of the chief priests: "He saved others; he cannot save himself" (15:31). Simon of Cyrene is conscripted to carry his cross, presumably because he is unable to carry it himself.

Jesus' only words from the cross in Mark accentuate his sorry state (15:34). He cries out in Aramaic, "Eloi, Eloi lema sabachthani?" ("My God, my God, why have you forsaken me?")—and like so many times before in Mark, is again misunderstood, as the bystanders think he is calling out for Elijah. This "cry of dereliction" is taken from the opening line of Psalm 22. Is the reader to envision Jesus reciting this psalm as death approaches? Can it be a coincidence that the author experiences a reversal and in the second half of this psalm praises the Lord for his deliverance (22:24: "he did not hide his face from me, but heard when I cried to him")? Mark allows the centurion at the foot of the cross to have the last word as Jesus takes his final breath: "Truly this man was God's Son" (15:39), joining the heavenly voice at the baptism and the transfiguration as the only speakers in Mark to voice an unqualified and uncorrected proclamation of his identity (1:11; 9:7). It seems fitting that Jesus is finally recognized for who he really is only in the moment of his most abject suffering.

## THE FIRST DAY OF THE WEEK AND THE END OF THE GOSPEL

Mary Magdalene and other women are the first to discover the empty tomb in all four gospels (Matt. 28:1–10; Mark 16:1–8; Luke 24:1–12; John 20:1–2). Because women were widely regarded (by men) as unreliable witnesses in the Greco-Roman world and were not allowed to testify in Jewish courts, their prominent role in the resurrection accounts is often viewed as a factor in favor of their historicity, as inventing this part of the story would only make it seem less credible to many readers. The women encounter a young man in a white robe who tells them not to be alarmed, as biblical angels often greet the humans to whom they have been sent with a message. He informs them that Jesus has been raised and instructs them to tell the disciples that he is heading to Galilee. Fleeing from the scene in terror, the news that God has vindicated his son by raising him from the dead does not immediately strike them as good. Based on the evidence of the most ancient manuscripts, most scholars believe the gospel concludes with Mark 16:8. If so, it ends as abruptly as it begins, and with a twist: On numerous occasions Jesus has told various characters to keep quiet about the marvelous events they have witnessed, only to be disobeyed again and again. Here, in the final lines of the story, the women have stumbled upon the most marvelous event of all and are told to spread the news, only this time "they [say] nothing"!

Is this how the gospel ends, not with a bang—as in the *Gospel of Peter*, when the moment of Jesus' exit from the tomb is described as taking the form of a sky-high cross that talks—but with a whimper, when even the good news that Jesus is risen fails to generate faith? Should readers give the women the benefit of the doubt since they are not granted a personal encounter with the risen Lord? The lack of closure compels the readers to reflect on the preceding narrative and, perhaps, contemplate their own place in its aftermath. This ending holds out promise of redemption even for those who fail in their first attempt at following Jesus (Lincoln 1989). In this sense, the ending sets the stage for a new beginning.

Not everyone is satisfied with this ending. Among the surviving manuscripts, there exists a version with a "shorter ending" appended to Mark 16:8, and a "longer ending" (16:9–20) appearing in most Bibles that has been the canonical version for most of Christian history. The awkward grammar of the ending at v. 8 and allusions to the resurrection (9:9; 14:28; 16:7) point to the possibility that the author intended to include a final coda. (It has also been suggested that the final leaf of the original manuscript has been lost, leaving the text incomplete.) A gospel without an appearance of the resurrected Jesus strikes many readers as anticlimactic. The longer ending supplies what is lacking in the shorter ending, perhaps having been added by another writer who had read Matthew and Luke. Mary Magdalene meets Jesus and brings the good news to the eleven. For this reason, she is often called the apostle to the apostles.

Those who believe, Jesus says, will not only cast out demons, speak in tongues, and heal the sick, but will also pick up serpents and drink poison without being harmed (16:15–18). Is this intended to be descriptive and applicable to the eleven alone, or is it prescriptive and therefore incumbent on all believers? A number of small churches in Appalachia elevate this text virtually to the level of a sacrament, encouraging their members as the Holy Spirit moves them to handle snakes as a sign of authentic faith. Given the nature of Jesus' commissioning, then, some readers may thus be perfectly content with one of the shorter endings.

# Matthew

| | |
|---|---|
| 1:1–2:23 | The genealogy, birth, and infancy of Jesus |
| 3:1–25:46 | Jesus' public ministry |
| 3:1–4:25 | Baptism, temptation, and proclamation of the Kingdom |
| 5:1–7:29 | The Sermon on the Mount |
| 8:1–9:38 | Deeds of power |
| 10:1–42 | The missionary discourse |
| 11:1–12:50 | Mounting resistance |
| 13:1–52 | The parable discourse |
| 13:53–17:27 | Confrontation, confession, revelation, and Passion predictions |
| 18:1–35 | The "Church" discourse |
| 19:1–20:34 | Questions and controversy |
| 21:1–22:45 | The triumphal entry and the cleansing of the Temple |
| 23:1–25:46 | The final discourse |
| 26:1–27:66 | The Passion Narrative |
| 26:1–16 | Conspiracy against Jesus and anointing at Bethany |
| 26:17–75 | Last Supper, betrayal, arrest, denial |
| 27:1–13 | Trial of Jesus and death of Judas |
| 27:14–66 | Crucifixion and burial |
| 28:1–20 | The Resurrection and the Great Commission |

By one informal measure—space devoted to it in the classic *Bartlett's Familiar Quotations*—the Gospel of Matthew has exercised a greater influence on the English-speaking world than any other book in the New Testament. Its outsized role in the church's teaching and preaching begins long before its translation into English or any other language. It usually appears at the head of canonical lists in the ancient church, and it is quoted more frequently than the other three gospels.

Jewish and Gentile Christians alike found in it a valuable witness to the life of Jesus. Its length and organization, including five substantial discourses, made it the most convenient and inclusive instrument for catechesis. Non-religious readers as well have found it to be a source of ethical, aesthetic, and even political inspiration. That is not to say that assessments of its legacy are uniform or uniformly positive. In short, Matthew's gospel furnishes admirers and critics alike with an embarrassment of riches.

Matthew is listed as one of the twelve apostles and identified as a tax collector (Matt. 9:9; 10:3; Mark 3:18; Luke 6:15; the tax collector in Mark 2:14 and Luke 5:27 is called Levi). The earliest discussion of Matthew's gospel mentions that he had compiled Jesus' teachings in Hebrew and "interpreted" them but leaves unclear if this is only a characterization of Matthew's literary style as "Jewish." If the author relies on Mark in writing his gospel, its date of composition would fall at a very late point in the apostle's life. While scholars are uncertain about the attribution of Matthean authorship, it is widely agreed that the writer is a Jewish Christian. Few Gentiles would have the facility with the Hebrew or Aramaic language evinced in the gospel or the familiarity with the political and ideological conflicts between various Jewish groups in the first century. The smooth Greek prose is that of someone with native proficiency, thus the author may be a Jew of the Diaspora. In Jesus' commendation of "every scribe who has been trained for the kingdom of heaven" (13:52), some scholars have discerned a sly self-description inserted by the author, but this is no more than an educated guess.

Palestine has been suggested as the location of the intended audience, though most scholars place them in Syria, the home of authors familiar with Matthew's gospel early in the second century such as Ignatius of Antioch. An Antiochene setting would fit with the consensus that the audience consists largely of Jewish Christians. Occasional indications of openness to God-fearing Gentiles may indicate their presence alongside Jewish believers (e.g., 4:15; 15:21–28, where the Canaanite woman successfully gets Jesus to throw "crumbs" to the "dogs" not of the house of Israel; and 28:19, where the disciples are sent to "all nations"). Antioch was home to a large Jewish population, and the Jewish Christian community there was divided over the extent of Torah-observance required of

Gentile converts (Acts 11:19–30; Gal. 2:11–19), a concern that may be reflected in debates about the law in Matthew.

Author and audience alike are embedded within the robust sectarian milieu of first-century Judaism. Judea and Galilee in Jesus' day were divided between rival parties. The Pharisees placed a special emphasis on the implementation of Mosaic law in all areas of life. The Sadducees oversaw affairs at the temple in Jerusalem. The Zealots sought political independence from Rome, and while they did not constitute a formal "party," their willingness to achieve their ends through armed struggle augmented their influence. And in the desert near the Dead Sea, the Essenes viewed all other groups as having fatally compromised the ancestral faith. After the destruction of the temple in 70 CE and the exodus of many Jews from Jerusalem, the intramural quarrels continue in the synagogues of the Diaspora as well as in Palestine. Christians enter the fray as one more Jewish sect participating in the debates that shaped Jewish life. With the Sadducees, Zealots, and Essenes relegated to the margins of Jewish society, the Christians with their Jesus-centered piety and the Pharisees with their claim to be Moses' successors as custodians of the law were the primary rivals vying for supremacy in Jewish religious affairs late in the first century. This atmosphere accounts for the prominent role played by the Pharisees in Matthew as well as for the rancor which characterizes their clashes with Jesus. The author's purpose in telling the story of Jesus as he tells it is to expound and validate their claim that Jesus is the Messiah whose life, death, and resurrection usher in the kingdom of heaven in accordance with the Scriptures, and that his mission and the mission he bequeathed to his disciples represent not the abolition of the law but its consummate fulfillment (5:17).

In addition to this political and religious context that is reflected in the text, Matthew's use of sources indicates a date of composition in the 80s. He relies on Mark's gospel, written ca. 70, and is in turn alluded to by writers early in the second century. By means of redactional analysis of his use of Mark, his incorporation of sayings material from "Q" shared with Luke, and the addition of distinctive material found nowhere else (conventionally designated "M" material) at the beginning, in the middle, and again at the end of his gospel, it is possible to appreciate his attempts at accomplishing his literary and theological objectives.

## THE BIRTH AND INFANCY OF JESUS

The first and most obvious addition that Matthew has made to Mark is the nativity account that takes up the first two chapters. None of the stories have parallels in the other gospels. The only shared material is in the genealogy (Matt. 1:1–17), which is found also in Luke but with numerous differences. While it may not be the most effective way to grab the reader's attention, the genealogy situates Jesus, "the Messiah, the son of David, the son of Abraham," within the long history of Israel from the patriarchs, through the monarchy and the Babylonian exile, and down to the time of his "father" Joseph. Its structure also insinuates that Jesus was born at an auspicious moment in that history. Most surprising is the inclusion of five women. Do they have anything in common? Tamar, Rahab, Ruth, and Bathsheba risk the taint of impropriety (of a sexual nature), but in so doing they play crucial roles in Jesus' family history and also foreshadow Mary's role in the story of Jesus' unusual birth.

Mary plays a smaller role in Matthew's nativity story than does Joseph (1:18–25). To her future husband's consternation, she is found to be with child prior to their marriage. Early critics of Christianity spread the rumor that Mary had been raped by a Roman soldier named Panthera (Origen, *Cels.* 1.32; in his epic *Jerusalem*, William Blake has Joseph forgive Mary when she admits to an illicit affair). An angel comes to Joseph in a dream before he can end their betrothal to allay his fears, inform him that the child is conceived "from the Holy Spirit," and prophesy that they will name him Jesus, "for he will save his people from their sins" (the Hebrew name *Yeshua* means "the Lord saves"). Matthew then comments with the first of fourteen "fulfillment citations." This term refers to the author's habit of narrating an event from Jesus' life and then employing a variation of the formula "all this took place to fulfill what had been spoken by the Lord/written by the prophet," followed by a quotation from the Hebrew Bible (Soares-Prabhu 1976). Similar formulas are used on occasion elsewhere (e.g., Mark 14:49; John 12:38) but not with the same consistency. It is not the only literary device by which the fulfillment theme surfaces in the text but it is certainly the most conspicuous. Any study Bible will identify the biblical texts quoted by Matthew in the footnotes, enabling the reader to examine them in their original context and assess the extent to which he is presupposing and building on it, ignoring it, or creatively reconceptualizing it for literary or theological purposes and in accordance with themes and motifs in evidence elsewhere in the gospel.

Specifically, the author states that the birth of Jesus fulfills Isa. 7:14 ("Look, the virgin shall conceive and bear a son, and they shall name him Emmanuel"). This is odd for multiple reasons, beyond the obvious ones having to do with biology. It is often pointed out that Matthew here quotes from the Septuagint, which renders the Hebrew *almah* (young woman) as *parthenos* (virgin), thus attaching the notion of sexual inexperience to the original term that lacks it. In this way, it is argued, the doctrine of the virgin birth results from a translation error that Matthew overlooks in his reliance on the Greek version and in his zeal to portray Jesus as the Christ by applying messianic prophecies to his biography. But this analysis itself overlooks more complicated aspects of the text. First, Isa. 7:14 was not considered a messianic prophecy by contemporary Jews. Second, if Matthew was not limiting himself to traditional prooftexts, then he presumably could have adduced any text of his own choosing, and yet he chooses one that on its face seems to be decisively disconfirmed in short order. That is to say, the prophecy states that "they shall name him Emmanuel" (1:23), and two verses later the narrator reports that they "named him Jesus"! It is not because but in spite of the name that he chooses Isa. 7:14. He must have found something else of significance in it, namely, the mention of the virgin conceiving. He matches the Scripture to his view of Jesus and not the other way around. Modern readers may mistakenly assume that a miraculous birth was either necessary or sufficient for proving the messianic status of Jesus. And the Isaiah text by itself would constitute weak evidence for the claim that Jesus was virginally conceived unless, that is, one already thought he was virginally conceived before reading it. Why the early Christians believe this about Jesus is unclear. Matthew's narrative indicates he is not inventing it but, rather, reflecting a pre-existing conviction held by some Christians before he writes his gospel (Brown 1973: 61–66).

It is not the Scriptures but a star in the east that points the Magi to the newborn king (2:1–12). Parallels in this episode to David and Moses contribute to the scriptural texture of Matthew's emerging Christology. Bethlehem, the city of David where the king was anointed by Samuel, is the site of his birth, unsettling the Idumean ruler Herod, who had been appointed "king of the Jews" by the Romans in 40 BCE. Feigning a desire to offer him worship, Herod tries unsuccessfully to enlist the Magi in his attempt to find the prophesied king. Before they resume their journey—celebrated in the poetry of W. B. Yeats and T. S. Eliot and described in legends recounted by Marco Polo—they pay homage to Jesus. On the basis of the number of gifts they bring, Christian tradition usually assumes there were three of them and gives them various names, most commonly Caspar, Melchior, and Balthasar.

Another angel warns Joseph to seek refuge in Egypt to avoid the murderous rage of Herod at being duped by the Magi (2:13–18). Many scholars doubt the historicity of the Slaughter of the Holy Innocents, as Herod's policy of killing all the boys in Bethlehem under two years old is commonly known, suggesting that the story is a haggadic midrash on the Moses story in which Matthew offers creative "commentary" on Scripture in story form. It is indeed difficult to imagine such a horror going unremarked by contemporaries until one recalls that the demography of first-century Bethlehem would make the number of deaths in any such massacre quite small—perhaps as few as ten—and not the inflated figures found in Byzantine tradition. Liturgical commemoration of "Childermas" often features hymns such as the "Coventry Carol" celebrating the Holy Innocents as the first Christian martyrs, and the main character in Albert Camus's *The Fall* says that Jesus allows himself to be crucified since they had been murdered in his place.

When the family returns to Israel upon hearing of Herod's death and settles in Galilee at Nazareth (2:19–23), Matthew follows Mark's narrative and moves forward in time to the appearance of John the Baptist preparing the way for Jesus.

## THE PUBLIC MINISTRY OF JESUS: FROM THE JORDAN TO JERUSALEM

The public ministry of Jesus begins, as in all four gospels, with his encounter with John the Baptist (3:11–17). It is in this episode that the reader sees the first of many Matthean tweaks made to Mark's narrative. Matthew describes John's reluctance to baptize Jesus, protesting that their roles should be reversed. Submitting to the baptism of John might be seen as an acknowledgement that the Baptist is the master and Jesus is the disciple, an awkward implication given Jesus' status for Matthew's readers which this exchange may be meant to address. This potential embarrassment is considered strong evidence in favor of its historicity, since the early church would not have made up an episode requiring additional explanation. Acts (18:24–25; 19:1–7) reports that there were followers of John who had never heard of Jesus, and as early as the second century, their respective followers could view one another with mutual suspicion. Devotees of John the Baptist included the Mandaeans, who practiced a heterodox form of Judaism and regarded as holy writ the eighth-century *Book of John*. This text features combative dialogues in Aramaic between John and Jesus, who is presented as an apostate aiming to create a new religion. In Matthew, by contrast, John agrees to baptize Jesus when he explains that it is necessary "to fulfill all righteousness."

Matthew expands Mark's temptation scene by adding the familiar back-and-forth between Jesus and Satan (4:1–11). Prior to the temptation, Jesus is conspicuously passive. At the baptism scene, he is largely acted upon and spoken about, and in his only lines he insists on being baptized by John. It is under the influence of the Holy Spirit that Jesus finds his voice. Satan phrases the temptations as conditional clauses—"If you are the Son of God" (4:3, 6)—and his allusions to Scripture give Jesus the occasion to prove his identity and demonstrate his bona fides as an authoritative interpreter of Torah, a posture he will assume in Matt. 5:17–48. Early commentators draw parallels between Jesus' time in the wilderness following the baptism with the story of Elijah (1 Kgs. 19:8), but it is more often Moses to whom he will be likened throughout the gospel.

Each of the Synoptic Gospels introduces the public phase of Jesus' career in roughly the same manner. Jesus returns from his time in the wilderness ready to begin his ministry in earnest, preaching a message of repentance in preparation for the kingdom of heaven, calling disciples to follow him, and healing the sick. Matthew expands the Markan narrative by inserting five major discourses (5:1–7:29; 10:1–42; 13:1–52; 18:1–35; 23:1–25:46). Most of the teaching in these discourses is classified as Q or M material.

(1) *The Sermon on the Mount* (5:1–7:29). Few speeches ever delivered have reached a more far-flung or diverse audience than the

Sermon on the Mount. John Winthrop and his fellow Puritans strove to live out Jesus' teachings as they founded the Massachusetts Bay Colony in the hopes it would be a shining "city upon on a hill" (5:14). Leo Tolstoy was profoundly moved by his reading of the Sermon, which led him to embrace a form of Christian anarchism and to regard any faith not guided by its literal commands as a form of "Pseudo-Christianity." Mahatma Gandhi likewise drew on the injunction to "turn the other cheek" (5:38–39) in formulating his doctrine of non-violent resistance, saying that he wished Christians paid more attention to the teachings of Jesus here than to Paul in his letters. Dietrich Bonhoeffer looked to the Sermon as an antidote to "cheap grace" and as the inspiration for a life of radical discipleship. Hong Xiuquan claimed to be God's younger son and to have secured the blessings announced by his older brother in the Beatitudes by establishing a utopian community with its capital at Nanking early in the Taiping Rebellion (1850–1864), one of the bloodiest civil wars ever fought.

Whether it was delivered in its current form or compiled by the author, countless readers have turned to it for guidance even as they have disagreed as to its essential nature (Greenman *et al.* 2007). Is it closer to the "original" than Luke's "Sermon on the Plain" (Luke 6:17–49)? Does it constitute a new law that functions for Christians as Torah does for Jews? Is it a political manifesto or does it concern purely spiritual matters? Do its principles apply only to individuals or should they guide affairs of state? If the former, are Jesus' commands to be taken literally and by all would-be disciples, as a guide to attaining the perfection that characterizes their heavenly father (5:48)? Or do they merely represent "counsels of perfection" that lead the believer in the pursuit of a holy life in imitation of Christ but are not strictly obligatory for salvation? Does Jesus set out an impossible standard by design, so as to bring to light human weakness and thus accentuate the need for grace and the justification that comes only by faith? Are its stringent requirements so thoroughly informed by an eschatological outlook that they amount to an "interim ethics" never intended to apply to human relations over the long run?

Jesus begins his inaugural address with a series of Beatitudes, statements describing dispositions toward God or fellow humans that make one "blessed" or "happy" (5:1–12; the Vulgate translation *beatus* is the source of the traditional terminology and not the fact that Jesus commends various "attitudes" adopted by his followers). Many of the Beatitudes manifest the theme of reversal seen later in Matthew (20:26–28; 23:11): the meek and poor inherit kingdoms, the mourners receive comfort, the hungry are filled. Of special note is the way in which the qualities lauded at the Sermon's outset correspond to those required for admission to the temple (e.g., Ps. 15:1–5; 24:3–6). Just as participation in the Jewish liturgy presupposes moral uprightness, so also does life in the kingdom ushered in by Jesus. Furthermore, the Beatitudes illuminate Matthew's socio-cultural context as well. That mercy (Matt. 5:7) is highly prized by Jesus is seen in his repeated references to Hosea 6:6 (cf. Matt. 9:13; 12:7), a text also cited in rabbinic texts that describe Jewish worship after the destruction of the temple. Later warnings about persecution (10:16–23; 23:34–36) also suggest that Matthew's readers would have welcomed the consolation promised in the concluding Beatitudes (5:10–11).

Although it has become a cliché to refer to Matthew as "the Jewish Gospel," the image of Jesus going up on a mountain—where so many other momentous events take place (e.g., the temptations, the transfiguration, and the Great Commission)—and, after the manner of Moses, proceeding to issue authoritative instruction in the form of five substantial texts suggests that there is some merit to this characterization. Unlike Moses at Sinai, however, Jesus does not receive the law but, rather, reveals its decisive interpretation. Matthew's readers would almost certainly have heard the charge that Christians nullify Torah in their belief and worship. Jesus' declaration that he has come not to abolish the law and the prophets but to fulfill them speaks directly to this accusation (5:17; the theory that 5:19 contains a veiled critique of Paul and his "law-free" mission to the Gentiles is intriguing but without a firm basis). Jesus actually heightens the demands of the Jewish law in the six "antitheses" that follow (5:21–48), each time saying "you have heard that it was said" and quoting Scripture before proceeding to issue authoritative commentary on the text with the formula "but I say unto you." No passage more vividly illustrates Matthew's Christological presentation of Jesus as a "new Moses."

The rest of the Sermon contains instruction on such matters as almsgiving, fasting, and prayer, including the version of the Lord's Prayer most commonly recited over the centuries (6:9–13; the KJV relies on manuscripts that add the final line drawn from

1 Chron. 29:11, reflecting a form of the prayer in circulation when the *Didache* was written at the end of the first century). Jesus seeks to inculcate an ethos of radical trust and dependence on God that, when adopted, will banish anxiety (6:25–34). Well-known phrases abound: e.g., "do not let your left hand know what your right hand is doing" (6:3); "lay not up for yourselves treasures upon earth, where moth and rust doth corrupt" (6:19 KJV); "Take therefore no thought for the morrow . . . Sufficient unto the day is the evil thereof" (6:34 KJV); "pearls before swine" (7:6).

(2) *The Missionary Discourse* (10:1–42). This discourse begins with a list of the Twelve whom Jesus has summoned to perform miracles and proclaim the good news but also warned about the hostility they will meet. He sends them out "like sheep into the midst of wolves," but they are to be "wise as serpents and innocent as doves" (10:16). They are not to be surprised at the upheaval their preaching will cause even within their own families. "I have not come to bring peace," he says, "but a sword" (10:34). Neither should they be afraid because they will be rewarded in heaven if they steadfastly bear witness to Jesus.

Many scholars see in Matt. 10:23 a key insight into the historical Jesus' self-consciousness. He tells the disciples that they "will not have gone through all the towns of Israel before the Son of Man comes." If this refers to Jesus' "second coming" spoken of in the early church, its apparent non-occurrence is a sign that the church did not fabricate this saying. It might also indicate that Jesus saw himself as ushering in a new age and yet died, deluded and unsuccessful in achieving his objectives. Only Matthew records this statement. Is this how the author understood the matter, and if so, did he see it as a failed prediction? Was his community in the 80s still in eager expectation of an imminent Parousia? Or did Jesus have in mind a different set of events that would transpire? The apocalyptic imagery in the fifth discourse raises the same interpretive questions.

(3) *The Parable Discourse* (13:1–52). Any doubts John the Baptist may have entertained about Jesus' identity as "the one who is to come" are put to rest by the reports of his miracles and his message, as well as the mixed reception he has been given (11:2–19). The positive and negative reactions to Jesus provide a subtext of many of the parables that comprise Matthew 13. Matthew excises only a few of Mark's

parables and also shares several in common with Luke (e.g., Matt. 7:16–20, 24–27; 11:16–18; 18:12–14; 22:1–10; 24:45–51; 25:14–30). Additional parables that appear only in Matthew, both in this discourse and elsewhere, include:

- The Wheat and the Tares (13:24–30). Jesus provides a point-by-point allegorical interpretation of this parable in response to a request from the disciples (Matt. 13: 36–43). In the setting of the early church, it represents an attempt at understanding why some of Jesus' fellow Jews responded to the preaching of the gospel and others did not. It has also been invoked in arguments for religious toleration and against compulsion in spiritual matters on the grounds that only God can sort out true from false belief.
- Hidden Treasure (13:44). One of the briefest of Jesus' parables, it sounds a similar note as the Pearl of Great Price. Whether or not the buyer of a field is entitled to keep any treasure found in it was a subject of rabbinic commentary. Whether the potential buyer is obliged to inform the seller about the treasure has been a subject of ethical debate. Whether such questions might miss Jesus' point merits consideration from a literary and theological perspective.
- Pearl of Great Price (13:45–46). Medieval interpreters frequently take the pearl to represent chastity or the monastic life more generally. One part of the Mormon canon of Scripture, entitled *The Pearl of Great Price*, contains stories about Abraham and Moses as well as a "retranslation" of Matthew 24. John Steinbeck's novel *The Pearl* is often regarded as a parable that is in turn based on this parable.
- The Fishing Net (13:47–48). Jesus' explanation that the good and bad fish will be sorted out "at the end of the age," when angels will separate the evil from the righteous, anticipates the apocalyptic urgency of the Sheep and the Goats.
- The Unmerciful Servant (18:23–35). This parable is similar in theme to the Parable of the Two Debtors in Luke 7:41–43. It immediately follows Peter's question and Jesus' reply that he should be prepared to forgive a brother "seventy times seven" times and is often considered a dramatization of Jesus' command to forgive in Matt. 6:14–15. Considering the enormous size of the

servant's debt, the fact that he is handed over to be tortured until it is repaid is harrowing.

- The Laborers in the Vineyard (20:1–16). Insofar as the landowner is the central character, some interpreters prefer to call this the Parable of the Good Employer. In Christian theology as well as in the hadith of Islamic tradition, the most popular interpretation of this parable has to do with periods of history and dispensations in God's dealings with humanity. It has also been applied to relations between Jews and Gentiles in God's providence, compared thematically to the Prodigal Son (Luke 15:11–32), and brought to bear on discussion of socioeconomic issues. The final line—"the last will be first, and the first will be last"—recapitulates the theme of reversal found in the Beatitudes. Whether "first" and "last" are meant chronologically or hierarchically is unclear.

- The Two Sons (21:28–32). Jesus tells this parable to convict the chief priests and elders of hypocrisy and bad faith. It is one in a series of controversy stories pitting Jesus against the Jewish leadership in Jerusalem.

- The Wedding Feast (22:11–14). Many scholars speculate that vv. 11–14 may have originated as a separate parable that was joined to vv. 1–10, which parallels Luke 14:16–24. The treatment of the guest ejected into "the outer darkness" for not wearing the proper clothing has bewildered interpreters. He is among the "many [who] are called" but not among the "few [who] are chosen." John Calvin interprets this pronouncement in connection with the doctrine of predestination.

- The Wise and Foolish Virgins (25:1–13). This parable, also known as the Ten Bridesmaids, was one of the most popular throughout the medieval period, presented often in the form of a mystery play. Early interpreters frequently connect it to the Song of Solomon, reading the parable through the lens of the marriage metaphor for the covenant relationship between God and Israel. Manuscripts that add "when the Son of Man comes" at the end of v. 13 indicate that early copyists were cognizant of the eschatological context in which it appears. Depictions of the virgins in stone adorn many cathedrals (e.g., Notre-Dame, Amiens, Strasbourg), and Bach's cantata *Wachet auf* ("Sleepers Awake") sets to music an older hymn based on the parable.

- The Sheep and the Goats (25:31–46). This is the last of Jesus' teachings before the Last Supper narrative commences. It highlights the importance of what come to be called corporal works of mercy. The emphasis on the treatment of "the least of these" is central to the Social Gospel movement. Numerous parallels with the missionary discourse in Matt. 10:1–42 suggest that Jesus may be thinking primarily of the disciples he has sent out to preach the gospel rather than the poor in general.

One might add other parabolic images and comparisons to this list (e.g., 7:6, 15, 16–20). Many are explicitly said to illustrate some aspect of the kingdom of heaven. Matthew appears to blunt somewhat the sharp edge of Jesus' saying about the purpose of the parables in Mark (Matt. 13:13; Mark 4:12).

(4) *The "Church" Discourse* (18:1–35). This discourse opens with the disciples' question about who will be the greatest in the kingdom of heaven. Jesus upends their expectations by replying that they must become like children and proceeds to outline a community ethic that prioritizes humility and mercy. Yet even the best of intentions will not completely prevent disputes from arising among the brothers and sisters in Christ in Matthew's audience. The process for resolving conflicts in the community in Matt. 18:15–20 follows the stipulations for judicial procedures laid out in Deut. 19:15 and later informs protocols relating to excommunication and reconciliation. Of the four gospel authors, only Matthew (16:18; 18:17) has Jesus refer to a "church" (*ekklēsia*). The status of the church is more exalted than one might expect from Jesus' comments on relations within the community. A local assembly of believers becomes the site of something more sublime when Jesus says, "For where two or three are gathered in my name, I am among them" (18:20). His statement recalls rabbinic texts that describe the *Shekinah*, the divine presence, as dwelling wherever two or three men sit together to discuss Torah (*m. 'Abot* 3.2–3). In effect, Matthew identifies Jesus with the *Shekinah*, articulating in a different mode the claim that Jesus is Emmanuel, "God with us" (1:23).

This is an astonishing claim not only at the level of Christology but of ecclesiology as well. Ecclesiology is the formal term for theological reflection on the nature of the church. Jesus says that the church's decisions on such matters as the granting of forgiveness for wrongdoing will be binding on earth and in heaven (18:18; cf. John 20:23), echoing in almost identical words the charge he gives to Peter two chapters earlier at Caesarea Philippi. After Peter confesses Jesus as the Messiah, Matthew makes a critical addition to the episode as it appears in Mark 8:27–29. Jesus congratulates him for his perspicuity and adds:

> You are Peter [*Petros*], and on this rock [*petra*] I will build my church, and the gates of Hades will not prevail against it. I will give you the keys of the kingdom of heaven, and whatever you bind on earth will be bound in heaven, and whatever you loose on earth will be loosed in heaven.
>
> (Matt. 16:18–19)

Jesus's response, involving a bilingual pun on Peter's name, is regarded by Roman Catholics as the clearest biblical warrant for the disciplinary functions and teaching office exercised by the papacy. Protestants prefer to interpret the "rock" on which the church is built not as Peter himself but the faith made manifest in his confession. In the symbolism of the keys, which become a standard element in Petrine iconography and in popular presentations of Peter standing guard at heaven's pearly gates, many scholars discern an allusion to the ancient Israelite practice of the king granting authority to a prime minister who, as holder of "the key of the house of David," is deputized to make binding decisions on his behalf (Isa. 22:20–23).

Peter's elevation is part of a larger pattern wherein Matthew "rehabilitates" the imperceptive disciples featured in Mark and depicts Jesus looking ahead to prepare trustworthy leaders for the church that will come together after his death and resurrection. While Matthew does not entirely eliminate their failures, they fare somewhat better in his narrative. The disciples appear to comprehend the parables and to recognize Jesus as the Son of God, and many references to their lack of understanding and hardness of heart have been deleted (13:52; 14:33; Mark 6:52; 8:17; 9:6, 10). By entrusting them with the power to bind and loose and with the mission to teach the nations in the gospel's closing lines, the Matthean Jesus licenses teachers qualified to guide the church through internal conflict and in its theological clashes with the scribes and Pharisees in the years after his death.

(5) *The Final Discourse* (23:1–25:46). Prior to the "apocalyptic discourse," which immediately precedes the events of Jesus' final night before the crucifixion, Matthew includes a lengthy attack on the scribes and the Pharisees that features some of the harshest rhetoric in the New Testament (23:1–37). They have just tested him with a question about "the greatest commandment" (22:34–40). Rabbinic commentary is replete with discussion of the relative importance of the "light" and "heavy" commands in Torah, of which there are 613 according to Jewish tradition (248 positive injunctions and 365 prohibitions). While it represented a certain democratizing impulse, the eagerness of the Pharisees to extend certain aspects of the law to the whole population nevertheless may have been experienced as a burden by the people of the land. Jesus proceeds to excoriate them for their failure to match their words with deeds. Accusations of hypocrisy were a standard component of religious and philosophical polemic in the first century, as was the charge that one's opponents were lovers of glory (23:5–7, 13, 23–30; Johnson 1989). Intra-Jewish debates from this period later included in the Mishnah suggest that Jesus was not the only critic of ostentation in matters of piety.

In the first section of the apocalyptic discourse (24:1–36), Matthew largely follows Mark 13 in focusing on the signs that will portend the coming of the Son of Man in the end-times. To this material he has added sayings and parables that stress the vigilance as they await the Parousia (24:37–25:46). When will it arrive? No one knows, "neither the angles of heaven, nor the Son, but only the Father" (24:36). Because of this uncertainty, it is all the more crucial that they remain always ready. Maintaining a robust spirit of eschatological expectation may have proven difficult in a post-70 Jewish milieu wary of the apocalyptic leanings of the groups that had fomented rebellion and invited the wrath of the Romans. The final parable in the discourse suggests that, for Matthew, readiness consists not in speculating about the timetable for the Son of Man's return but in cultivating acts of mercy.

The Passion narrative begins with Matthew noting that Jesus had finished his teaching (26:1). That the author intends to depict Jesus in the guise of a rabbinic teacher is amply demonstrated by the manner in which these five discourses contribute to the gospel's overarching literary structure. And yet he suggests that it is a mistake to view him as merely a great teacher and nothing more. While Markan characters consistently and indiscriminately refer to Jesus as "Teacher" or "Rabbi," curiously it is his enemies who call him "Teacher" in Matthew, and only Judas Iscariot addresses him as "Rabbi" (26:25, 49). Nowhere does he play the part of the rabbi propounding noble ethical truths more eloquently than in the Sermon on the Mount, but to overlook the Christological implications of Jesus' repeated assertion of his prerogative to supersede Moses as an interpreter of the law is to miss the forest for the trees.

Matthew's multifaceted Christological portrait does not come fully into focus until the Passion account runs its course (Matera 2001: 121–49). The author follows the Markan sequence, omitting very little and adding only a few episodes. The conspiracy to kill Jesus and Judas' plan to betray him, the anointing at Bethany, the Last Supper, the prayer in Gethsemane, the arrest, the trial before Caiaphas the high priest, and Peter's denial closely adhere to the Markan source in content and detail, though with unique touches that cohere with Matthean themes. Jesus forbids his disciples from resisting the mob that has come to arrest him since, he says, he could call on God to send twelve legions of rescuing angels were he not intent on fulfilling the Scriptures (27:50–54; the writer of the hymn "Ten Thousand Angels" says he later learned that "Seventy-Two Thousand Angels" would have been more accurate). This intimation of power complements the royal image implicit in the homage paid by the Magi (2:12), the many references to Jesus as "Son of David" (1:1; 9:27; 12:23; 15:22; 20: 30–31; 21:9, 15; 22:42), and his assumption of "all authority" in the Great Commission (28:18). An account of a repentant Judas attempting to return the blood money and committing suicide when he is rebuffed likewise illustrates the divinely ordained nature of the events surrounding Jesus' death (27:3–10). Later writers that portray Judas in a more positive light as the only disciple that truly understands Jesus and is willing to play an indispensable role in salvation history, such as Jose Luis Borges ("Three Versions of Judas") and Robert Graves (*King Jesus*), disregard Jesus' remark about his betrayer that "it would have been better . . . not to have been born" (26:24).

Recurring self-references to the Son of Man (16:27–28; 17:12, 22; 20:18, 28; 26:2, 24, 45) remind the reader that, on the way to his enthronement, the Son of David must nevertheless walk a path of suffering. That suffering takes place at the hands of the Romans after he is handed over by the Jewish authorities. Prompted to action after a disturbing dream (later re-imagined in a long poem by Charlotte Brontë), Pilate's wife warns her husband to "have nothing to do with that innocent man" (27:19). When the crowds reject his proposal to release Jesus and call for Barabbas instead, Pilate "washes his hands" of Jesus' blood (27:20–24).

Should the reader treat this depiction as a negative comment on Pilate's cowardly evasion of responsibility? To the contrary, it is often argued that Pilate is portrayed sympathetically by Matthew in order to shift the blame to the Jews. Positive assessments emerge in the patristic period and later, especially in the Ethiopian and Coptic churches where he and his wife are venerated as saints, and in Mikhail Bulgakov's surrealist *The Master and Margarita*, where he dotes on his dog and suffers from debilitating migraines. But older sources paint a picture of Pilate as a hard-nosed Roman governor who looks quite different from the vacillating figure anxious to placate the Jews under his rule at the trial (e.g., Josephus, *Ant.* 18.85–90; *J. W.* 2.175–177). In an earlier incident reported by Josephus (*J. W.* 2.169–174) in which he had offended the sensitivities of the Jews of Jerusalem by introducing engraved golden shields, however, Pilate actually backs down for fear of unduly antagonizing the populace and causing an uproar that would cause trouble for him in Rome by revealing his corruption in other areas (cf. Philo, *Legat.* 302). Although many details cannot be confirmed, first-century sources lend credence to the general account provided by Matthew.

The response of "all the people" to Pilate—"His blood be on us and on our children!" (27:25)—has come to be known as the blood curse. Its legacy is an unhappy one. It has been invoked through the centuries to justify persecution of the Jews as "Christ-killers" guilty of deicide. Matthew may be interpreting the events of 70 CE in Jerusalem as the consequence visited on the children of those who had called out for the death of Jesus. He was not the only Jew to search for a theological explanation for this unparalleled catastrophe, nor was he alone in blaming other Jews for it. But since his gospel has survived, his explanation has remained available to those who would misinterpret it as a statement of the responsibility of all Jews at all times for Jesus' death. It may also be that Matthew sees in the cry of the people an unwitting double entendre (Cargal 1991). Far from calling down a perennial curse on themselves, in Matthew's telling they may be, unawares, bearing witness to the truth of what Jesus had said about his "blood of the covenant" poured out "for many for the forgiveness of sins" (26:28; John 11:50–52 similarly sees Caiphas "prophesying" in spite of himself when he says that "it is better . . . to have one man die for the people than to have the whole nation destroyed").

To Mark's reference to the splitting of the temple curtain at the moment of Jesus' death, Matthew adds that, as a result of an earthquake, "many bodies of the saints who had fallen asleep were raised" (27:51–54). Ezekiel's vision of the dry bones coming back to life may be the inspiration for this apocalyptic imagery insofar as it offered a portent of a new beginning (Ezek. 37:1–14). Whereas return from exile is the new beginning announced by the prophet to Judea, in the case of Jesus and of the saints who emerge from their tombs, the fulfillment of this oracle will be more literal. At the sight of these remarkable phenomena, the centurion and his companions declare, "Truly this man was God's Son!" Their confession foreshadows the positive response of the Gentiles to whom Jesus sends the disciples with the good news in the Great Commission (Dahl 1976: 49). Having remained faithful to his calling as the Son of God to the very end, Jesus will be vindicated "on the third day" (2:15; 4:1–11; 14:33; 16:16; 26:63–66; 27:40–43).

## THE RESURRECTION: FROM THE EMPTY TOMB TO THE END OF THE AGE

Matthew comes closer than the other canonical gospels to depicting the moment of the resurrection. An earthquake occurs when the women come to the tomb and an angel "like lightning" descends from heaven to roll back the stone. As in Mark, the angel tells them to share the good news with the disciples in Galilee, but the women in Matthew, though afraid, leave with great joy. Jesus appears to them as they are on their way to deliver the message. Matthew also reports that the guards who were frightened by the angel told the chief priests of what they had seen. The chief priests devise one of many explanations to account for the rise of the resurrection faith, bribing the guards to say the body had been stolen.

The eleven finally encounter Jesus in the last five verses of the book (28:16–20). Their meeting is somewhat awkward. "When they saw him, they worshipped him," it says, "but some doubted." What did they "doubt"? That it was indeed Jesus before their eyes? That they should worship him? The verb (*distazō*) is used earlier when Peter briefly follows Jesus walking on the water but is admonished ("You of little faith") when he sinks (14:31). It can also mean "hesitate." Are they hesitant to approach him because, since their last meeting, they had all abandoned him? Their previous mountainside rendezvous with Jesus, at the transfiguration (17:1–8), similarly left the disciples simultaneously worshipful and confused.

Jesus moves quickly to focus their attention on the task at hand (28:19–20). With "all authority in heaven and on earth," he commands them:

> Go therefore and make disciples of all nations, baptizing them in the name of the Father and of the Son and of the Holy Spirit, and teaching them to obey everything I have commanded you. And remember, I am with you always, to the end of the age.

This mandate, traditionally called the Great Commission, brings the gospel to its conclusion.

The theological and literary significance of this ending is three-fold: (1) the baptismal formula employed in many Christian denominations is drawn from Jesus' instructions in this text, attested as early as the end of the first century in the *Didache* (7.1–3). It has also been cited as an early expression of the doctrine of the Trinity; (2) the Great Commission has served as a rallying cry for evangelistic undertakings around the world, especially after the World Missionary Conference held at Edinburgh in 1910. The disciples are now to make disciples of others, and patristic writers record various traditions about the disciples and the geographic regions they evangelized. Jesus' instructions here also mark a pivot of sorts, from preaching exclusively to "the lost sheep of the house of Israel" (10:5–6) to spreading the good news to "all nations," including Gentiles (cf. 23:13–14). The sending out of the disciples to the nations reverses the direction of witness found in Matt. 2:1–12, where the Magi come from far away to pay homage to the baby Jesus; and (3) the conclusion echoes the nativity accounts in one other way. Whereas the naming of Jesus in Matt. 1:23 is connected to the oracle of Isa. 7:14 and the name "Emmanuel," which, the narrator helpfully explains, means "God with us," Jesus' final words reassure the disciples, "I am with you always." The gospel thus begins and ends with the proclamation that the presence of God is in some sense specially mediated in the person of Jesus.

# Luke-Acts

| | |
|---|---|
| Luke 1:1–2:52 | The birth and childhood of Jesus |
| 3:1–9:50 | Jesus in Galilee |
| 3:1–4:13 | Baptism, genealogy, and testing |
| 4:14–30 | Rejection at Nazareth |
| 4:31–9:50 | Preaching, confrontation, and deeds of power |
| 9:51–19:27 | The travel narrative |
| 19:28–21:38 | Jesus in Jerusalem |
| 19:28–48 | The triumphal entry and the cleansing of the Temple |
| 20:1–21:4 | Mounting opposition |
| 21:5–38 | The final discourse |
| 22:1–23:56 | The Passion narrative |
| 22:1–13 | Conspiracy against Jesus and Passover preparations |
| 22:14–62 | Last Supper, prayer in Gethsemane, betrayal, arrest, denial |
| 22:63–23:25 | Trials before Pilate and Herod |
| 23:26–56 | Crucifixion and burial |
| 24:1–53 | The Resurrection and the Ascension |
| Acts 1:1–8:3 | The birth of the Church: growth and resistance |
| 1:1–26 | The Ascension and reconstituting the Twelve |
| 2:1–47 | Pentecost |
| 3:1–5:42 | Spreading the word in and around Jerusalem |
| 6:1–7 | Friction in the Messianic community |
| 6:8–8:3 | The testimony of Stephen |
| 8:4–15:35 | From Jerusalem to the Gentiles and back |
| 8:4–40 | Spreading the word in Samaria |
| 9:1–31 | The conversion of Saul |

*(continued)*

| | |
|---|---|
| *(continued)* | |
| 9:32–12:25 | Peter's preaching and the response of the Gentiles |
| 13:1–14:28 | Paul's first missionary journey |
| 15:1–35 | The Jerusalem Council |
| 15:36–28:31 | From Jerusalem to Rome |
| 15:36–18:21 | Paul's second missionary journey |
| 18:22–21:16 | Paul's third missionary journey; ministry in Ephesus |
| 21:17–23:35 | Conflict in Jerusalem |
| 24:1–26:32 | Trials in Caesarea |
| 27:1–28:31 | Journey to Rome |

Little is known about one of the most important authors of the New Testament, identified as Luke in references to and manuscripts of the third gospel in the second century. A "Luke" is mentioned in passing as a trusted co-worker of Paul in the letters (Col. 4:14; 2 Tim. 4:11; Philem. 24). Attempts to demonstrate that Luke "the beloved physician" is indeed the author of the gospel have occasionally focused on the usage of medical terminology, though the prevalence of animal terms has led others to observe waggishly that if the author was a doctor, he must have been a veterinarian. Byzantine tradition regards him as the first painter of icons, having produced images of Mary as well as Peter and Paul. (There are even ancient and medieval paintings of Luke painting the Virgin.) It is his literary artistry, however, that has had the larger impact. That legacy consists of the eponymous gospel and also the Acts of the Apostles. This two-volume work, conventionally designated Luke-Acts, comprises approximately one-fourth of the New Testament. Furthermore, Acts provides the earliest and most popular narrative purporting to describe the life of the early church in the first years after the resurrection of Jesus. (Few scholars endorse the theory that Luke also wrote the Pastoral Epistles as a third volume of his magnum opus.)

Differences in theological emphasis and expression and in biographical detail lead many scholars to doubt that Luke is the true author. Indeed, Luke nowhere evinces any awareness of Paul's letters. In the preface of the gospel (1:1–4), the unnamed author indicates that he was not an eyewitness to the events surrounding Jesus' ministry. Acts, on the other hand, includes a number of episodes referred to as the "we" passages, where the author recounts travels of Paul in the first person plural (16:10–18; 20:5–16; 21:1–18; 27:1–28:16), which seems to imply that he is a participant in at least a portion of the story he is telling. Whoever wrote the gospel also wrote its sequel, be it Luke or an anonymous author later in the first or early second century. They share a common literary style, thematic emphases, and dedicatee named in their opening lines. Given the weight attached to claims of apostolic testimony, witnessed in works in the name of Peter, Thomas, James, John, and others, the attribution of Lukan authorship in the absence of any other compelling reason for putting the name of a non-apostle on the two-volume work leads many scholars to give the good doctor the benefit of the doubt. The author writes in excellent Greek and is usually thought to be a Gentile that may have been attracted to Judaism before his conversion to Christianity. Beyond this, little can be said with certainty. The preface in Luke 1:1–4 supplies a few more clues to his vantage point on the events he narrates. As with the other gospels, here the author will be referred to as Luke if only as a matter of convenience.

Questions of authorship are naturally connected to questions about dating. Unless there is a significant chronological gap between the writing of the gospel and of Acts, the earliest possible date of composition is the early- or mid-60s, when early traditions place Paul's death under Nero. Paul is alive and well in Rome at the conclusion of Acts. Reasoning that Luke does not record Paul's death because it has not yet occurred, some scholars posit the mid-60s as the latest Acts could have been completed. This conflicts with other analyses that the gospel must be dated later because of its reliance on Mark, written ca. 70 CE. An early dating presupposes that a primary purpose of Acts is to provide a comprehensive account of Paul's life and that Luke's silence about his death therefore implies that it has not yet taken place. Paul is certainly a major character in Luke's narrative, but he is part of the larger story that begins in Judea and will not end in Rome but will extend "to the ends of the earth" (Acts 1:8). Some scholars date Luke-Acts well after the turn of the century, but the consensus is that it was completed in the 80s or 90s.

Were it not joined with Acts, discussion of the gospel's literary genre would include little more than the considerations involved with Matthew, Mark, and John. More than anything, Luke-Acts is an example of ancient historiography (Aune 1987: 77–115). Rather than simply record events, Luke attends to their connectedness by making explicit how one event necessarily leads to another. Most conspicuously, it is "necessary" that Jesus suffer and die and not a tragic mistake (Luke 9:22; 13:3; 22:37; 24:7, 26, 46; Luke's Jesus uses the verb *deî* in reference to his mission far more often than Matthew and Mark). Luke resembles other Greco-Roman and Hellenistic Jewish historians such as Thucydides, Dionysius of Halicarnassus, and Josephus in his liberal use of speeches that explicate these historical dynamics. By crafting rhetorically sophisticated speeches that fit the character and occasion, Luke is able to reiterate important themes, interpret key episodes, and offer unobtrusive commentary on the significance of the events recounted in the surrounding narrative through the voice of such characters as Mary, Zechariah, Anna and Simeon, Peter, Stephen, and Paul. Luke's work is also distinguished by its attention to chronology. His story does not take place "once upon a time" but, rather, in the midst of contemporary events at particular places and times. The story of Jesus is firmly rooted in the "non-biblical" world, and Luke takes pains to synchronize the birth of Jesus, the appearance of John the Baptist, and the itineraries of Peter and Paul with reference to the tenures of emperors, tetrarchs, high priests, and various Roman functionaries so that ancient and modern readers alike are able to situate them within a "public" history.

The opening preface is perhaps the most formal literary sign that Luke conceives of his task along the lines of other ancient historians (1:1–4):

Since many have undertaken to set down an orderly account of the events that have been fulfilled among us, just as they were handed on to us by those who from the beginning were eyewitnesses and servants of the word, I too decided, after investigating everything carefully from the very first, to write an orderly account for you, most excellent Theophilus, so that you may know the truth [*asphaleia*] concerning the things about which you've been instructed.

John mentions his purpose in writing (20:31), but Luke is the only one of the Synoptic Gospels to state his aims explicitly. Luke's preface provides critical insights into his audience and objectives.

What does the reader learn from this preface? First, Luke acknowledges that he is not the first to take up his subject in writing and that he has read "many" of these accounts as part of his research. He does not say how many he has read, how long they were, which parts of his story they paralleled, or who wrote them. Mark is among these accounts, as is Q or whatever source Luke shares with Matthew. Second, although he does not explicitly state what he thinks of these other accounts, one may infer that he finds them lacking in some respect. After all, there is little reason to produce such a substantial work if the job has already been done satisfactorily. Perhaps his intent to write an "orderly account" reflects some discontent with the way in which the story has heretofore been told. Third, all he says about the "events" about which he is writing is that they "have been fulfilled among us." He has learned about them from eyewitnesses, implying that he was not himself present "from the beginning." That these events "have been fulfilled" intimates that Luke sees them as the realization of promises and prophecies. The "us" among whom they have been fulfilled, moreover, refers to Luke and his reader(s), therefore he is not limiting his story to the days of Jesus' ministry but to current events, so to speak. His story will not end with the death and resurrection but will continue with the story of the early church in the ensuing years. Fourth, he is addressing Theophilus, a common Greek name among Jews and Gentiles. If Luke is playing with etymology, this may be a way of saying that his work is for any "lover of God." More likely, Theophilus is Luke's literary patron who is taking responsibility for the copying or distribution of his work to a broader audience. As he has been "instructed," it seems that he is already a Christian or undergoing catechesis.

Most importantly, Luke says that he wants to provide *asphaleia* concerning the contents of that instruction. Many versions render this term "truth," which gives the misleading impression that Luke fears his readers have been deceived. He might have used another word, *alētheia*, that he uses elsewhere and more literally means "truth (as opposed to lies)," but instead he uses a word that means "certainty" or "firmness." If his aim is to provide certainty, then understanding

Luke's purpose involves discovering the nature of the doubts he senses on the part of his readers. Insofar as Luke seeks to offer an explanation or defense of the instruction they have received in the form of a historical narrative, his work belongs to the genre of apologetic historiography (Sterling 1992: 311–93).

But what are those doubts and whence do they arise? Does Luke want to supply a brief for Paul's defense in Rome, where he is awaiting trial at the end of Acts? Is he writing an apology for Christians in Rome or in the wider empire, defending them against suspicion that their religion is socially subversive? Is he distinguishing them from the Jews who had recently fomented a rebellion and thus alleviating any fears that they posed a threat to the *Pax Romana*?

Aspects of Luke-Acts touch on each of these concerns. More fundamentally, however, Luke is cognizant of a theological challenge that might unsettle any Christian reader, whether Jewish or Gentile. At stake is nothing less than the integrity of God. The proclamation that God had acted to redeem Israel through a son, a messiah, who dies and rises from the grave was hardly what most Jews in the first century were expecting. Is God, then, an utterly unpredictable and unreliable deity whose appeal to Gentiles signals a concomitant rejection of Israel? The gospel would then be bad news for Jewish believers but also, if less obviously, for Gentiles who had placed their hopes in the God of Abraham, Isaac, and Jacob. Luke writes to reassure his readers that God has kept his promises made of old that not only would Abraham and his progeny be blessed, but that in him "all the families of the earth shall be blessed" (Gen. 12:3). The precise form of these blessings was the subject of vigorous debate in the Second Temple period, and the final clause of God's pledge often received less attention than the others. Jews and Gentiles often appear to have required little encouragement to think of their relations with God as separate but equal at best, as one sees in Acts and in Paul's letters (e.g., Romans 9–11). By re-narrating Israel's history, often in the speeches of characters such as Stephen and Paul (Acts 7; 13), Luke aims to demonstrate that the gospel has gone out to the Jews first but that the incorporation of Gentiles by God is not an afterthought in the plan of salvation. Throughout history, Jews and Gentiles alike have responded to God in faith and obedience as well as strayed from the path or ignored the call to obedience. This history continues in the story of Jesus and absorbs the reader in the "present" of the late first century.

In Luke's telling, the fulfillment of God's promises to Abraham takes place in continuity with the birth of the church that grows and spreads under the guidance of the Holy Spirit given at Pentecost (Acts 7:17; 13:23, 32; 26:6).

Concerns such as these were unavoidable wherever Theophilus called home, be it Antioch, Rome, or somewhere within the orbit of the Pauline mission in Greece among Gentiles who had received the good news. Theology ultimately counts for more than geography in situating Luke's audience and discerning his purposes in writing.

## THE GOSPEL

An analysis of Luke's editorial shaping of his narrative produces a greater appreciation of his socio-cultural context and of his authorial aims. Like Matthew, he develops the narrative inherited from Mark by augmenting it at the beginning, in the middle, and at the end, most substantively in the form a sequel that follows the movement started by Jesus for twenty-eight more chapters as it spreads throughout the Mediterranean.

### THE BIRTH AND CHILDHOOD OF JESUS

Luke's preface is only a brief introduction to the stories that take up the first two chapters. Nearly every element of every scene is unique to the author and thus labelled "L" material (Brown 1977: 235–499). Luke begins slightly earlier than the other gospels, with the parents of John the Baptist (1:5–25). Zechariah and Elizabeth are "righteous before God" but childless. When Zechariah enters the temple to perform his priestly duties, the angel Gabriel appears to tell him that his wife will bear a son who will go out with "the spirit and power of Elijah" to "make ready a people prepared for the Lord." He is struck speechless for his disbelief, and Elizabeth subsequently conceives.

Gabriel's speaking role is briefer in Luke than in Islamic tradition, where he is said to have dictated the entire Qur'an to Muhammad, but he makes the most of the lines he is given in the Annunciation (1:26–38). This episode has been depicted in sacred art, most famously by Fra Angelico, and also used as a type-scene, as in the Satanic parody at the conclusion of the 1968 film *Rosemary's Baby*. Gabriel appears to Mary and greets her in words that become the opening to one of the most frequently recited prayers in Christendom, the Hail Mary (in Latin, *Ave Maria*), which corresponds to the Douay-Rheims version: "Hail, full of grace, the Lord is with thee." Anyone who has heard the text set to music by Bach or Schubert would agree that Dante chooses wisely in making it the first thing his narrator hears upon entering heaven. Mary learns that she will bear a son who will be called "Son of the Most High, and the Lord God will give to him the throne of his ancestor David . . . and of his kingdom there will no end" (1:32–33). The humble nature of the birth contrasts not only with the glorious fate foretold for the offspring but also with other, less placid stories of divine parentage from Greek mythology perhaps familiar to Luke's Gentile readers, a theme explored in verse form by Oscar Wilde ("Ave Maria Gratias Plena").

"How can this be," Mary asks, "since I am a virgin?" Her perplexity is understandable. Christian tradition extrapolates both backward and forward from Mary's virginal state. It is often claimed Mary remains perpetually a virgin and that Jesus' siblings mentioned in the gospels (Matt. 13:55–56; Mark 6:3) are cousins or the children of Joseph from a previous marriage. Not only does her virginity aid her in avoiding sin, it is also claimed—mostly within Catholic tradition but also affirmed by Martin Luther—that Mary was preserved from the taint of original sin when her own parents conceived her, a doctrine known as the Immaculate Conception. The second-century *Protevangelium of James* shows that ancient readers understood Gabriel's words in a literal rather than some symbolic sense in its depiction of a midwife performing a gynecological exam and confirming that her virginity was intact. To the angel's explanation that "nothing will be impossible with God," soon-to-be mother Mary acquiesces, speaking words of wisdom, "Let it be with me according to your word" (1:38).

At the Visitation (1:39–46), an otherwise unremarkable meeting takes a propitious turn when the child in Elizabeth's womb leaps at the sound of Mary's voice. That these prenatal gymnastics are no accident is confirmed when the narrator ascribes the event to the agency of the Holy Spirit, which appears more than fifty times in Luke-Acts. Elizabeth's exclamation (KJV: "Blessed art thou among women and blessed is the fruit of thy womb") will also become part of the Ave Maria, making her the first of many generations to call Mary "blessed" (cf. 1:48). Even more audacious is her address to Mary as "mother of my Lord," employing a divine title for Jesus under the influence of the Holy Spirit.

Mary's response resembles many of the psalms of praise attributed to David (e.g., Pss. 33, 113, 117). The Magnificat has had a place in the liturgy of the Western church since the sixth century, and its text has been set to music by Vivaldi, Telemann, and Mozart, among many others. The first half of the hymn focuses on the marvelous work God has done for Mary, and the second half broadens the horizon. The final lines feature a motif that recurs throughout Luke-Acts: God's help for "his servant Israel . . . according to the promise he made to our ancestors, to Abraham and to his descendants forever." Mary recognizes that she has entered the unfolding drama of God's fidelity to Abraham and his seed (1:72–73; 3:8; 19:9; Acts 3:25; 7:17).

Friends and family celebrate the "great mercy" shown to Elizabeth when she gives birth to John the Baptist, thereby fulfilling Gabriel's prediction and confirming Mary's declaration about those who fear the Lord (1:14, 50, 58). After his voice returns, Zechariah's hymn, the Benedictus (1:68–79), answers the question they pose: "What then will this child become?" He praises God for the marvelous deeds he is about to perform for Israel in raising up a savior from the line of David "as he spoke through the mouth of his holy prophets from of old" (1:70). God "has remembered his holy covenant, the oath sworn to our ancestor Abraham," again alluding to the promises made to the patriarchs (Gen. 22:16–17; Jer. 11:5; Mic. 7:20). John will be "prophet of the Most High," the last in a long line of heralds preparing for the arrival of the Messiah, who will be called "Son of the Most High" (Luke 1:32; 16:16).

Luke goes to great lengths to situate the birth of Jesus in the context of world history (2:1–7). The "events that have been fulfilled among us," according to Luke (1:1), do not happen outside of human history but through it. Although it is impossible to confirm the administration of a census under Quirinius corresponding to the timeline suggested in Luke 2, regional variations in imperial policy and gaps in bureaucratic recordkeeping lead many historians to reserve judgment on the reliability of Luke's cursory description. The nativity itself is recounted with striking simplicity. Any particulars receive less emphasis than the significance various characters see in it as a fulfillment of prophecy.

Mundane details in the narrative nonetheless furnish patristic writers with material with which to counter Gnostic claims that Jesus only appeared to become a man and that his was not an actual, fleshly body.

An angelic choir accompanies the densely Christological news delivered to the shepherds in the fields that there is "born this day in the city of David a Savior, who is the Messiah, the Lord" (2:11). Their brief song, the Gloria in Excelsis (2:14), adds to the musicality of Luke's nativity account. Like the Benedictus, it is used in the Matins service in the Book of Common Prayer as well as in well-known Christmas carols.

Eight days later, Mary and Joseph take Jesus to the temple to be circumcised. There they are met by two elderly Jews, Simeon and Anna. The scene serves an important function in Luke-Acts (2:25–40). Circumcision had been instituted as a sign of the eternal covenant between God and Abraham, and it becomes a point of contention in Acts. Because it is one of Luke's objectives to demonstrate that the messianic faith is in continuity with Israelite tradition and not a radical departure, it is important to show that it is acknowledged from the outset by pious Jews. Simeon's canticle, the Nunc Dimittis (2:29–32), looks back over a lifetime of waiting for "the consolation of Israel" and forward to God's salvation, prepared in the presence of all peoples, a light for revelation to the Gentiles." Anna likewise departs the temple speaking of Jesus "to all who were looking for the redemption of Israel" (2:38).

With these and so many other testimonies echoing in her ears, Mary contemplates what they portend (2:19). Her wonder increases after a Passover visit to Jerusalem from their home in Nazareth when Jesus is twelve (2:39–51). Dante Gabriel Rosetti ("Ave") is one of many poets who ponder what Mary knows about her son and when she knows it. The story of the child prodigy teaching the teachers is the only event recorded in the canonical gospels between Jesus' infancy and the start of his ministry. No other aspect of Jesus' life has invited more creative elaboration in the attempt to fill in this biographical gap. From the second-century *Infancy Gospel of Thomas*, which depicts a five-year-old *enfant terrible* who smites anyone who displeases him, to medieval legends alluded to in Blake's "Jerusalem" of Jesus traveling to England with Joseph of Arimathea, to more recent esoteric speculation that similarities between his teachings and those of Buddhism and Hinduism are explained by teenage sojourns in India and Tibet, the history of Jesus' "missing years" demonstrates that popular imagination abhors a vacuum.

## FROM THE MANGER TO THE CROSS

Luke makes the transition to the story of Jesus as an adult by turning again to John the Baptist and his activity in the region of the Jordan (3:1–22). Between the baptism and the temptation in the desert, he inserts a genealogy that traces Jesus' lineage back further than does Matthew, who stops at Abraham (3:23–38). By following it all the way back to Adam, Luke broadens the spatial and temporal horizon of his story and places Jesus in the context of a universal history that reaches back before and extends beyond the formation of Israel as a people. After the temptation, he returns north to Galilee to begin his ministry.

Very broadly, Luke follows the Markan plotline while Jesus is in Galilee, with some additions and the omission of most of the stories in Mark 6:45–8:26. In terms of Luke's Christology, the most telling expansion of shared material is in the rejection at Nazareth (4:16–30; cf. Mark 6:1–6). Jesus' reading of the Torah at the synagogue on the Sabbath is narrated in cinematic detail. The text is from Isa. 61:1–2:

> The Spirit of the Lord is upon me, because he has anointed me to bring good news to the poor. He has sent me to proclaim release to the captives and recovery of sight to the blind, to let the oppressed go free, to proclaim the year of the Lord's favor.

As the assembly looks on, he adds a comment that strikes them as presumptuous (4:21): "Today this scripture has been fulfilled in your hearing." Other characters in the nativity and resurrection accounts speak of Jesus as fulfilling prophecy. To his claim to be the Lord's anointed prophesied in Isaiah, Jesus adds a response that makes explicit Luke's view that he is himself a prophet as well, albeit one without honor among his own (4:24). By comparing himself to Elijah and Elisha, he makes the further point that the Israelites' rejection of the prophets prefigured the Galileans refusal to recognize him. Their subsequent attempt to throw him off a cliff shows that they grasped his meaning. (The healing of the widow at Nain in Luke

7:11–17, found only in Luke, parallels the story of Elijah in 1 Kgs. 17:8–16 and elicits the admiration of the people, who say "A great prophet has risen among us!") As Elijah and Elisha were received by non-Israelites, so also will Jesus be received by Gentiles. Luke will enhance this portrait of Jesus as the righteous prophet rejected by his own people in the travel narrative, in the Passion, and in the sermons in Acts (Luke 13:33; Acts 3:22; 7:37).

The prophetic aspect of Lukan Christology is accentuated in the Sermon on the Plain (6:20–49), so called because it is delivered "on a level place" and contains several of the sayings found in the Sermon on the Mount. Luke includes only four Beatitudes (vv. 20–23), which differ from their Matthean parallels in their emphasis on the present. For example, whereas Matthew's Jesus blesses the poor "in spirit" and those who hunger and thirst for righteousness, Luke's Jesus simply addresses "the poor" and those who are hungry and weeping "now." Paired with the corresponding woes pronounced on the rich and those who are full and laughing "now," the Lukan Beatitudes emphasize God's displeasure with the oppression of the poor by the wealthy characteristic of the message of the prophets as well as the motif of reversal seen in the Magnificat (Isa. 10:1–4; Amos 2:6–7; 5:10–13; Luke 1:51–53).

Following the second of three Passion predictions (9:22, 43–45; 18:33), Jesus solemnly "set[s] his face" to journey south because, as he will explain on the way, "it is impossible for a prophet to be killed outside of Jerusalem" (9:51; 13:33). Readers of Mark find Jesus teaching in Galilee at the end of chapter nine, only to begin chapter ten and find that he has already arrived in Judea. Luke inserts a lengthy travel narrative here and periodically reminds the reader that Jesus is in transit (9:51–19:27; cf. 13:33–34; 17:11; 18:31). This journey provides additional narrative space for Luke to develop his portrait of Jesus as the "prophet like Moses" (Deut. 18:15; Acts 3:22–23; cf. Moessner 1989).

Most of the material in the travel narrative is either shared with Matthew or distinctively Lukan, with very little drawn from Mark. Unique miracle stories depict Jesus attracting followers from among the people and at the same time provoking further hostility from Jewish leaders (13:10–17; 14:1–6; 17:11–18). A more prominent feature of the travel narrative is the inclusion of numerous parables. Throughout the gospel, Luke retains most of Mark's parables and also shares many in common with Matthew. Any reckoning of Luke's unique parables would include the following, of which all but one appear in the travel narrative:

- The Two Debtors (7:41–43). This parable is embedded in the Lukan version of the anointing of Jesus by the sinful woman (7:36–50). The conception of sins as debts owed to God is commonplace in early Judaism.
- The Good Samaritan (10:25–37). Along with the Prodigal Son, this is perhaps the most famous of all the parables. Although the lawyer who poses the question that prompts Jesus to tell it is "testing" him and seeks "to justify himself" after Jesus initially responds by quoting the *Shema* (Deut. 6:5), the matter of who qualifies as "neighbor" is a legitimate one discussed at length in rabbinic commentary on Lev. 19:18. Its traditional title has been used in the names of charitable organizations and laws providing legal protections for bystanders who give aid in emergency situations, and social psychologists invoke it in explaining the phenomenon of "diffusion of responsibility." It has been interpreted as an allegory relating the history of salvation with Christ as the Samaritan and as a critique of racial prejudice. The tension it reflects between Judeans and Samaritans is present also in John's story of the Woman at the Well (John 4). Benjamin Britten's *Cantata misericordium* celebrating the Red Cross's centenary sets the parable to music.
- The Friend at Midnight (11:5–8). This parable underscores the need for persistence in prayer emphasized in the Lord's Prayer that immediately precedes it (11:1–4), as does the Unrighteous Judge (18:1–8).
- The Rich Fool (12:16–21). A question from the crowd about familial conflict related to inheritance elicits this parable. Jesus addresses what he sees as an underlying issue—preoccupation with wealth as a misplaced priority—rather than any legal angle. His explication of the Unjust Steward would seem to apply equally to this parable: "You cannot serve God and mammon" (16:13). The advice to "eat, drink, and be merry" (v. 16) appears here, though on the lips of the fool who equates the possessions he has stored up with his "soul."

- The Barren Fig Tree (13:6–9). Figs and fig trees are often used to symbolize Israel in oracles of judgment (Jer. 24:10; Ezek. 17:9; 19:12–14; Hosea 9:10). The warning of its destruction here echoes John the Baptist's warning that "the ax is laid to the root" of every tree "that does not bear good fruit" in the form of repentance (Luke 3:8–9).

- The Lost Coin (15:8–10). This is the second—after the Lost Sheep in 15:3–7—in a series of three parables on the theme of "lost and found."

- The Prodigal Son (15:11–32). This is the longest of Jesus' parables and one of the best known, even if many readers are unable to define "prodigal." (It means wasteful or extravagant.) Is the moral drawn from the actions of the younger son? the older son? the father? William Wordsworth, Christina Rossetti, Rudyard Kipling, Rainer Maria Rilke, Elizabeth Bishop, and other poets have re-imagined it from the perspective of different characters. Modern authors from Franz Kafka (*Homecoming*) to Thomas Wolfe (*You Can't Go Home Again*) have spun engrossing tales out of its central motifs. Theologians have plumbed its depths, from Ambrose, who cites it in defending reconciliation for repentant sinners against Novatian, to John Paul II, whose encyclical *Dives in misericordia* takes it as a point of departure for a meditation on divine mercy. Artists have focused on different points in the story. Most focus on the dissolute living, the pigpen, or the reunion, none more affectingly that Rembrandt. Beginning with Cain and Abel, the theme of sibling rivalry is a perennial one in the biblical tradition.

- The Unjust Steward (16:1–8). No parable in the New Testament has tested the ingenuity of interpreters or produced more divergent readings than this text, sometimes called the Dishonest or Shrewd Manager. Is the main character intended as a positive or a negative example? Is Jesus commending fraudulent business practices? Is he praising the steward's cleverness or prudence in the use of money? Is Jesus being ironic? Does the parable reflect a sense of eschatological urgency, that is, does it have to do with time and not money? Has something been lost in translation or in the text's transmission? Is it directed at the Pharisees and tax collectors who are said to be present? Do any of the characters represent God or Jesus?

- The Rich Man and Lazarus (16:19–31). No other parable features a character with a proper name. This text has figured in debates about the immortality of the soul, the existence of Purgatory and limbo, and the possibility of repentance after death. Thomas Aquinas, Jonathan Edwards, and other Christian writers have seen in it an instance of "the abominable fancy," the idea that the happiness of those in heaven consists partly in contemplating the punishment of the wicked in hell. The final line, where Father Abraham tells the rich man that his brothers, "if they do not listen to Moses and the prophets, neither will they be convinced if someone rises from the dead," provides literary foreshadowing of the unbelieving response to the good news that Luke's readers would have witnessed.
- The Unrighteous Judge (18:1–8). Sometimes this parable is called the Importunate Widow. It contains elements of sly humor in the use of a boxing term (*hypōpiazō*, "to give a black eye") to describe the widow's "bothering" behavior in v. 5 and in the judge's frank admission in his interior dialogue that he has "no fear of God and no respect for anyone."
- The Pharisee and Tax Collector (18:9–14). Together with Jesus' characterization of his adversaries in Matthew 23, this parable is the reason "Pharisee" connotes self-righteousness in English.

Short or long, Luke has a knack for bringing together a collection of stories well told. He often indicates the audience in attendance for their performance, adding to the dramatic effect in the process.

A common thread running through many of the Lukan parables has to do with wealth and the use of one's possessions. In many instances, the thrust of the parable complements the warnings about greed found earlier in John the Baptist's instructions to those who come to him for baptism and in the woes from the Sermon on the Plain (3:10–14; 6:24–26). More generally, the teachings of Jesus and Luke's characterization of various figures suggest that he sees one's attitude toward possessions as an index of discipleship (Johnson 1977). The first disciples "leave everything and follow him" when Jesus calls them (5:11, 27). The centurion whose son Jesus heals is said to have demonstrated his love for the Jews by building them a synagogue (7:5). He tells the crowds who come to hear him, "None of you can become my disciple if you do not give up all your possessions" (14:33; cf. 18:18–25).

Allowing for an element of hyperbole—after all, it is difficult to practice the almsgiving he commands unless one has resources—this note in his teaching becomes a refrain. But it is not a simple ad hominem against the rich as irredeemably corrupt. Zacchaeus, the short man who climbs a tree to see Jesus, is a case in point (19:1–10). His response to Jesus' teaching is to promise that he will give half of his wealth to the poor and repay fourfold those whom he may have defrauded. Joanna, one of the many female characters appearing only in Luke, also provides a positive example. She is among the women who accompany the disciples from Galilee and "provide for them out of their resources," following Jesus to the cross and beyond (8:1–3; 23:49, 55–56; 24:10). Acts contains additional examples illustrating this pervasive Lukan theme that the disposition of one's wealth is expressive of an interior disposition relating to acceptance or rejection of Jesus as the Messiah.

The triumphal entry and the cleansing of the temple follow fast upon the conclusion of the travel narrative. As Jesus draws near to the city, he foretells Jerusalem's destruction in terms that are more detailed and less tinged with apocalyptic imagery than elsewhere (19:41–44). His prediction combines lament for the city with blame for rejecting the Lord's anointed. God will allow their enemies to prevail, he tells them, "because you did not know the hour of your visitation," which has already been identified with the appearance of Jesus (1:68–69; 7:16). Predictions of the temple's demise take up the first half of Jesus' final discourse in Luke 21:5–38. The second half of the discourse, however, has been interpreted as distinguishing the fall of Jerusalem from the events that will signal the cosmic cataclysm that will coincide with the Son of Man's appearance to usher in the end-times. Writing after 70 CE, Luke is aware that the latter does not immediately follow the former.

Why does Judas Iscariot betray Jesus to the chief priests and scribes? Satan is partly to blame, entering Judas after having left Jesus after the temptation "until an opportune time" (4:13; 22:3–6). Jesus obliquely mentions his betrayer at the Last Supper, which is longer than in Matthew and Mark and has the tone of a farewell discourse. The words of institution closely resemble the form they take in 1 Cor. 11:23–26. Just as the first covenant connected with the Exodus was sealed with sacrificial blood, so will the "new covenant" instituted by Jesus. The addition of the call to remembrance (22:19: "Do this in remembrance of me") further underscores the Passover dimensions of the scene. Remembrance is a pervasive motif in the Exodus story (Exod. 2:24; 12:14; 13:3; Deut. 16:3) as well as in the *Passover Haggadah*, in which Jews bring to mind the saving actions of God who has "remembered" the people.

Pilate is skeptical about the false charges brought by the Sanhedrin (23:1–7). He transfers Jesus to Herod when he learns that, as a Galilean, he falls under the tetrarch's jurisdiction. Only Luke records this appearance before Herod in the midst of Jesus' trial (23:8–12). This hearing provides another venue for emphasizing Jesus' innocence. Although Herod questions him and, like Pilate, has shown little compunction in the past about the arbitrary use of force against undeserving victims (9:9; 13:1–2), he does nothing more than mock him as the chief priests continue to level charges. When he sends him back he thus implicitly affirms Pilate's view that there is "no basis for accusation against this man" (23:4). Pilate twice more repeats this judgment in dialogue found in no other gospel (23:13–16, 20–22).

Protestations of Jesus' innocence continue while he hangs on the cross. One of the criminals crucified with Jesus joins in mocking him, but the other rebukes him because, while they are getting their just deserts, "this man has done nothing wrong" (23:39–41; this "good thief" is promised a place in Paradise and is later honored as St. Dismas, to whom prison chapels are often dedicated in remembrance of his repentance *in extremis*). This pattern culminates at the moment of his death. Matthew and Mark quote the centurion as saying, "Truly this man was God's Son" (Matt 27:54; Mark 15:39). In Luke, after witnessing the equanimity of his final moments—Jesus asks God to forgive his tormentors "for they do not know what they are doing" (23:34) and quotes from a psalm supplicating God to deliver the righteous from their enemies (31:6), "Father, into your hands I commend my spirit," but does not utter the cry of abandonment from Ps. 22:1—the centurion praises God and cries out, "Certainly this man was innocent" (23:47). The persistence of the motif comports with Luke's overarching portrayal of Jesus as a righteous but persecuted prophet.

By no means is this to say that Luke denies Jesus' sonship. To be sure, in Luke he is the Son of God, and also the Son of Man, the Son of David, and the Messiah. The thief's dying request—"Jesus, remember me when you come into your kingdom"—hints at two other titles applied to Jesus in Luke-Acts. In calling on Jesus to save him, he joins other Lukan characters who refer variously to both God and Jesus as "savior" (1:47; 2:11, 30; Acts 5:31; 13:23). The leaders and the soldiers ironically taunt him (23:35), but the thief recognizes his salvific power. It is somewhat surprising that he is the only character to address him, simply, as "Jesus," which means "the Lord saves." Although manuscripts that add "Lord" to his address in Luke 23:42 are not the earliest, the scribal addition is understandable. "Lord," *kyrios*, can be used in Greek as a term of honor, much like "sir," and thus its application to Jesus can be ambiguous, especially when used in direct speech. When the thief echoes the Lord's Prayer ("thy kingdom come") in his request, he appears to be approaching Jesus as someone worthy of extraordinary respect. Luke's consistent reference already in the gospel to Jesus as *kyrios* in narration demonstrates that it reflects the author's own vantage point more clearly than it does when it appears on the lips of his characters (e.g., 7:13; 10:1, 41; 11:39; 12:42; 13:15; 17:5–6; 18:6; 19:8; 22:61). That Jesus is "Lord" is a Christological perspective that becomes more manifest in Acts but already pervades Luke's version of the gospel (Rowe 2006).

## RESURRECTION AND ASCENSION

The story of the empty tomb differs in detail from the other Synoptic accounts, but presents the same general scenario. It is followed by a poignant story of two travelers on the road to Emmaus that is unique to Luke (24:13–35). Cleopas and an unnamed companion are discussing the recent events surrounding the death of the man they "had hoped . . . was the one to redeem Israel," when Jesus joins them (24:21). But they mysteriously do not recognize him; he had, after all, been through quite a lot, having been literally to hell and back the day before according to the Apostles' Creed. Gently chastising them for failing to see the crucifixion as part of a divine plan, "beginning with Moses and all the prophets," Jesus proceeds to "interpret to them all the things about himself in all the scriptures" (24:27). Only when they stop to share a meal are their eyes opened as he prepares it in a manner reminiscent of the Last Supper (24:30: "he took bread, blessed and broke it, and gave it to them"). No sooner do they recognize him "in the breaking of the bread" than he vanishes from sight, to appear later in the midst of the eleven. John Wesley echoes their language (24:32: "Were not our hearts burning within us while he was talking to us on the road?") in speaking of his "heart strangely warmed" on the occasion of his conversion at Aldersgate.

After convincing the disciples that he is not a ghost, Jesus "opened their minds to understand the scriptures" and again explains the necessity of his death so that "everything written about [him] in the law of Moses, the prophets, and the psalms" might be fulfilled (24:44–45). Notes from this crash course on salvation history have not survived. One may surmise that the many references and allusions to the Scriptures earlier in the gospel and in the expository speeches delivered in Acts derive from lessons not unlike the one depicted in this scene. Much of the New Testament constitutes an attempt to understand and explain how Jesus fulfilled biblical prophecies—many of which had never been regarded as messianic prophecies at all—in unexpected ways.

That they are "witnesses of these things" brings the reader back to Luke's statement in the preface that his research includes material handed down by eyewitnesses (1:2). Before they are to proclaim the good news, however, they are to wait in Jerusalem. "I am sending upon you what my Father promised," he says, "so stay here in the city until you have been clothed with power from on high" (24:49). His words will come true ten days later at Pentecost (Acts 1–2).

Only Luke-Acts describes the moment of Jesus' departure from the earth (Luke 24:50–51; Acts 1:6–11; Mark 16:19 includes the ascension in the "longer" ending). Allusions to the ascension occur elsewhere, and it is presupposed in texts that describe Jesus as exalted to heaven and seated at the right hand of the Father, in fulfillment of Psalm 110 (1 Tim. 3:16; Heb. 4:14; cf. Rom. 8:34; Eph. 1:20; Heb. 1:13; 8:1). According to the Hebrew Bible and extracanonical Jewish writings, Enoch, Abraham, Moses, Elijah, and Isaiah precede Jesus in ascending to heaven. For Luke, however, Jesus' place at God's right hand marks the inauguration of the kingdom declared earlier in the gospel (cf. Acts 2:24, 32–35). And when the disciples return to Jerusalem, "continually in the temple praising God," his story, which began with Zechariah serving in the sanctuary, comes full circle.

## THE ACTS OF THE APOSTLES: THE STORY CONTINUES

What might a sequel to the gospels of Matthew, Mark, or John have looked like had they thought to write one? Any such hypothetical works might have taken various literary forms, included otherwise unknown stories, and dealt with a wide range of theological issues. The question is of course unanswerable because only Luke tackled the project of chronicling the transition from the time of Jesus to the time of the church. And largely because his account is the first, it has functioned as the de facto "official" version. Even for scholars who believe it does not yield an accurate representation of the early years of the church find it difficult to avoid treating its framework as the starting point for telling that story. Many of the New Testament letters are written decades earlier than Acts and thus provide first-hand testimony to this period. Due to their literary genre, however, they are ill-suited to the task of writing a history. Scholars who place greater faith in Luke as a historian readily concede that his account is selective and heavily shaped by particular theological concerns. In the course of narrating the expansion of the movement from its origins in Galilee and Judea to Rome and points in between, he suggests answers to pressing questions pondered by Christians who came before and who will come after him.

That Acts has spawned many imitations and has been considered an ancient novel or even an epic are signs that he has executed his self-appointed task in a compelling fashion. In the first several centuries, there are the *Acts of Peter*, *Acts of Paul and Thecla*, *Acts of Thomas*, *Acts of Andrew*, *Acts of Pilate*, *Acts of Thaddeus*, and *Acts of Mark*, as well as such works as the *Martyrdom of Matthew* and the *Apostolic History of Pseudo-Abdias*, among many others, modelled on Acts or taking its episodes as points of departure for the creation of pious fictions intended to supply edifying entertainment. Peter and Paul are the main protagonists, with the former dominating the first half of the narrative and the latter taking center stage in the second half. Characters who play supporting roles receive top billing in many of these later writings. James and John accompany Peter as he preaches the gospel in the early chapters, but take the lead in such works as the second-century *Acts of John*, where John causes the Temple of Artemis in Ephesus to collapse in a showdown with its priests and uses his miraculous powers the next day to ward off an infestation of bedbugs, and the second-century *Apocryphon of James*, a letter in which James relates secret teachings he received from the risen Jesus before sending out the rest of the apostles to spread the good news. Stephen's status as Christian protomartyr is enhanced in the *Revelation of Stephen*, where he resembles an ancient Rasputin, dying only after being crucified, having molten lead poured in his ears and mouth and nails driven into his feet and heart, and then stoned. The evangelist Philip who converts the Ethiopian eunuch is often conflated with the apostle Philip, who travels with his sister Mariamne in the fourth-century *Acts of Philip* and converts a talking leopard and a talking goat with whom they celebrate a communion rite involving vegetables and water. The *Acts of Andrew and Matthias* tell of the adventures of these lesser-known apostles among cannibals, while the *Questions of Bartholomew* provides a transcript of Bartholomew's "interviews" with Jesus, Satan, and Mary on such subjects as the population of heaven, the fallen angels, and the nature of the virginal conception. (Mary demurs on the last question, explaining that fire would come out of her mouth and consume the world if she were to answer.) One of Paul's Athenian converts lends his name to a fifth-century Christian Neoplatonist philosopher now known as Pseudo-Dionysius the Areopagite. And Paul's co-worker Barnabas becomes the "author" of a second-century anti-Jewish epistle as well as a late-medieval gospel that "foretells" the coming of Muhammad by name.

This rich Lukan ensemble of the canonical book takes part in a drama that plays out across the Mediterranean, continuing the account of "all that Jesus did and taught from the beginning until the day when he was taken up to heaven" in a second volume dedicated to Theophilus (1:1–2). For forty days, he was "giving instruction . . . and speaking about the kingdom of God." Perhaps the reader is to understand that the apostles' speeches delivered later in Acts relay the details of this instruction.

Jesus' last command before his ascension, which has already been recorded in the gospel, is that the apostles wait in Jerusalem "for the promise of the Father" to be fulfilled when they are "baptized with the Holy Spirit" (1:4–5; cf. Luke 24:49). Jerusalem is the setting for the final five chapters of the gospel and the first seven chapters of Acts. The city serves as a fulcrum around which the story turns, as

Paul and others continually return there after venturing out further north and west (8:25; 9:26; 11:2, 29; 15; 19:21; 21:15–26). This literary technique further grounds the story of the church in the history of God's dealings with Israel by situating its birth in close geographic proximity to the site of so many other seminal events described in the Scriptures. Jesus deflects their question about the timing of Israel's restoration and again tells them that they will soon be endowed with power, the third explicit mention of the Holy Spirit in the first eight verses. The Holy Spirit, already more prominent in Luke than in the other gospels, will be a prominent presence in Acts. Just before Jesus ascends, he says that they will be his witnesses "in Jerusalem, in all of Judea and Samaria, and to the ends of the earth" (1:8). This final message, providing a rough table of contents for the book, stands as a prophecy that will be fulfilled in the succeeding narrative, thereby affirming his word as reliable and validating the mission to be carried out by the apostles.

## THE BIRTH OF THE CHURCH: GROWTH AND RESISTANCE

The disciples reassemble "in the upper room" (1:13) where they had been "talkin' with Jesus," to borrow the lyrics of the gospel classic made famous by Mahalia Jackson, and Peter gives the first of several speeches highlighting the fulfillment of prophecy through the Holy Spirit. This speech concerns the death of Judas (described differently in Matt. 27:5) and the necessity of replacing him (1:15–22). Newly reconstituted with the selection of Matthias, the Twelve thus emerge as yet another symbol of continuity with Israelite tradition. This sets the scene for the momentous events of Pentecost ten days later (2:1–41).

Pentecost is another name for the Jewish harvest festival Shavuot, the Feast of Weeks, which falls fifty days after Passover. It draws pilgrims from far and wide who come to Jerusalem to celebrate it. Various Jewish traditions associate its date with the appearance of the rainbow to Noah and the giving of Torah to Moses at Sinai, where in some midrashim the law is said to have divided into seventy tongues. In Acts 2, the place where the disciples are gathered is filled with "a sound like the rush of a violent wind," divided tongues of fire appear over them, they are filled with the Holy Spirit, and they begin to speak in other languages (2:1–4). Although some bystanders joke that they must be drunk, most of the "devout Jews from every nation" are amazed because they can miraculously understand in their own languages. Modern Pentecostalism takes its name from this account and has prominently featured the phenomenon of speaking in tongues since its birth at the Azusa Street Revival in 1906. It is often noted that the event is reminiscent of the confusion of tongues at Babel (Gen. 11:1–9), only in reverse, such that the divisions plaguing humanity since the time just prior to the call of Abraham are to be repaired in the foundation of the church.

Peter's speech is a tour de force (2:14–36). He announces that they are "in the last days" when Joel (2:28–32) prophesied that God would pour out the Spirit "upon all flesh" and that "everyone who calls on the name of the Lord shall be saved." He implicates his audience in the unjust execution of Jesus, but assures them that God has vindicated Jesus by raising him. In this way, Peter forcefully argues, the resurrection honors God's oath in Ps. 16:8–11 and the exaltation of Jesus to the right hand of his Father makes good on the pledge to David (2 Sam. 7:12–13) to put one of his descendants on his throne. Cut to the heart, the crowd asks what they should do and are told to repent and be baptized (2:37–38). According to Luke, 3,000 persons respond to his call. Through Peter's speech, Luke radically revises Jewish expectations by reinterpreting the promises made to Abraham as having their fulfillment in this very event made possible only by Jesus' death and resurrection (cf. 4:25). And while the audience here consists of other Jews, the availability of the promise not only to them and their children but also to "all who are far away, everyone whom the Lord our God calls to him" foreshadows the response of the Gentiles that will occupy much of Luke's story (2:33, 39).

Luke's description of the early community as devoted "to the apostles' teaching and fellowship, to the breaking of bread and the prayers" (2:42) is often invoked as a paradigm for life within the church. If nothing else, it is a reminder that Luke conceives of the messianic movement as social in nature rather than as a personal relationship with Jesus and nothing else. That they "had all things in common" and would sell their possessions and distribute the proceeds to members "as any had need" (2:44–45) is a sign for many readers that the early church was not only a social movement but a socialist or communist one. Assessing this claim, along with the view that any departure from this practice marks an ecclesial fall from grace, entails answering a number of questions. Is the portrait accurate or does it contain hyperbole? Was it compulsory or was it a voluntary response to the Spirit's promptings? Was it a short-term solution adopted in view of the exigencies of that time and place or was it intended as a long-term policy, and to what extent was it conditioned by waxing or waning expectations of the Parousia? How well it may have worked after the early days is uncertain in light of the Jerusalem church's poverty that Paul's collection was intended to alleviate (Acts 11:29; 2 Cor. 9:7). Whether or not Luke intends the account to function prescriptively, it certainly fits with his tendency in the gospel to view the disposition of one's wealth as an external sign of internal conversion. Barnabas and Ananias and Sapphira respectively present the first of numerous positive and negative examples of this notion in Acts (4:42–47; 5:1–11).

But the life of the community is not a purely internal matter. Accompanied by John, Peter goes out to the temple precincts where he performs healings as marvelous as those of Jesus and continues to preach the good news in terms that draw the ire of the Jewish leaders. Especially provocative is his assertion that "there is no other name under heaven given among mortals by which we must be saved" (4:12). Throughout this section and later with Paul, one sees the apostles re-enacting a pattern of giving prophetic witness, meeting resistance, and being vindicated. It is a dynamic Peter describes in his speeches about Jesus, who had previously told them that they would be persecuted but need not worry about their defense because he would enable them to endure (Luke 21:12–19). As Peter and his companions are imprisoned but then miraculously liberated (5:17–21), they experience Jesus' words coming to fruition in the presence of the people. The leaders are flummoxed. Gamaliel, a respected rabbi mentioned in the Mishnah, proposes an approach that is simultaneously pragmatic and theologically astute: let them be, he says, "because if this plan or this undertaking is of human origin, it will fail; but if it is of God, you will not be able to overthrow them" (5:38–39).

Complaints from Greek-speaking believers against Aramaic-speaking believers about the neglect of their widows in the community's food distribution shows that the idyllic harmony of the early days would not forever be exempt from long-standing ethnic tensions. Many scholars see this as evidence of a larger conflict that defined early Christianity, pitting a Jewish "Petrine" faction against a Gentile "Pauline" faction and only reaching a fateful compromise in the second century in the form of "early Catholicism." This thesis holds that this compromise was a negative development and that Acts attempts to conceal a less benign reality. Although it greatly oversimplifies the issue, relies too heavily on Hegelian dialectic to explain historical change, and requires a dating of Acts that is much later than what most scholars accept, it rightly calls attention to the social, theological, and cultural diversity that characterizes Christianity from the earliest stage.

To address the problem, the Twelve appoint deacons to oversee community affairs. One of the deacons is Stephen, who is accused of blasphemy and put on trial before the high priest. He pulls no punches in defending himself and his fellow messianists against the charge that they are in effect heretics or apostates from Judaism (7:1–53). On the surface, Stephen appears to ignore the charges against him. His concise overview of Israelite history as well as Paul's in Acts 13:16–41 should be read against the backdrop of other retellings of biblical history that were popular in the Hellenistic period. Such retellings are necessarily selective and have a particular slant or point the authors want to emphasize, as with the encomium to faith in Heb. 11:1–40. Stephen draws his audience—and Luke's—into Israel's history by focusing on the many detours along the way to the fulfillment of God's promises first made to Abraham. Readers may consult the dozens of references to the Hebrew Bible to discover what is accented or de-emphasized in moving from the original literary context to Stephen's speech.

The prediction of a "prophet like Moses" made by Moses himself in Deut. 18:15 is taken by Stephen not as referring to Joshua but to Jesus, "the Righteous One" (7:37–38; cf. 3:22–23). He accuses his accusers of forever opposing the Holy Spirit, just as their ancestors did, and asks a loaded question that seals his fate: "Which of the prophets did your ancestors not persecute?" Stephen's rhetoric, if a bit more heated when he calls them "betrayers and murderers," resembles that of Jesus in the rejection at Nazareth, where the audience attempts to kill him (7:51–53; cf. Luke 4:16–30). This time they finish the job. Stephen has a beatific vision as they drag him out to be stoned. He prays to Jesus, "receive my spirit," just as Jesus prayed to God on the cross, and also echoes Jesus when he asks, "Lord, do not hold this sin against them" (7:59–60; cf. Luke 23:34, 46). This scene is the clearest indication that Luke sees the protagonists in Acts as animated by the same Spirit at work in the life, death, and resurrection of Jesus.

Stephen's death halts the steady progress of the movement depicted in the first several chapters. Persecution of the church breaks out in Jerusalem, propelling its members into the countryside of Judea and Samaria for safety—the very region where the risen Jesus had said they would bear witness. With their enemies acting as unwitting catalysts, the reader thus recognizes this as only a temporary setback.

## THE RESPONSE OF THE GENTILES

Missionary successes in Samaria open the next chapter in the church's expansion (8:4–24). Among the converts of Philip, one of the deacons appointed in Acts 6, is a certain Simon, who offers to buy the power of handing on the Holy Spirit when Peter and John come to town. Simon Magus, as he is later called, becomes the nemesis of Peter in the second-century Pseudo-Clementine literature, after which Epiphanius and other patristic writers consider him the arch-heretic and father of Gnosticism (*Pan.* 21.7.2). His attempt to purchase miraculous power explains the etymology of the ecclesiastical sin of simony.

A positive example of the gospel's reception in Samaria is found in the Ethiopian eunuch (8:26–40). Is he a Gentile, a Jewish proselyte, or a God-fearer who has not fully converted to Judaism (Shauf 2009)? Luke does not say. That he is occupied reading the Hebrew Bible on his way back from worshipping in Jerusalem means that he is certainly no ordinary Gentile, though Luke will make much more of Cornelius' Gentile status in Acts 10–11. Castrati, however, were excluded from the Israelite assembly according to the Pentateuch (Deut. 23:1), and so neither was he an ordinary Jew. The passage he is reading is the Song of the Suffering Servant from Isa. 53:7–8 ("Like a sheep he was led to the slaughter"). In Jewish tradition, this figure is usually identified with Israel as a whole and it was not interpreted messianically prior to the New Testament. Philip's typological explanation of a text the Ethiopian does not understand and then vanishing follows the pattern of Jesus at Emmaus. He receives baptism and goes on his way, presumably back to Ethiopia, the figurative "ends of the earth" from a Greco-Roman perspective.

Saul's cameo at the stoning of Stephen develops into a major role with his conversion en route to Damascus (9:1–30), the most famous episode in Acts after the Pentecost event. Luke has Paul—as he is later called, with no explanation for the name change (13:9)—repeat the story twice more in defense speeches (22:4–16; 26:9–18). A favorite theme of artists, his experience has become a type-scene in world literature and popular culture, as in the 1980 movie *The Blues Brothers* where an ex-convict literally "sees the light" and embarks on "a mission from God." Johnny Cash saw himself as a latter-day Paul, redeemed from a sinful past, and drew on his biography in a novel about the apostle (*The Man in White*). Scholars debate the degree to which Luke may have embellished it and other aspects of his career (Lentz 1993). Although Paul in his letters never describes his blinding encounter with Jesus ("Saul, Saul, why do you persecute me?") exactly as he does here, he stakes his claim to be an apostle on a profoundly transformative experience with the risen Jesus (9:5; 1 Cor. 15:8–9). Ananias—not to be confused with the husband of Sapphira or the high priest who presides over Paul's hearings in Jerusalem and Caesarea (5:1; 23:2; 24:1)—is told by the Lord that Paul will be a "chosen instrument" to bring his name "before Gentiles and kings and before the people of Israel" (9:15). To the astonishment of new friends and foes alike, this is precisely what he begins to do shortly after the scales fall from his eyes.

Before Paul takes center stage as "apostle to the Gentiles" (Rom. 11:13), however, Peter has his own epiphany that facilitates outreach to non-Jews (10:1–48). At the same time as Cornelius, a God-fearing Roman centurion, Peter has a dream that eventually brings them together. In Peter's dream, he sees a large sheet filled with all manner of unclean animals and is told to "kill and eat." When he protests, he is told by a voice, "What God has made clean, you must not call profane" (10:15). He takes this as a sign, after hearing of Cornelius' dream, that "God shows no partiality, but in every nation anyone who fears him and does what is right is acceptable to him" (10:34–35). The Holy Spirit confirms Peter's interpretation of events when it falls on the Gentiles to whom he is speaking. Many scholars believe that God-fearers like Cornelius constitute the primary intended audience of Luke-Acts (cf. 13:43; 17:4).

Not everyone reacts enthusiastically to the news that the Holy Spirit had been poured out on the Gentiles. "Why did you go to uncircumcised men and eat with them?" ask some of the Jewish Christians in Jerusalem (11:2–3). In abbreviated form, Peter then recapitulates the account of how the Spirit had come upon the Gentiles just as it had on the Jews "at the beginning" (11:4–17). His critics are silenced, if only for a time. The movement spreads to Antioch, where Paul and Barnabas spend a year teaching and, the narrator notes, the disciples were first called "Christians" (11:26). Back in Judea, Herod initiates a persecution that results in the death of James the brother of John. Still, according to one of Luke's periodic summaries, "the word of God continued to advance," by ordinary and extraordinary means (12:24; cf. 2:43–47; 4:32–37; 8:1–2; 9:31).

Resistance comes from sundry false prophets and sorcerers, and also from rank-and-file members of the Jewish community as well (13:4–12, 44–51; 14:19). So severe is this resistance that on multiple occasions Paul announces that he is shaking the dust off his feet and suspending his mission to fellow Jews (13:46, 51; 18:6). Yet when he enters a new town, he continues to go straight to the synagogue (14:1–7; 17:1–9, 10–14; 19:8–20). Unbelieving Jews do not share Paul's conviction that Jesus was the Messiah. Within the messianist community, however, Christ-believing Jews take issue with any relaxation of the law's requirements for non-Jews, though they do not object to the baptism of Gentiles or doubt their receipt of the Holy Spirit in the parley concerning Cornelius in Acts 11. Their stance is understandable: does not devotion to the son of the God of Israel, the Messiah foretold in the Jewish Scriptures, obviously entail observance of the Jewish law, even for Gentiles? Does not the burden of proof fall on those who answer "no"? The underlying issues do not go away, as more and more Gentiles respond to Paul's preaching.

The "Apostolic Conference" convened ca. 49 CE in Jerusalem addresses this pressing question (15:1–35). It is a watershed moment in the history of early Christianity. Is it the same event as Paul's awkward conflict with Peter over protocols for table fellowship with the uncircumcised described in Gal. 2:1–14? Historians who attempt to coordinate the theological implications and biographical details of the two accounts are divided on the question (Dibelius 1956). At stake is the basis on which Gentiles can be admitted to Christian fellowship.

Must they in essence become Jews in order to become Christians? James, the brother of the Lord, presides over the affair which features testimony from Peter, Paul, and Barnabas. Their deliberations sift the claims of Scripture and experience and contemplate the relationship between belief and practice in arriving at a compromise between those who would impose all of Torah's demands on Gentile converts and those who would do away entirely with the requirements of circumcision and kashrut. Like other speakers in Acts, James finds a precedent for Gentile inclusion in Scripture (Amos 9:11–12). The council's decision sets the new faith on a course that will eventually diverge from mainstream Judaism in such a way and to such a degree that they form separate religions.

## FROM JERUSALEM TO ROME

With the rejoicing of the Gentiles upon learning of the council's decision, one might expect the Gentile mission to move forward with all haste. But Paul returns to Antioch and other cities where he had already preached and recruits Timothy, whom he circumcises (16:2). He crosses over to Europe in response to a vision and soon runs afoul of the authorities. It is not the last time Paul will be taken into custody for disturbing the peace (16:19–24; 24:26–27). He is chased out of Thessalonica by a band of hired thugs, but receives a warmer reception in the synagogue at Beroea until the Jews of Thessalonica hear of his whereabouts. For his own safety, Paul is then spirited away and unceremoniously dumped in Athens, the intellectual capital of the classical world.

Paul's speech delivered there at the Areopagus is the most famous in Acts after those of Peter and Stephen (17:16–34). It has been read variously as a quintessential expression of a natural theology emphasizing metaphysical and ethical principles shared by all peoples, as a prototypical Christian sermon aimed at Gentiles, and as a perennial meditation on the relationship between faith and philosophy. With more references to Greek poets than to Jewish Scripture, it addresses an audience that, to an extent, stands for the cultured world of the Greeks and Romans. Juxtaposed alongside the exuberant pagans at Derbe and Lystra in Acts 14 who mistake Paul and Barnabas for Hermes and Zeus after their healing of a lame man and attempt to offer them sacrifices, the cool response of the Athenians makes a less than flattering impression on the reader.

The Athenians are depicted as busybodies, interested in other people's affairs but averse to introspection. Their apparent misconstrual of "Jesus and the resurrection (*anastasis*)" as a deity and his female consort is in line with the busybody's prurient interest in sex. Their reaction to the speech's conclusion is even more telling. Nothing peculiarly Christian has been said in vv. 23–29, which resonate with Stoic ideas about the gods and the universe. But in the peroration of the speech he makes more exclusivistic claims (17:30–31):

> While God has overlooked the times of human ignorance, he now commands all people everywhere to repent, because he has fixed a day on which he will have the world judged in righteousness by a man whom he has appointed, and of this he has given assurance to all by raising him from the dead.

Having just heard the only genuine "news" in the speech, the audience suddenly loses interest. The sins of others are more interesting than their own, which Paul calls on them to contemplate.

From Athens Paul travels to Corinth, where he stays for eighteen months (18:1–17). Perhaps it is the lackluster response of the Athenian philosophers that leads him to go back to basics in his proclamation to the Corinthians, preaching "Christ crucified" instead of "lofty words of wisdom" even though it is "foolishness to Gentiles" (1 Cor. 1:23; 2:1). Gallio joins the parade of Roman officials reluctant to get entangled in internecine squabbles when Jews bring Paul before his tribunal. (Luke's reference to Gallio's tenure as proconsul of Achaia enables scholars to date many of the events in Acts with specificity.) Paul's subsequent stay in Ephesus lasts nearly three years (19:1–41). He speaks in synagogues and lecture halls, heals the sick, and casts out evil spirits. Silversmiths organized by Demetrius causes trouble for Paul because, his preaching having turned so many people away from idol worship, their profit margin has shrunk and their patron deity Artemis has been dishonored. Paul is rescued from the mob by the town clerk, but leaves town for a while in case civic passions flare again. His emotional farewell speech to the Ephesian elders gathered at Miletus recalls Jesus' discourse in which he predicts his own impending trials in Jerusalem and warns them of false teachers (20:17–35).

Jerusalem turns out to be no safer (21:17–23:30). Rumors that Paul subverts the Jewish law have circulated in advance of his return. Violent protests erupt when he is accused of entering the temple with Gentiles in tow (21:27–40). Defense speeches delivered before various audiences take up a significant portion of the rest of the book (Porter 1999: 151–71). On the temple steps, Paul is shouted down but not before he can repeat his conversion story (22:1–21). Before the Sanhedrin, he drives a wedge between the Pharisees and Sadducees in attendance by strategically mentioning a disputed theological doctrine—the resurrection—whereupon the Pharisees absolve him of wrongdoing (23:1–10).

A conspiracy to kill Paul, who had earlier invoked the protections afforded by Roman citizenship, leads to his transfer to Caesarea. The charge made by the prosecution that he is "an agitator among all the Jews throughout the world" is formulated to capture the attention of Roman officials wary of political unrest (24:5; cf. 21:38). Felix, the procurator of Judea, appears satisfied by Paul's defense, but nevertheless leaves him in prison for two years as a favor to the Jews and likely in the hopes of extorting a bribe (24:10–27). To avoid being sent back to Jerusalem by Festus, Felix's successor, Paul appeals his case to the emperor (25:1–12). His appeal is granted, but before his departure he has one final opportunity to share his story. This time the audience is Herod Agrippa II, the great-grandson of Herod the Great (26:1–23).

The series of Pauline speeches serves three related functions in Luke's narrative. It displays the literary fulfillment of prophecies made by Jesus before and after his resurrection that his followers would bear witness to him before kings and rulers (Luke 21:12; Acts 9:15). It rebuts the theological charge of novelty and reiterates that the Christian message consists of "nothing but what the prophets and Moses said would take place" (26:22). And it provides ample opportunity for various characters to proclaim the innocence of Paul individually and of the broader messianic movement in the face of accusations that it is seditious. By demonstrating its continuity with Judaism, Luke can at the same time obviate any legal problems that might ensue if it were to be denied status as a *religio licita*.

Despite experiencing shipwreck, starvation, and snake bite, Paul makes landfall and soon comes to Rome (27:1–28:14). Since he is greeted by believers, it is clear that Paul did not introduce Christianity to the capital of the empire. Yet his arrival, against all odds, provides a final example of the providential spread of the faith to the ends of the earth. Paul is under house arrest for two years and is able to receive visitors and continue preaching to the Jews. The results are mixed at best. He interprets the situation, as do other New Testament texts, with reference to Isa. 6:9–10 (Acts 28:25–27; cf. Matt. 13:14–15; John 12:40). Widespread Jewish rejection of the gospel, he says, was always part of God's plan. Whether it will ever be thus, he does not say. The ending is therefore somewhat bittersweet, notwithstanding the receptiveness of the Gentiles to whom Paul preaches "with all boldness and without hindrance" (28:28–31; a twenty-ninth chapter of Acts in a spurious manuscript first published in 1871 imagines a Pauline journey to Britain where the apostle meets ancient Druids and preaches to one of the "lost tribes" of Israel on the future site of St. Paul's Cathedral).

Luke appears as a character in the 1955 sword-and-sandal epic *The Silver Chalice*, loosely based on the *Acts of Peter*, and remarks that "every Christian you meet is a man who's changed his mind or else he wouldn't be a Christian." Insofar as they are all converts to Christianity, Luke's readers have all made turns, albeit from different directions. It would be a mistake to read the conclusion of Luke-Acts as a supersessionist prediction that only Gentiles will listen to the good news. Even if Gentiles exceed Jews in raw numbers within the church when Luke is writing, it is difficult but important to keep in mind the demographic reality that the vast majority of both Jews and Gentiles in the first century do not respond affirmatively to the apostles' preaching. Both groups thus represent faithful "remnants" in the ongoing story of the formation of God's people, in the church and under the auspices of the Holy Spirit.

# John

| | |
|---|---|
| 1:1–18 | Prologue |
| 1:19–12:50 | The Book of Signs |
| 1:19–51 | Calling of the disciples |
| 2:1–5:47 | Working wonders in Galilee, Samaria, and Judea |
| 6:1–71 | The Bread of Life |
| 7:1–10:42 | Living Water, the Light of the World, and the Good Shepherd |
| 11:1–57 | The Raising of Lazarus |
| 12:1–50 | The anointing at Bethany and the entry into Jerusalem |
| 13:1–20:31 | The Book of Glory |
| 13:1–38 | The Last Supper and the foot washing |
| 14:1–17:26 | Jesus' farewell discourse |
| 18:1–19:42 | The Passion narrative |
| 18:1–19:15 | Arrest, denial, and trial |
| 19:16–42 | Crucifixion and burial |
| 20:1–31 | Resurrection |
| 21:1–25 | Epilogue: The risen Jesus in Galilee |

The Gospel of John is a tour de force. No one else in the early church tells the story of Jesus in quite the same way. From antiquity it has been recognized as the most distinctive of the canonical gospels. Clement of Alexandria refers to it as the "spiritual Gospel" (Eusebius, *Hist. eccl.* 6.14.7) at the same time that the Gnostic writer Heracleon is composing a commentary on it, the first devoted to a document that will become a part of the Christian canon. The Johannine Jesus thus contains multitudes, appealing equally to heretics and the orthodox. His story begins before the foundation of the world (1:1–5) and ends with the declaration that the world is too small for the libraries needed to do it justice (21:25).

Even as Matthew, Mark, and Luke supply most readers with the broad outlines of Jesus' biography, it is quite often John that gives him voice. Rivalled only by his Matthean counterpart, John's Jesus has made an enormous impact on the Christian idiom and, in particular, on the English language, especially by way of the King James Bible. "Born again" believers of the Evangelical persuasion think of themselves as having undergone the spiritual rebirth demanded by Jesus in his conversation with Nicodemus (3:3), which also includes what may be the most widely quoted verse in the Bible—"For God so loved the world, that he gave his only begotten Son, that whosoever believeth in him should not perish, but have everlasting life" (3:16). The man born blind (9:1–38) utters what will become one of the most famous lyrics in the most famous of all Christian hymns, "Amazing Grace" (". . . was blind, but now I see"). Those caught in corrupt legal systems have taken heart at Jesus' proclamation that "the truth shall set you free" (8:32). Others in the depth of despair and anxiety have been comforted by his words to the disciples he would soon leave, "Peace I leave with you, my peace I give unto you . . . Let not your heart be troubled, neither let it be afraid" (14:27). Enemies of hypocrisy are fond of quoting his instruction to let the one "without sin . . . cast the first stone" at the woman caught in adultery (8:7), undeterred by its absence from the most reliable manuscripts. Writers as diverse as John Paul II (in the title of his encyclical *Ut Unum Sint*) and Friedrich Nietzsche (in the title of his last book, *Ecce Homo*) have borrowed Johannine phraseology that has passed through the Vulgate (17:21; 19:5). John's Jesus is not only a man of many words but of many deeds as well. He turns water into wine (2:1–11), raises Lazarus from the dead (11:1–44), and endows his disciples with the Holy Spirit (20:21–23), yet he is not above performing humbler tasks such as washing his disciples' feet and preparing breakfast for the fisherman whose ample catch he has made possible (13:1–17; 21:9–14).

None of the four gospels explicitly names their author or includes footnotes enabling readers to check their sources. The Fourth Gospel comes closer to revealing its author's identity than the other three. In the closing scene, the author identifies "the disciple whom Jesus loved" as the one "who is testifying to these things and has written them," adding, "and we know that his testimony is true" (21:20–24).

The shift from third- to first-person pronouns for the last two verses of the book, however, makes it unclear whether this constitutes an outright confession that the "Beloved Disciple" is himself the author of the Fourth Gospel or simply the authoritative source for the traditions that have gone into its composition. The Beloved Disciple, strangely, is never named (13:23; 19:25; 20:2; 21:7). Through comparison with the Synoptic Gospels, one may infer that this title refers to the Apostle John, son of Zebedee and brother of James, the disciple who reclined next to Jesus at the Last Supper, notwithstanding conspiracy theories popularized by Dan Brown in *The Da Vinci Code* asserting that Mary Magdalene was actually the Beloved Disciple. Most scholars believe the author was a disciple of this John, writing possibly from Ephesus, where early church traditions say that John settled either with Jesus' mother or shortly after her death. Eastern Orthodox Christians celebrate the Translation of St. John the Theologian because, according to the *Synaxarion*, his disciples found his tomb in Ephesus empty. The Johannine Letters are usually attributed to the same circle, if not to the same hand responsible for the gospel. Revelation was traditionally associated with the same John but is now thought to come from a different writer of the same name.

## DATE, AUDIENCE, OCCASION

While his identity may remain somewhat veiled, the author helpfully provides clues about his audience, his context, his self-consciousness as a participant in the revelatory process whereby "we have seen his glory, the glory as of the Father's only Son, full of grace and truth" (1:14), and his purposes in writing. Neither Matthew nor Mark states his purposes in writing a gospel, and Luke declares his intentions in his opening preface. John waits until near the end (20:30–31). He admits that he has been selective in the events he has chosen to recount, and in spelling out his criterion for inclusion he reveals his purpose:

> Now Jesus did many other signs in the presence of his disciples, which are not written in this book. But these are written so that you may come to believe that Jesus is the Messiah, the Son of God, and that through believing you may have life in his name.

Are the "other signs" simply other miracles, or is he thinking of other sorts of deeds? Is he referring to omitted episodes appearing in the Synoptic Gospels? It may drive many readers to distraction to learn that John possesses a treasure trove of stories about the life of Jesus and that he deliberately leaves much or even most of them out.

Furthermore, there is a textual ambiguity even in this seemingly straightforward declaration. A one-letter variant in the ancient manuscripts results in a tense change in the verb "believe" (*pisteu[s]ēte*). Depending on the manuscript one trusts, it may thus be translated either "might believe" (i.e., "come to have faith") or "may believe" (i.e., "continue to have faith"). The implications for the intended audience should be obvious. Opting for the former yields an intended audience of non-Christians in whom John seeks to awaken belief. Opting for the latter yields an intended audience of Christians already in the fold, so to speak, whose faith the author wants to sustain and deepen. It is instructive to re-read the gospel with an eye trained on the ways in which the narrative comports with one or the other of these options. In either case, John's ultimate hope for his readers' salvation is expressed in the final clause.

Throughout the gospel, the author subtly inserts himself into the narrative in a way that draws attention to its post-Easter perspective. In summarizing the cleansing of the temple, which the Fourth Gospel places at the beginning of Jesus' public ministry rather than near the end, John notes that the disciples would later connect Jesus' actions to specific biblical prophecies and that they would only understand the true import of his promise to "raise up" the temple after he was raised from the dead (2:14–22). Likewise, at the triumphal entry into Jerusalem in John 12, the disciples "did not understand these things at first," but "when Jesus was glorified" they could perceive that the Scriptures were written about him. As late as Easter morning, at the very entrance to the empty tomb, the Beloved Disciple himself "did not understand the scripture, that he must rise from the dead" (20:8–9). In addition to these asides remarking on the internal state of certain characters, many of the memorable lines attributed to Jesus in ostensible dialogue with other characters (e.g., 3:16) may just as plausibly be read as the author's own commentary explaining the significance of the interaction. The imperceptiveness of the Twelve, which invites comparison with the portrayal of the disciples in Mark, appears to be inevitable in the Fourth Gospel and not worthy of condemnation.

The unbelieving response of other characters, however, is not excused, and this characterization is a key to understanding the context of the Fourth Gospel's composition (Culpepper 1983: 125–32). Above all, it is "the Jews" (*hoi Ioudaioi*) who are portrayed as the implacable foes of Jesus throughout the text. Whereas Matthew, Mark, and Luke refer to "the Jews" on only a handful of occasions, John does so several dozen times (e.g., 1:19; 2:18; 5:10; 9:18; 18:31; 19:42). From the outset, the reader is told that Jesus "came to what was his own, and his own people did not accept him" (1:11). The subsequent narrative vividly dramatizes this lack of faith. "The Jews" criticize him for healing on the Sabbath and begin plotting his death, "because he was not only breaking the Sabbath, but was also calling God his own Father, thereby making himself equal to God" (5:16–18; 7:1). Later, when they attempt to stone him, they explain that it is for blasphemy, "because you, though only a human being, are making yourself God" (10:31–33). When Pilate says he sees no crime he has committed, "the Jews" answer that according to their law, "he ought to die because he has claimed to be the Son of God" (19:7). Their mutual animosity is most palpable in their argument about Father Abraham (8:39–59). Both Jesus and "the Jews" claim to be the true heir of Abraham and children of God, but Jesus rejects their claim: "You are from your father the devil" (8:44). Many of Jesus' followers are afraid to be associated with him because of what the Jews may do to them (7:10–13; 19:38). The specific threat is spelled out in John 9:22, where it is reported that "anyone who confessed Jesus to be the Messiah would be put out of the synagogue."

It would perhaps be unsurprising to find such starkly different religious perspectives were Jesus himself not one of "the Jews." Jesus observes Jewish festivals such as Sukkoth, Hannukah, and Passover (2:13; 5:1; 7:14; 10:22; 12:1), and is called a Jew by other characters (4:9; 18:35; 19:3, 19). Lest one presume that Jesus' Jewishness is merely incidental, in his conversation with the woman at the well he says that "salvation is from the Jews" (4:22). Further complicating John's depiction of the Jews is the appearance of several Jewish characters who believe in Jesus or, at the very least, are willing to give him the benefit of the doubt rather than immediately assume that he is demon-possessed (8:31; 9:16; 10:19–21; 11:45; 12:11). Those at the Jewish festivals who are said to fear speaking openly about Jesus on account of "the Jews" (7:10–13) are themselves presumably Jewish. Therefore, in some sense, not all of "the Jews" are to be numbered among "the Jews."

To solve this puzzle, it has been suggested that the many positive or neutral references to *hoi Ioudaioi* are better translated not as "the Jews" but as "the Judeans" when it refers to Jesus' enemies, as it is clearly only a subset of all Jews that oppose him. (Many scholars believe that *hoi Ioudaioi* designates a group of Jewish leaders opposed to Jesus and responsible for his death, but that there is no ideal way of reflecting this distinction through translation.) This is an imperfect solution that nevertheless attempts to clarify the author's orientation and purpose in writing a gospel. His familiarity with the geography of Judea, with Jewish customs, and with interpretations of the Bible common among both Hellenistic and rabbinic Jewish writers suggests that John identifies as a Jew—or has, perhaps, until recent developments have made him feel like an outsider—engaged in ongoing intra-Jewish debate about the faith traditions of Israel, not entirely unlike the situation reflected in Jesus' polemic against the Pharisees in Matthew 23. His audience may also include Samaritans and Gentiles, who look forward to a coming day when they will worship "neither on this mountain nor in Jerusalem" (4:21). When the author mentions the threat of Christ-believers being put out of the synagogue (9:22; 12:42; 16:2), he uses a term, *aposynagōgos*, that appears nowhere else in contemporaneous Greek literature. Although there is hostility between Jesus and some of his fellow Jews during his lifetime, the scenario envisioned by John is more indicative of circumstances near the end of the first century and later when Christian claims about Jesus put them beyond the pale of acceptable belief about God in the view of most Jews for the way they are perceived to compromise the strict monotheism enjoined by Torah. John and his readers may have recently experienced ostracism on this basis. The Fourth Gospel, then, should be understood as part of a defensive attempt to carve out an identity for a community of Christ-believers that is undeniably rooted in Judaism in its symbolism and the sources informing its theology, yet also distinct from the religion practiced by most Jews by virtue of the place occupied by Jesus in its worldview and worship (Brown 1966: lxx–lxxix).

Unfortunately, when it is read out of context, as it has been for much of Christian history, the Fourth Gospel has the capacity to foster anti-Semitism (Kysar 1993). In its radically dualistic imagery—featuring contrasts of spirit with flesh, light with dark, life with death, and truth with falsehood—"the Jews" are consistently associated with the negative aspect. Insofar as Jesus' enemies are condemned for their lack of belief rather than on the basis of their racial background, "anti-Semitic" is an anachronistic label for its bitter polemic, even the charge that the Jews are the spawn of Satan (8:44). Properly speaking, it is more accurate to employ the term "anti-Jewish," though when the text is read by Gentiles this distinction has often made little difference. In this vein, John was the gospel featured most prominently in *Die Botschaft Gottes* (*The Message of God*), a dejudaized abridgement of the New Testament produced in 1940 by the Institute for the Study and Eradication of Jewish Influence on German Church Life (Heschel 2008: 106; its editor excised John 4:22—"salvation is from the Jews"—and called on the church to ban sermons based on it).

Answers to these questions about the Fourth Gospel's purpose, historical context, and intended audience are closely related to the question of dating. Tensions between early Christian groups and the larger Jewish community worsen as time passes. The vitriol on display in the Fourth Gospel indicates that relations may have deteriorated to the point that the author and his fellow Christ-believers have been ejected from the local synagogues (9:22; 16:2). Dating the deterioration of these relations is difficult since any such break likely occurred at different times in different locations, progressing more rapidly after the destruction of the temple in 70 CE. The *Birkat ha-minim*, a Jewish "benediction against the heretics" usually dated to 85 CE, has been interpreted as a jab at Christians, though there is no reason to think it was composed specifically as a response to the Fourth Gospel. John's "high" Christology no doubt contributed to the break, and many scholars posit that the development of the idea that Jesus was divine would have taken several decades. Yet the image of a pre-existent, quasi-divine Christ appears already in Paul (Phil. 2:6–11).

The one thing that can be said with confidence is that the Fourth Gospel was written no later than ca. 125 CE, the date of a papyrus fragment ($P^{52}$) containing an excerpt from John 18 discovered in Egypt in 1920. Backing up for the time needed for the text to be copied and circulated, most scholars date the gospel to the last decade of the first century.

More effort has been expended in determining a relative dating for the Fourth Gospel by comparing it with the Synoptic Gospels, which is in turn dependent on the literary relationship between the former and the latter one assumes. There are two primary options when it comes to the literary relationship. Either (1) John is familiar with one or more of the Synoptic Gospels or the traditions behind them, in which case it is thought that the author is writing to correct or supplement their narratives and understandings of Jesus; or (2) John is totally independent from the Synoptic tradition, even if their stories follow parallel narrative arcs: John the Baptist appears announcing the coming of Jesus, who works wonders and dispenses moral and theological wisdom, attracts disciples and provokes opposition, dies on the cross, and rises on the third day. With an abundance of source material (21:25), John could have composed his account with minimal overlap. If John is to some extent dependent on the Synoptic Gospels, then it must be later. How much later is harder to say. For example, if one accepts the consensus that the Synoptic Gospels are written forty or fifty years after the death of Jesus, it seems arbitrary to place John a decade or two later on the basis of its high Christology, as if a certain understanding of Jesus required six or seven decades to develop but would have been unthinkable in only four or five. On the other hand, if the Fourth Gospel is independent of the Synoptic Gospels, then one may date it early—few scholars posit a pre-70 date—or as late as 100 CE. Those who place it later nonetheless recognize that it may contain historical reminiscences that predate the Synoptic accounts and may even derive from eyewitnesses who are knowledgeable about Jewish customs and the environs of Jerusalem.

## JOHN AND THE SYNOPTIC TRADITION

However one construes the literary relationship between John and the Synoptic Gospels, there are numerous differences in terms of their structure and content (Smith 1980): (1) where and when Jesus conducts his ministry in John; (2) who appears and what happens along the way; and (3) how Jesus is portrayed—each area affords an opportunity for comparison with the Synoptic Gospels.

(1) John and the Synoptic Gospels differ in relation to time and space. First, how long does Jesus' ministry last? Everyone "knows" that Jesus dies at the age of thirty-three. But the New Testament never says so. To arrive at this number, one must start with the notice in Luke 3:23 that Jesus begins his public ministry when he is about thirty. If one were to plot the events described in the Synoptic Gospels on a timeline, it would be possible to fit the entire story into a single year. Not so with John, with its references to multiple celebrations of Passover and other Jewish feasts (2:13; 6:4; 12:1; 18:28), which implies a ministry of about three years. By combining the two, the result is a three-year ministry ending with Jesus' death at thirty-three. Furthermore, the Johannine timeline seems to indicate that Jesus' climactic final visit to Jerusalem begins during the Jewish festival of Sukkoth in the fall and lasts several months instead of a single week (7:1). Perhaps John does not share Luke's scruples about composing an "orderly account" (1:1, 4), or it may be that his ideas about how things fit together do not conform to normal chronological categories (cf. the frequent references to Jesus' "hour" in 2:4; 4:23; 5:25; 7:6, 8; 12:27). Second, John's narrative unfolds in a slightly different geographic setting. Most of the story told by the Synoptic Gospels takes place in Galilee before shifting south to Judea for the last week of Jesus' life. By comparison, much more of John takes place in Judea, in and around Jerusalem, with relatively few events of consequence taking place elsewhere.

(2) The Fourth Gospel features a distinctive cast, including a number of characters who appear in none of the other canonical gospels but who enjoy a thriving post-biblical career. Nathanael (John 1:45–52), initially skeptical that anything good can come from Nazareth before Jesus salutes him as a "true Israelite," is identified in the thirteenth-century Nestorian *Book of the Bee* as one of the infants who survives the Slaughter of the Holy Innocents. Nicodemus (3:1–21; 19:39), the furtive Pharisee who visits Jesus by night and later assists Joseph of Arimathea in preparing Jesus' body for burial, lends his name to one of the most popular noncanonical texts of the Middle Ages, the fourth-century *Gospel of Nicodemus* which describes the "Harrowing of Hell" between Good Friday and Easter, and appears prominently in Michelangelo's Florentine *Pietà*. The Samaritan Woman at the Well (4:7–42) becomes Saint Photini in

the Orthodox Church after she converts her five sisters, two sons, and Nero's daughter to Christianity and is martyred by being thrown down a dry well shaft. The woman caught in adultery (7:53–8:11), often (mis-)identified as Mary Magdalene, becomes the prototype for Hester Prynne in Hawthorne's *The Scarlet Letter*. Lazarus (11:1–57), according to Eastern Orthodox tradition, flees in a leaky boat to the island of Cyprus (or Marseilles, according to the thirteenth-century *Golden Legend*) where he serves as bishop, so disturbed by the sight of unredeemed souls during his brief sojourn among the dead that he never again laughs for the final thirty years of his life. The soldier who pierces Jesus' side (19:34) with the "Spear of Destiny" coveted by Hitler for its alleged powers is later christened Saint Longinus and played by John Wayne in *The Greatest Story Ever Told*.

In addition to these figures, many of the characters John shares with the other gospels appear in unique scenes or receive special narrative treatment. John the Baptist supplies one of the Fourth Gospel's dominant Christological motifs in hailing Jesus as "the Lamb of God who takes away the sins of the world" (1:29, 36) as well as the title— in Latin (*Agnus Dei*)—of the incipit to the pre-Communion prayer in the Mass. Mary's maternal nudge leads to the first revelation of Jesus' glory and to the disciples' faith in him at the Wedding at Cana (2:1–11). Peter receives a special three-fold charge from Jesus ("Feed my sheep") and has his own martyrdom foretold (21:15–19). Although he ultimately addresses him as "My Lord and my God," Thomas earns his "dubious" sobriquet when he refuses to believe that Jesus is risen until he is presented with tangible proof, a moment of incredulity never more graphically depicted than by Caravaggio (20:24–29; according to medieval traditions, he was also inconveniently absent for the Assumption of Mary). Pontius Pilate's dialogue with Jesus (18:28–19:16) is much more detailed than in the Synoptic Gospels, including one of the most famous rhetorical questions in history—"What is truth?" (18:38). And the Beloved Disciple himself takes responsibility for Jesus' mother and becomes her "son," and later outruns Peter to the empty tomb (19:25–27; 20:1–9).

Several other scenes are found only in the Fourth Gospel. Much of Jesus' Galilean ministry in John 2–4 is unique to John, as are the healing of the lame man at the pool of Bethesda (5:1–18), the Bread of Life discourse and its aftermath (6:22–71), various disputations with Jewish authorities (7:1–52; 8:12–59), the Good Shepherd discourse (10:1–42), the plot against Lazarus (12:9–11), the footwashing (13:1–38), and the farewell discourse (14:1–17:26). But there are other points at which, on the hypothesis that he is familiar with the Synoptic Gospels, John feels that less is more. Left out of his narrative are such characters as Joseph, Herod Antipas, the rich young man, and the Canaanite woman. Pivotal scenes from the Synoptic Gospels are also absent. Stories about Jesus' birth and childhood are missing, as are the temptation, the Sermon on the Mount/Plain, the transfiguration, Peter's confession at Caesarea Philippi, the institution of the Lord's Supper, and Jesus' prayer in Gethsemane. The Johannine Jesus performs no exorcisms, and while he uses figurative language, his teachings never take the form of parables.

(3) John's portrait of Jesus is informed by a distinctive Christological vision (Schnackenburg 1995: 219–94). A striking aspect of this portrayal is the manner in which Jesus talks about himself in lengthy discourses rather than arguing with his opponents about the law. The Synoptic Jesus punctuates his serial appearances in relatively concise episodes with brief, frequently cryptic sayings. Readers may be forgiven for their failure to recognize Jesus for who he is, all the more so when he speaks of himself in the third person as the Son of Man. Everyone in the Fourth Gospel, by contrast, is in on the so-called Messianic Secret, as Jesus does nothing to conceal his identity. For example, he can be evasive on the question of his messianic status in the Synoptic Gospels, but he responds unambiguously to the Samaritan woman when she mentions the coming of the Christ, saying, "I am he, the one who is speaking to you" (4:26).

Most conspicuously, Jesus utters seven "I Am" sayings employing a specific metaphor to describe himself that are related thematically to the scene where it appears. In many cases, these self-referential metaphors echo passages in the Hebrew Bible where they are associated with God (Exod. 16:1–36; 33:13; Ps. 23:1–4; Isa 5:1–7; 40:3; 42:6–7; Ezek. 34:11–16). These seven statement are:

- "I am the Bread of Life" (John 6:35, 41, 48, 51). This metaphor and the accompanying discourse, appearing in conjunction with the miracle of the loaves and fishes, are often cited in debates about the "real presence" in the Eucharist. Medieval hymns often extend it by making Mary's womb the "oven" in which it was baked.

- "I am the Light of the World (8:12). Large golden lamps were lit at the temple in the Court of Women during Sukkoth (7:2); thus Jesus claims to embody the festival's meaning.
- "I am the Gate for the Sheep" (10:7, 9). Often translated "the Door," this metaphor emphasizes Jesus' role in admitting those who, like Peter (21:15–18), will "feed his sheep."
- "I am the Good Shepherd" (10:11, 14). The earliest and most popular examples of Christian art are thought to be symbolic representations of Jesus the Good Shepherd found in Roman catacombs. Gentiles are the "other sheep" (10:16) who will hear Jesus' voice, though Mormons have interpreted this as refer- ring to a contingent of Jews who migrated to North America ca. 600 BCE and Jehovah's Witnesses see it as a reference to the majority of believers who will live forever on a remade earth rather than in heaven.
- "I am the Resurrection and the Life" (11:25). Before raising their brother Lazarus, Jesus tells Mary and Martha that he makes present the general resurrection anticipated in the future by the faithful.
- "I am the Way, the Truth, and the Life" (14:6). Critics of Christian exclusivism are uncomfortable with Jesus' explanatory gloss, "no one comes to the Father except through me."
- "I am the True Vine" (15:1, 5). Those who "abide" in Jesus are the "branches" that bear fruit.

At several other points Jesus makes emphatic "I am" (*egō eimi*) state- ments without any predicate (4:26; 6:20; 8:24; 13:19; 18:5–8). Many translations obscure this element of Johannine style by rendering it in a variety of ways in order to smooth the English syntax. This habit unintentionally conceals the way in which this unusual grammati- cal construction—adding the personal pronoun *egō* is unnecessary in Greek—constitutes an allusion to the divine name, YHWH, in the Hebrew Bible. The most famous instance is when Moses encounters God in the burning bush in Exod. 3:14 and, when he asks his name, is told, "I AM WHO I AM . . . say to the Israelites, 'I AM has sent me to you'."

Is this reading too much theology into the author's syntax? After all, *eimi* is the most commonly used verb in the Greek language.

But sometimes "to be" is not "to be" in the ordinary sense. Jesus' argument with Jewish leaders in John 8 confirms the suspicion that his peculiar language serves to express the author's "high" Christology. When Jesus says that Abraham rejoiced over his coming, the Jews remark that this is impossible since he is not even fifty years old. Jesus replies, "Very truly, I tell you, before Abraham was, I am" (8:58). Should he not have said, "before Abraham was, I was"? The awkward syntax is no accident, and the implicit claim to divinity does not go unnoticed by the Jews, who pick up stones to stone him. They are not such sticklers for proper grammar that they would put him to death for using the wrong verb tense.

With its emphasis on Jesus' divine qualities, John's high Christology is manifest in many other ways as well. In the opening verse, he is identified as the Word of God who was not only "with God" in the beginning but "was God" (1:1). He assumes prerogatives normally reserved for God and states that one's response to the Son is indicative of one's response to God (3:18, 36–36; 8:19; 12:47–48). Jesus' role in this relationship is often described as that of an envoy: "Whoever believes in me believes not in me but in him who sent me. And whoever sees me sees him who sent me" (12:44–45; cf. 5:30; 11:42; 17:8; 20:21). Jesus is unique in that he is sent "from above." He tells Nicodemus, "No one has ascended into heaven except the one who descended from heaven" (3:13; 6:33, 38; 17:16; 18:36–37). In similarly unequivocal terms, he tells the Jews, "You are from below, I am from above; you are of this world, I am not of this world" (8:23). From these texts, in which Jesus appears to descend from heaven and almost hover above the earth without ever quite planting his feet on the ground, one can surmise what attracted Gnostic and Valentinian writers to the Fourth Gospel. The worry expressed in the Johannine Letters about the "antichrist" who denies that Jesus has come in the flesh as a human being (2 John 7) but not, apparently, that he was divine likewise comes into clearer focus. The Johannine Jesus states his supernatural claims most succinctly in response to the Jews at Hannukah who want to know if he is the Messiah: "The Father and I are one" (10:30). This terse reply may admit multiple interpretations. That the Jews again attempt to stone him shows that they understand it as tantamount to a claim of equality with God well before Thomas addresses the risen Jesus as "My Lord and my God" (20:28).

Alongside the highest Christology of any book in the New Testament, John juxtaposes poignant glimpses of Jesus' humanity. Notwithstanding expressions of the intimate relationship believers enjoy with Jesus in such popular hymns as "What a Friend We Have in Jesus," it is only in the Fourth Gospel that Jesus is said to be their friend (15:13–16). In the Beloved Disciple, he not only has a friend but, as it were, a best friend. He lowers himself to the point of washing his disciples' feet. He can become angry, passive-aggressive, and argumentative. In the Bible's shortest verse, he even weeps (11:35), though nowhere does he laugh, as he does in Gnostic texts such as the *Second Treatise of the Great Seth* or the *Apocalypse of Peter* where "the living Jesus" laughs at the ignorance of onlookers who suppose it is he who is nailed to the cross. Simultaneously "low" and "high," John's Christology informs patristic theologians in articulating the notion of a hypostatic union in which the full humanity and full divinity of Jesus partake in one and the same substance. Perhaps no other text supplied more fodder for Christological controversy before and after Nicaea than the Gospel of John.

Many scholars place little trust in John as a source for the teachings of the historical Jesus, especially when compared with the Synoptic Gospels. Those who are more confident in its historical value concede that while it may not preserve unedited the very words he spoke (*ipsissima verba*), it nonetheless presents a faithful rendering of the very voice (*ipsissima vox*) of Jesus that reliably transmits the thrust of his proclamation. Do Jesus, the other characters, and the narrator of the Fourth Gospel simply make explicit what is contained in the Synoptic tradition but remains only implicit? Alternatively, does the Fourth Gospel interpret the significance of Jesus in ways that Jesus and his followers would consider alien or repugnant? Disentangling the historical from the theological dimensions of these questions is no easy task. A brief overview of the narrative may help clarify whether they are the right ones to ask.

## IN THE BEGINNING

John's high Christology is conspicuous from the outset: "In the beginning was the Word [*logos*], and the Word was with God, and the Word was God" (1:1; the New World Translation of the Jehovah's

Witnesses resists the Trinitarian reading of this verse by rendering the last clause "and the Word was a god"). If the prologue (1:1–18) were set to music, one could easily imagine the trumpets from Richard Strauss's *Also Sprach Zarathustra* blaring in accompaniment to the word "God" and again in a higher key at the announcement in John 1:14 that "the Word became flesh." Jewish tradition accommodates subordinate agents in creation such as the personification of Wisdom (Prov. 8:22–31; Sir. 24:1–12) and the pre-existent Logos adapted from Plato and the Stoics by Philo of Alexandria (*Fug.* 101), but nothing quite so startling as the identification of this agent with God, who grants to all who believe in him "power to become children of God" (1:12). Irenaeus develops this theme when he says that God "became what we are in order to make us what he is" (*Haer.* 5), as does, in a different way, Lorenzo Snow in the famous Mormon couplet, "As man now is, God once was;/As God now is, man may be." The doctrine of the Incarnation expressed here poses a major stumbling block for both Jews and Muslims who view it as a grave violation of strict monotheistic imperatives. Appropriation of the prologue's language ranges from the light to the very dark. Envious Frenchmen deployed John 1:14 in mocking the loquacious philosopher David Hume's corpulence, muttering as he entered the room, "And the Word became flesh." On a more chilling note, Hermann Hoyer entitled his 1937 painting of Hitler speaking to a small group of admirers in the early days of the Nazi Party "In the Beginning was the Word."

With the use of so many verbs in the past and perfect tense, the prologue conveys the sense of a fait accompli. He "was in the world . . . and lived among us," but still "the world did not know him." Jesus is not named until v. 17 and does not enter until v. 29, well after John the Baptist is introduced. The reader wants to know more about the Word, but the priests and Levites appear obtuse in their desire to know only about John, who deflects their questions and points to "one who is coming after" (1:27). Titles for Jesus proliferate quickly. By the end of the first chapter, he is referred to as "the true light," "the Word," "God," "Rabbi," "Messiah," "Son of God," "Son of Man," and "King of Israel"—as if no single descriptor can adequately capture the identity of "the only Son." Their precise significance is unclear unless the reader is willing, like the disciples, to "come and see" (1:39, 46). The stage is thus set for the revelation of his glory.

## THE BOOK OF SIGNS

Scholars customarily divide John into two major sections, the Book of Signs (1:19–12:50) and the Book of Glory (13:1–20:31). Beginning at the Wedding at Cana in chapter two, the Book of Signs includes seven miracles. Four of the seven are unique to John:

- Water into Wine (2:1–11). Whereas many paintings of this episode, such as that of Veronese, depict it as a decadent affair, the Roman Catholic Church teaches that Jesus' attendance sanctified the institution of marriage. Taking place "on the third day" after a sequence of four previous days (cf. 1:1, 29, 35, 43), many interpreters see it as a re-enactment of the seven-day creation and a statement that Jesus continues the work of the creator.
- The Healing of the Royal Official's Son (4:46–54; cf. Matt 8:5–13; Luke 7:1–10). After an initial rebuke—"Unless you see signs and wonders you will not believe" (4:48)—Jesus responds to the official's request by performing a "long distance" miracle.
- The Healing of the Lame Man (5:1–18). Because it is missing from the earliest manuscripts, Bibles now omit the explanation in John 5:4 about the healing effects available to the first person in the pool after its surface was periodically disturbed by an angel.
- The Feeding of the Five Thousand (6:1–14; cf. Matt. 14:13–21; Mark 6:32–44; Luke 9:10–17). This is the only miracle recorded in all four gospels. This sign precedes the Bread of Life discourse and features parallels with the story in Exod. 16:1–36 of God's provision of manna in the desert.
- Walking on the Water (6:16–21; cf. Matt. 14:22–27; Mark 6:45–51). In counting the signs, some scholars omit this episode from the list and instead count the crucifixion or resurrection as the seventh.
- Healing the Man born Blind (9:1–41). The awkward question of the disciples—"who sinned, this man or his parents, that he was born blind?" (9:2)—has factored into theological debates about the relationship of sin to sickness and disability. From antiquity, this text has been used as a reading for catechumens preparing for baptism.

- The Raising of Lazarus (11:1–44). In *The Greatest Story Ever Told*, the raising of Lazarus occurs to great fanfare, with an arrangement of Handel's "Hallelujah" chorus playing in the background. Although the scene is more than a little melodramatic, it captures the climactic tone of the ending of the Book of Signs.

John alone refers to these marvelous deeds as "signs" (*sēmeia*), and states that he has chosen these out of many others he might have described specifically to produce or sustain faith that Jesus is Messiah and Son of God (20:30–31).

Fondness for synonyms does not account for John's terminology on this point. To be sure, a sign looks like a miracle. John discusses their function and lays stress on what they signify. They are meant to engender or deepen belief (2:11, 23), yet signs are neither necessary nor sufficient for producing it (12:37). Jesus commends Thomas for his belief after seeing his wounds, but implies that "those who have not seen and yet have come to believe" are more blessed (20:29). The signs reveal his glory, foreshadowing in some cases the ultimate glorification to occur on Good Friday and Easter. The signs can have symbolic value pertaining to specific groups, as when the healing of the blind man accentuates the spiritual blindness of the Pharisees (9:39–41). More often they serve to signify or manifest God's active presence in the world (5:17–21).

These signs help to illustrate the nature of the "life" Jesus brings into existence and makes possible for humans (1:4; 3:15–16; 4:14; 5:40; 6:33). It is "eternal" and "abundant" (6:40; 10:10). It is furthermore described in several passages not as a future hope but a present reality (3:36; 5:24; 6:47, 54), leading many scholars to characterize the Fourth Gospel as embracing a "realized eschatology" (Dodd 1953). Passages placing Jesus' salvific action in the future are less common (6:39, 44; 14:3). The temporal ambiguity of the Synoptic refrain that "the kingdom of God is at hand" (Mark 1:15; Luke 21:31) is to a degree preserved in John (5:25: "the hour is coming, and is now here"; 6:54: "Those who eat my flesh and drink my blood have eternal life, and I will raise them up on the last day") even if the pendulum tends to swing from the future back toward the present in the dialectical relationship between the "already" and the "not yet."

The last of the seven signs, the raising of Lazarus, is the most awe-inspiring. Among the Jewish leadership opposed to Jesus it also inspires fear at the possible Roman response to the resulting growth of his following (11:45–53). In plotting his death, they in fact hasten the moment of his glorification when he is "lifted up" on the cross. Caiaphas, the high priest, unwittingly becomes a mouthpiece for Johannine theology when he explains that "it is better . . . to have one man die for the people than to have the whole nation destroyed" (11:50). With this development, Jesus winds down his public ministry and John makes the transition to the Book of Glory.

## THE BOOK OF GLORY

The Book of Glory narrates the Last Supper and Jesus' farewell discourse to his disciples, followed by the Passion and Resurrection accounts. This sequence of events leads up to the "hour" at which the Father glorifies the Son "with the glory that [he] had . . . before the world existed" so that the Son may in turn glorify the Father (17:1–5; cf. 13:31–32; 14:13; 15:8; 16:14).

John makes the transition by noting that it was Passover and that "Jesus knew that his hour had come to depart from this world and go to the Father" (13:1). This final meal with his disciples occupies considerably more space than it does in the Synoptic Gospels. It begins with the footwashing (13:1–11), which assumes a symbolic significance equal to that attributed by Matthew, Mark, and Luke to the meal of bread and wine itself. Jesus performs this humble act of hospitality as an example of how to fulfill the "new commandment" he has given his followers—"love one another" (13:34; 15:12; cf. 1 John 2:7–11)—and it is re-enacted in many churches on Maundy Thursday. They will need to love one another because "the world" will hate them, as it has hated him (15:18–25; 17:14). To be called Jesus' "friends" and not his "servants" is at the same time heartening and also sobering since it comes on the heels of his definition of true friendship: "No one has greater love than this, to lay down one's life for one's friends" (15:13–15).

However much Jesus prepares his disciples in advance, his departure is sure to bring uncertainty. So as not to leave them orphaned, he promises to be with them forever through the offices of the Paraclete (14:15–24). Variously translated as "Advocate," "Helper," or "Comforter," the *paraklētos* is described as "the Spirit of truth" and identified as the Holy Spirit which, Jesus says to his disciples, "will teach you everything, and remind you of all that I have said to you" (14:17, 26; cf. 12:16). Inasmuch as Jesus in the Fourth Gospel is "the truth" (14:6), it is difficult to distinguish him from the Paraclete. And while John nowhere articulates the doctrine of the Trinity in a formal manner, any attempt at tracking relations between and among the Father, Son, and Paraclete—the Paraclete "abides" in the disciples, Jesus is "in" the Father, the disciples are "in" Jesus, and Jesus is "in" the disciples (14:17–20)—yields some appreciation for the church's arrival at that conclusion. As they are unable to understand all the things Jesus says to them while on earth, it is all the more crucial that this "Spirit of truth" will guide them into the truth (16:12–13). Jesus' solicitude for his disciples is evident in the "priestly prayer" (17:1–26) in which he contemplates the self-sacrifice he is soon to make.

The Passion account in John (18:1–19:42) aligns much more closely with the Synoptic Gospels than do earlier portions of the narrative. As he does elsewhere, the author nonetheless tells the story in a distinctive way. Elements found in the other gospels are missing such as Simon of Cyrene bearing the cross for Jesus, the cry of dereliction ("my God, my God, why have you forsaken me"), the darkness over the land, the rending of the temple curtain, and the comment of the centurion at the moment of his death.

More intriguing than what is missing is what John includes that the other evangelists do not, all the more so as it reflects the characteristic emphases of Johannine Christology. The Johannine Jesus is not a taciturn figure who impotently suffers the indignities heaped on him by his enemies. Even in dire straits, he exhibits a level of control consonant with his status as "one with the Father." He possesses preternatural knowledge of the past, present, and future and acts accordingly (18:4; 19:28). Before Judas can identify him, he gives himself over to the officers who come to apprehend him. He engages in a spirited discussion with Pontius Pilate about the nature of his kingship that leaves the Roman prefect agitated and indecisive. From the cross, he makes arrangements for the care of his grieving mother (19:25–27). At the moment of his death, he displays consummate equanimity, declaring, "It is finished," thus making good on his earlier pledge to lay down his life only when he is ready to do so (19:30; cf. 10:18).

Historical considerations suggest that the Johannine Passion narrative extends the ovine symbolism associated with Jesus in the opening chapter, where John the Baptist calls him "the Lamb of God who takes away the sin of the world" (1:29, 36), through the closing chapters. The Synoptic Gospels appear to place the death of Jesus on Passover (Nisan 15), which makes the Last Supper a Seder meal (Mark 14:12). But whereas John agrees by placing the crucifixion on Friday, he refers to that day as "the day of Preparation for Passover" (19:14), which would make Passover fall on Saturday. Why is this significant? In John, Jesus dies just as the lambs are being sacrificed to celebrate Passover. Which timeline is correct, John's or that of the Synoptics? Strong arguments can be made for both sides, and scholars have made ingenious attempts at reconciling them (Humphreys 2011). Does John manipulate the calendar to affirm a view of Jesus he already holds, or was it the fact that his death coincided with the ritual that leads him to apply the title "Lamb of God" to Jesus? Whatever the case, it is clear that imagery associated with the paschal lamb—including the detail that Jesus' legs do not need to be broken to hasten his death (19:31–36), which makes his death conform to the requirement that sacrifices be without blemish (Exod. 12:46; Deut. 17:1)—pervades John's portrait of Jesus and expresses the notion that his death was "for the people" (3:16; 11:50; 15:13; 18:14). Just as Jesus is both shepherd and a lamb, he acts as both priest and perfect sacrifice.

On the first day of the week, Mary Magdalene is the first person to discover the empty tomb. Apart from this, nearly every component of the resurrection accounts is unique to John. Chapter 20 recounts appearances of the risen Jesus in Jerusalem. Returning to the tomb after reporting the news to the other disciples, Mary Magdalene mistakes the risen Jesus for the gardener and is told not to "touch" or "hold on to" him before he ascends to the Father (20:11–18). Jesus then appears to the other disciples, breathes the Holy Spirit on them, and authorizes them to forgive sins (20:19–23). Thomas must wait a week before he meets Jesus, and in addressing him as "my Lord and my God" (21:28) he arrives at the point where the reader began in John 1:1, with the announcement that "the Word was God."

Many scholars believe John 21, recounting appearances in Galilee, was added slightly later by another writer. Like Mary Magdalene,

Peter and the other fisherman do not at first recognize Jesus. The Beloved Disciple is the first to do so. After they haul in a large catch of fish, they join Jesus on shore for breakfast. (The precise number of fish—153—has generated several numerological theories as to its purported significance, none terribly persuasive.) Jesus' three-fold command to Peter to "feed [his] sheep" and subsequent prediction of his death suggests that following Jesus in the role of shepherd will lead to a similar ending (21:15–19). Between Peter the pastor and the Beloved Disciple, who stands as a witness and interpreter of Jesus' life, Jesus has made provision for the rest of the community of believers, whom he sends out into the world he came to save (20:21; cf. 3:16–17; 17:15–23).

# 3

## THE LITERATURE OF THE NEW TESTAMENT

### Letters

When, in addition to the Hebrew Bible, the church recognized twenty-seven writings as authoritative for matters of faith and practice, it took an unusual step. Most religions do not include letters in their canons of Scripture. And for good reason. Letters ostensibly belong to the category of occasional literature; that is, they are prompted by and written for particular occasions. In addition to the twenty-one New Testament books in epistolary form, Acts and Revelation have letters embedded in their narratives. Anyone other than the original addressees is in essence reading these letters over their shoulders. The pitfalls are obvious. Not privy to the specific circumstances that generated the correspondence, there is the ever-present danger that later readers will misunderstand allusions made by the authors and construe their remarks out of their primary context. The possibility of misinterpretation is so great that some observers are tempted to declare the entire enterprise of reading the letters for guidance in the present illegitimate in principle, especially insofar as the original authors did not envision a broader readership.

Even those who have little interest in their contemporary application worry that sufficient material for reconstructing the situation of the authors and audiences is lacking.

But one uncontested fact suggests that reading the letters 2,000 years after they were first delivered is not wholly inappropriate: unlike most letters from antiquity, these have been preserved for posterity, and not by accident, like many of the papyrus documents from Oxyrhynchus and other trash heaps in Egypt. The original readers must have seen fit to save, circulate, and permit their reproduction, or else it is highly unlikely that they would have survived. They must have felt that the contents possessed some relevance for other settings. The Colossians (4:16) and Laodiceans were even instructed to exchange letters they had received and read them in their respective congregations, perhaps indicating the author's design to address audiences beyond the original recipients.

More transparently than any other writings, the letters disclose the transcendent hopes as well as the day-to-day realities of the earliest Christians, even earlier than they called themselves "Christians" and thought of their movement as belonging to a religion apart from Judaism. They differed from other Jewish sects in acclaiming Jesus of Nazareth as the Messiah. While his death and resurrection were key turning points in history, the precise significance of this fact was not always self-evident. That they mattered was not in dispute; precisely how they mattered—for issues ranging from dietary practice and sexual ethics to political involvement and family arrangements—was the vital question. The letters show the authors working out answers at both the theological and practical levels, often in contentious dialogue with their audiences. Modern readers must reconstruct the perspectives of the latter from the responses of the former, a complicated task given that the authors were not thinking of furnishing the resources for accomplishing it. Of special importance is their commitment to re-reading the Hebrew Bible through the lens of their profoundly transformative experience of Jesus (Moyise 2012). They make use of hermeneutical strategies common among both Jewish and Greco-Roman writers, but often focus on texts and traditions that were not typically deemed messianic prophecies— again testifying to the impact made by Jesus, who was taken to be the key to understanding the Scriptures rather than being defined or limited by conventional expectations and interpretations.

Although the early church is distinctive in the status it accorded to a collection of letters, by no means were they the only ones to make use of the letter genre for religious or philosophical purposes. The letter is one of the literary genres from antiquity still in use today and therefore the obstacles to interpreting them are not as great as with others, such as the gospel narratives or Revelation. Handbooks from ancient Greece and Rome delineate a wide range of letter types (e.g., friendly, paraenetic, grieving, thankful, congratulatory) and the informal "rules" for their composition (Malherbe 1977). Much surviving correspondence was produced as part of the official business of government bureaucracies. Other documents function as do letters today between friends and family. Stoic, Epicurean, and Cynic philosophers also produce a body of letters of a more refined literary quality to perpetuate their founders' teachings, to attract followers, to explain their own doctrines or disparage those of their rivals, and to encourage their fellow philosophers to conduct their affairs in a manner consistent with their convictions. Cicero, Seneca, Porphyry, and others write many such letters, which often resemble essays more than ordinary missives. The New Testament letters fall at various points on a continuum between the formal (Romans, Hebrews) and the informal (Philemon, 2–3 John). Even at their most formal, however, one ought not to read them as if they were systematic formulations of early Christian theology. While they undeniably contain material that is by any reckoning theological in nature, it would be a mistake to expect a level of precision, organization, and comprehensiveness as one finds in Aquinas or Calvin. Making sense of the letters requires the interpreter to determine which aspects are contingent on particular social-historical circumstances, and which aspects can be generalized or understood by means of judicious cross-cultural analogies.

The most consequential of the early Christian letter writers is the Apostle Paul. Thirteen letters are attributed to Paul. Hebrews was included among his letters prior to the Reformation, 2 Peter mentions his letters, and the Letter of James is sometimes interpreted as a response to Pauline teachings. The letter becomes a standard vehicle for transmitting or contesting Christian doctrine due in no small part to the popularity of his writings. It has even been suggested that the notion of a specifically Christian canon of Scripture begins in the middle of the second century as a response to the ten-letter Pauline canon of Marcion, an influential teacher who rejected the Hebrew Bible and is branded a heretic by Irenaeus and Tertullian. Around this time one begins to see other letter collections emerging, associated with such figures as Clement of Rome, Ignatius of Antioch, Polycarp of Smyrna, as well as Gnostic texts like Ptolemy's *Letter to Flora*. Apocryphal letters also appear, such as *3 Corinthians*, the *Epistle of Barnabas*, and a series of anodyne exchanges purportedly between Paul and Seneca, the Roman philosopher and advisor to the emperor, Nero, who would eventually have Paul beheaded and force Seneca to commit suicide in the mid-60s.

Apart from the Acts of the Apostles, which provides a selective, second-hand account of Paul's ministry, no texts have survived that would fill in the gaps inevitably left by the letters. It is doubtful that apocryphal texts such as the *Acts of Paul and Thecla* contain much biographical information that is reliable. It is nevertheless possible for scholars to agree on a few basic facts about his life. He is raised in Tarsus, located in modern-day Turkey. A Greek-speaking Jew of the Diaspora, he aligns himself with the Pharisees and occupies himself with interpreting the Torah and plumbing its depths for belief and practice (Acts 26:5; Phil. 3:5). He turns at some point from persecuting followers of Jesus to proselytizing on their behalf, proclaiming the message that "Christ redeemed us from the curse of the law by becoming a curse for us" and that "everyone who calls on the name of the Lord"—a title he used for both God and Jesus—"shall be saved" (Rom. 10:13; Gal. 1:13–24; 3:13). He does not see himself as converting to a religion different from Judaism, yet most Jews of his day do not share his belief that Jesus is "the end of the law" who, as the Messiah, ushers in the last days and "rescues us from the wrath that is coming" (Rom. 10:4; 1 Thess. 1:10). This clash of convictions becomes integral to the dynamic by which Judaism and what comes to be called Christianity go their separate ways beginning in the latter part of the first century.

Critics of Paul appear among Jewish and Jewish-Christian groups very early, accusing him of nullifying the role of the law in maintaining a covenant relationship with the God of Israel. A few centuries later, Muslim sources condemn him for introducing the blasphemous notion of Jesus' divinity. For these and many other reasons, his latter-day detractors frequently refer to him as the founder of Christianity, expressing their view that the centuries-long development of the Christian faith has in fact been a tragic corruption of the religion taught by Jesus in the form of a backhanded compliment (Meeks and Fitzgerald 2007: 395–419). Although such exaggerated claims pin too much responsibility on a single individual, it is true that the history of the church would look quite different without the indelible Pauline stamp it bears. His writings are the source of many signature concepts embraced by most Christians on such matters as sin, the Holy Spirit, and salvation. He was the most zealous champion of the mission to the Gentiles, the success of which resulted in a cultural ethos that would never have developed had the church remained predominantly Jewish. Finally, his policy of establishing churches in the cities he visits rather than simply convincing individuals that Jesus had risen from the grave and would soon return to judge the living and the dead helps to imbue Christianity with a communal sensibility that has no doubt contributed to its longevity.

Arguments about Paul's legacy are related to literary-historical arguments about authorship. While doubts about the authorship of his letters are exceedingly rare until the nineteenth century, it is now widely believed that some of the New Testament letters may be pseudonymous. Of the thirteen letters attributed to him, scholars have no doubts that seven are in fact written by Paul. These seven "undisputed" letters are:

Romans
1–2 Corinthians
Galatians
Philippians
1 Thessalonians
Philemon

A majority of scholars believe that the other six are written by his devotees, perhaps as a transparent fiction intended to perpetuate his teachings and apply them to new situations in the years after his death (Beker 1991). These "disputed" or deuteropauline letters are:

Ephesians
Colossians

2 Thessalonians
1–2 Timothy
Titus

Scholars who question the authenticity of these letters point to: (1) difficulties in reconciling Paul's missionary itinerary in Acts with personal details gleaned from his letters; (2) differences in language and style from the undisputed letters; and (3) apparent theological inconsistencies between the disputed and undisputed letters. Scholars who are less inclined to reject the traditional attributions note that: (1) Acts is neither first-hand nor a comprehensive account of Paul's career; (2) that subjective assessments of style often fail to notice the way in which an author's language can greatly vary based on purpose, audience, and subject matter; and (3) that "inconsistencies" can often be a function of the interpreter's ignorance of context and that, more-over, authors sometimes change their minds. The issues raised by each of these texts will be discussed below, in the sections devoted to the disputed letters.

As an authorial personality, Paul looms larger than anyone else in the New Testament and leaves a literary footprint equaled only by Luke, whose two-volume narrative devotes considerable attention to the apos-tle's affairs. So great is his influence that the other epistles are often relegated to the margins. The anonymous Letter to the Hebrews is often overlooked as a theological tour de force, especially among Protestant interpreters, in part because of the determination that it does not belong to the Pauline corpus. The seven remaining letters are grouped together as the General or Catholic Epistles, so-called because they appear to address a broader (Grk. *katholikos*, "universal") audience rather than individual churches.

James
1–2 Peter
1–2–3 John
Jude

This terminology dates to the fourth century (Eusebius, *Hist. eccl.* 2.23.25), and the collection as a whole may have been intended to complement the Pauline collection. Many interpreters regard them as pseudonymous products of the late-first and early-second century. Whether their attention to false teaching, the church as an institution, faith as a "deposit" of tradition, and other concerns mark them as representative of post-apostolic "early Catholicism"—nomenclature normally intended as pejorative by those who employ it—remains a matter of debate.

The order in which the letters are treated varies from scholar to scholar. A chronological treatment might be ideal if only the task of placing them in their order of composition were not a matter of ongoing disagreement among scholars. They are discussed here in their canonical sequence, which appears to be based mainly on their length. That they are interpreted as individual letters on their own terms is more important than the order in which they are interpreted.

## SUGGESTIONS FOR FURTHER READING

The body of scholarly literature devoted to the letters is large and ever-expanding, with Paul receiving the lion's share of this attention. M. D. Hooker, *Paul: A Short Introduction* (Oxford, UK: Oneworld, 2003), is one of many concise, accessible introductions to the main issues in the study of Paul. Other reliable guides include C. J. Roetzel, *The Letters of Paul: Conversations in Context* (4th ed.; Louisville, KY: Westminster John Knox, 1998); L. E. Keck, *Paul and His Letters* (2nd ed.; Minneapolis, MN: Augsburg-Fortress, 1988); T. R. Schreiner, *Interpreting the Pauline Epistles* (2nd ed.; Grand Rapids, MI: Baker, 2011); and, for particular attention to Paul's theology, V. Wiles, *Making Sense of Paul: A Basic Introduction to Pauline Theology* (Peabody, MA: Hendrickson, 2000). Raymond F. Collins, *Letters That Paul Did Not Write* (Collegeville, MN: Liturgical Press, 1988), focuses on Hebrews and on the deuteropauline letters. J. Murphy-O'Connor, *Paul: A Critical Life* (New York: Oxford University Press, 1996), uses Paul's letters to shed light on his upbringing, education, and missionary career. D. A. Campbell, *Framing Paul: An Epistolary Biography* (Grand Rapids, MI: Eerdmans, 2014), follows a similar procedure but arrives at a chronology that diverges from that of most contemporary scholars. W. A. Meeks and J. T. Fitzgerald, eds., *The Writings of St. Paul* (2nd ed.; New York: Norton, 2006), include the annotated text of all the Pauline letters along with brief introductions, followed by excerpts from Augustine, Luther, Nietzsche, and many other writers that demonstrate the apostle's enormous influence, as well as ancient texts inspired by Paul and criticizing Paul. Scholarly treatment of several of the controversial issues raised by the letters may be found in M. D. Given, ed., *Paul Unbound: Other Perspectives on the Apostle* (Peabody, MA: Hendrickson, 2010).

A useful tool for comparing Paul's teachings on various subjects, with the relevant sections of the letters laid out in parallel columns, is F. O. Francis and J. P. Sampley, *Pauline Parallels* (2nd ed.; Philadelphia, PA: Fortress, 1984). J. P. Ware, *Synopsis of the Pauline Letters in Greek and English* (Grand Rapids, MI: Baker, 2010), includes parallels among the disputed as well as the undisputed Pauline letters. N. Elliott and M. Reasoner, eds., *Documents and Images for the Study of Paul* (Minneapolis, MN: Fortress, 2011), collect primary documents from the first-century world inhabited by Jews, Greeks, and Romans. J. P. Sampley, ed., *Paul in the Greco-Roman World: A Handbook* (Harrisburg, PA: Trinity Press International, 2003), examines cultural conventions, literary devices, and social customs of Paul's world in order to understand how his readers would have made sense of his writings. H.-J. Klauck, *Ancient Letters and the New Testament: A Guide to Content and Exegesis* (Waco, TX: Baylor University Press, 2006) highlights the literary genre of the letter in ancient Greece and Rome to reveal the distinctive conventions, forms, and purposes of the New Testament letters.

K. H. Jobes, *Letters to the Church: A Survey of Hebrews and the General Epistles* (Grand Rapids, MI: Zondervan, 2011), provides an overview of the content of the non-Pauline letters, while H. Bateman IV, *Interpreting the General Letters: An Exegetical Handbook* (Grand Rapids, MI: Kregel, 2013), introduces the reader to the finer points of exegetical method using examples from these writings. R. P. Martin and D. G. Reid, eds., *Dictionary of the Later New Testament & Its Developments* (Downers Grove, IL: InterVarsity, 1997), contains entries and bibliographies for a wide range of topics related to the study of Hebrews and the General Epistles.

# Romans

Paul's longest letter is also his most influential, both inside the church and in its impact on the broader culture. Written from Corinth near the end of his Aegean mission to a community he has long wished to visit (1:9–13), Romans resembles a formal theological treatise more than his other letters. Yet it is sent to a flesh-and-blood group of believers whose circumstances shape the message it conveys. The immediate occasion for writing Romans is Paul's plan to travel westward to Spain to spread the gospel among the Gentiles at the edge of the known world (15:20–29). En route, he hopes to stop in Rome for spiritual and logistical support. With no centralized meeting place, the Christian community meets in private homes where Paul's messenger (probably Phoebe mentioned in Rom. 16:1) may have read the letter on multiple occasions for different gatherings.

His grand project of uniting the Gentiles in faith with Jewish believers, however, is not an uncontroversial one. Despite the fact that many members of his network have travelled to or from the empire's capital (16:1–23), most of the Christians there have never met him and may have reservations about endorsing his mission.

There would be no need for such a detailed elaboration of his view that Jews and Gentiles alike are made righteous by faith and not by works of the law if everyone accepted it as a matter of course. The audience likely includes both Jews (4:1: "our ancestor according to the flesh") and non-Jews (11:13–32: "you Gentiles"). Paul devotes so many of his arguments to the objections of a Jewish interlocutor (e.g., 2:17–3:8; 9:1–5) that it seems unlikely to be merely a rhetorical device for countering purely hypothetical challenges. The relationship between these two groups is a concern that runs through the letter from beginning (1:2–6) to end (16:26).

Rome was home to a large Jewish population long before the birth of Christianity. Suetonius (*Claud.* 25.4) reports that in 49 CE the Emperor Claudius expelled the Jews from the city after a disturbance of the peace having to do with a certain "Chrestus." If this is an instance of imperial authorities garbling the name of a foreign cult leader—"Christus"—it would suggest that, as in many other locales, the Christian community in Rome emerged out of and often in conflict with the Jewish community there and that outsiders frequently made no distinction between the two (Brown and Meier 1983: 100–2). According to Acts 18:2, Priscilla and Aquila, the missionary couple greeted by Paul in Rom. 16:3, are said to be among the exiled Jews. When Claudius dies in 54 CE, Jews begin to return, but in their absence Gentile influence within the church has expanded. Tensions between the two sectors had theological and social dimensions, reflected respectively in the plea of Romans 9–11 for them to recognize each other as siblings in Christ and the exhortations to live in harmony in Rom. 14:1–15:13.

Although the audience is predominantly Gentile, Paul builds his arguments on a scriptural foundation. And read from one perspective, Scripture itself can make it difficult to conclude that Jews and Gentiles are equal in God's eyes. Impartiality (2:11) may strike many readers as an ideal attribute for a deity to possess. Worshippers of a given deity, however, may understandably hope for special blessings, and Yahweh's selection of Israel as his "chosen people" (Deut. 7:6; 14:2) might seem to compromise any claims to impartiality. More crucially, the charge of favoritism may be seen as an accusation of injustice. The opening salvo of Paul's argument thus puts the Jew–Gentile relationship front and center in his defense of the righteousness (*dikaiosynē*) of God. The gospel is:

> [t]he power of God for salvation to everyone who has faith, to the Jew first and also to the Greek. For in it the righteousness of God is revealed through faith for faith, as it is written, "The one who is righteous will live by faith."
>
> (Rom. 1:16–17, quoting Hab. 2:4)

The good news, then, is that God's impartiality is demonstrated by the fact that both Jews and Gentiles are eligible for salvation, albeit on different timetables. But in Rom. 1:18–32, Paul turns immediately to the bad news, so to speak, by describing the way in which "the wrath of God is revealed from heaven against all ungodliness." "There will be anguish and distress for everyone who does evil" he states (2:9), "the Jew first and also the Greek." Any Gentiles invoking their ignorance of the law as exculpatory are informed that they have no excuse because their own instincts prove it is "written on their hearts" (2:1, 14–16). Paul here subscribes to a version of general revelation or natural law wherein any individual is able to intuit the existence of God and of a basic moral code incumbent on all persons to uphold, without the aid of special revelation. In other words, Gentiles may not have received the Torah, but reason, conscience, and observation of the natural world provide an adequate basis for knowledge of God. While this idea is common among Stoics, Paul baptizes it in such a way that later Christian thinkers will regularly build on it in developing their theological systems. Paul's articulation of it has become controversial due to his use of homosexual behavior as a prototypical case of denying the inherent human knowledge of the creator.

Jewish readers may wonder whether their election as God's people brings any advantage, if it is the case that the law and its ordinances are unnecessary for pleasing God (3:1–8). Paul does not fully answer the question at this point beyond insisting that Israel was indeed blessed in a special way and that its subsequent faithlessness cannot "nullify the faithfulness of God" (3:3). Up to this point, Jesus has been largely absent from Paul's argument. His role in the revelation of God's righteousness becomes clearer in Rom. 3:21–26: "apart from the law, [it] has been disclosed . . . the righteousness of God through faith in Jesus Christ for all who believe. For there is no distinction, since all have sinned and fall short of the glory of God." Through his sacrifice on the cross, God "justifies the one who has faith in Jesus."

Scholars are divided on the proper translation of a key phrase, *pistis Iesou/Christou*. Should it be read as an objective genitive (= "through faith in Jesus/Christ") or as a subjective genitive (= "through the faith or faithfulness of Jesus/Christ")? Put differently, is it the faith of the individual in the person and work of Jesus that puts the relationship with God on the right footing, or is it Jesus' own faithfulness that accomplishes justification? The two readings are not mutually exclusive and may involve only a difference in emphasis. Paul's own emphasis in Rom. 3:27–31 is upon the fact that God is the God of Jews and Gentiles alike, who will be justified on the same basis—faith—and that this is not contrary to the law (Hays 1997).

It is this doctrine of justification by faith and what it reveals about God that Martin Luther has chiefly in mind when he says he lost Christ in his study of scholastic theology but found him again in Paul. To demonstrate that his teaching accords with the law and the prophets and is not a spurious innovation, Paul cites the example of Abraham (Rom. 4:1–25; cf. Gal. 3:6–18). He quotes Gen. 15:6—Abraham "believed God, and it was reckoned to him as righteousness"—and points out that this pronouncement was made prior to the covenant of circumcision was sealed and was therefore not contingent on adhering to a law that would not arrive until much later. God's purpose was to make Abraham "the ancestor of all who believe without being circumcised" (4:11). The divine promise to Abraham "depends on faith, in order that [it] may rest on grace and be guaranteed to all his descendants," thus fulfilling God's pledge in Gen. 12:3 to make him a great nation and to bless all the families of the earth through him (4:16).

By emphasizing the role played by a single historical figure in effecting reconciliation for all humanity, Paul embraces the "scandal of particularity" on which many of his readers have stumbled. Even more bewildering to Christianity's critics is his parallel assertion that "sin came into the world through one man" (5:12). Adam is the "one man" Paul has in mind. Catholic theologians often rely on Augustine's interpretation of this verse in defending the doctrine of original sin, the idea, closely related to the Calvinist notion of total depravity, that all humans possess a congenital predisposition to evil. Proponents of the doctrine believe that, however grim, it affords the most realistic accounting of human nature, while those who deny it often regard its consequences in areas as diverse as law, sexuality, education, and psychology as mostly pernicious (Jacobs 2008).

Happily, while "one man's trespass led to condemnation for all," where sin increased, "grace abounded all the more" (5:18–20). But if divine grace is the response to human fault, "Should we continue in sin in order that grace may abound?" (6:1). The rhetorical device Paul employs is known as diatribe, a style of debate popular among Greek and Roman orators. The speaker voices the hypothetical questions of an imaginary interlocutor and then proceeds to clear away the fallacious reasoning that underlies anticipated objections. Paul's "reply" here, as at other points where he uses the diatribe (3:1–2; 6:15; 7:13; 11:1, 11) is emphatic: "By no means!" Drawing a faulty conclusion from the working of God's grace will result in the readers remaining slaves to sin.

Many interpreters believe that Paul's cri de coeur in Rom. 7:4–25 over his inability to meet the demands of the Torah—"I do not do what I want, but I do the very thing I hate" (7:15)—may be a similar example of speech in character and not a transparent guide to his attitude toward the Mosaic law (Stowers 1994; whether the "character" in question is a Gentile God-fearer, Adam in Genesis 3, backsliding Israel in Exodus 32, or sinful humanity has proven a more difficult question to answer). This view is a response to longstanding interpretations associated with Augustine and Luther that regard Paul as the "wretched man" (7:24) speaking about his personal experience in a quest for liberation from a guilty conscience. Luther's understanding of the Christian as *simul iustus et peccator*, simultaneously justified and still a sinner, is based on this passage. Scholars aligned with what is known as the "New Perspective" on Paul believe that traditional readings assume a caricature of Second Temple Judaism as a legalistic religion of "works righteousness" and contend that the "I" throughout Romans 7 cannot be the apostle speaking autobiographically, either pre- or post-conversion, since this would imply a negative view of the law that was unthinkable for a devout Jew (Dunn 1983). Both sides of the debate agree that Paul is seeking to clarify the relationship between the law and sin. He rejects the notion that the law is itself sinful, since it was given by God (7:7). The law creates an awareness of sin even as it is ultimately incapable of neutralizing sin's power by itself. It is only through the death of Jesus that "the just requirement of the law might be fulfilled" and sin's power might be nullified, thus freeing the believer to live "according to the Spirit" (8:3–4).

This does not mean that the Christian life will be free from struggles, but the pessimism of chapter seven gives way to optimism by the end of chapter eight: "If God is for us, who is against us?" Paul asks, only to answer his own question by affirming that nothing—not death or angels or rulers or anything else in creation—"will be able to separate us from the love of God in Christ Jesus our Lord" (8:31, 38–39).

Is it nonetheless possible to alienate oneself from God? The anguish one hears in Rom. 9:1–5 raises this very question. As Paul contemplates the ambivalence of his fellow Jews toward his preaching, he feels compelled to pre-empt the charge that "the word of God [has] failed." One can easily imagine non-Christian Jews remarking that Paul's message implicitly accuses God of infidelity in breaking the promises to Israel that it would be his "treasured possession out of all the peoples" (Exod. 19:5). After all, why else would it receive such a lukewarm response unless it was God's express desire, in purportedly acting "apart from the law" through Jesus, to operate in such a way that so much of Israel would find it repugnant? In response to the specious claim that "God has rejected his people" (11:1–2), Paul makes an appeal, replete with scriptural allusions, to Jews and Gentiles to acknowledge that they both belong to the people of God on the same terms.

Calvinists have long understood Romans 9–11 to be the definitive statement of the doctrine of predestination, the idea that God ordains certain individuals for salvation and others for damnation regardless of any choices they may make. The "elect" are incapable of resisting God's offer of salvation or falling from grace, and those not among the elect may do nothing to merit salvation. Numerous verses support this view (e.g., 9:11, 14, 18: "So then he has mercy on whomever he chooses, and he hardens the heart of whomever he chooses"). Arminian interpreters point out that there are just as many texts that seem to offer support for the view that humans have free will and that, while salvation is a gift, all have the opportunity to accept God's grace (e.g., 10:4, 9, 12–13: "Everyone who calls on the name of the Lord will be saved," quoting Joel 2:32).

However fundamental the questions it raises may be, the debate about predestination in Romans 9–11 neglects Paul's emphasis on God's dealings with both individuals and groups of people over the winding course of Israel's history. He swerves back and forth between hope (11:26) and seeming despair (11:7) over the fate of Israel, and between encouragement and admonition for any Gentiles tempted to gloat on the erroneous assumption that they have replaced the Jews as God's people (11:13–24). Paul's comment that "it depends not on human will or exertion, but on God who shows mercy" (9:16) at first glance seems to express a Calvinist sentiment, but "it" appears to denote "God's plan of election" (9:11) since neither salvation nor damnation are mentioned in the context. God "elects" or chooses specific individuals or groups to play special roles in his plan without any obvious regard for their moral worthiness. He has mercy on some and "hardens" others, allowing Israel to "stumble," though not "so as to fall" (11:11). Paul concedes that God's plans are mysterious—"How unsearchable are his judgments and how inscrutable his ways!"—but celebrates the outcome, affirming that "God has imprisoned all in disobedience so that he may be merciful to all" (11:32–33).

After eleven chapters of dense exposition, Paul turns from the indicative to the imperative in Rom. 12:1 (ESV): "I appeal to you therefore . . . to present your bodies as a living sacrifice, holy and acceptable to God, which is your spiritual worship." The transformation of their minds will empower them to discern God's will in their dealings with one another and with those outside the community who may persecute them (12:2–21). The possibility that such persecutors might include the state is not entertained in Rom. 13:1–7 as seriously as it will be just a few years after they read his letter. Only occasionally is the intersection of religion and politics as manifest as one sees here, where Paul states that every person should be "subject to the governing authorities; for there is no authority except from God, and . . . therefore whoever resists authority resists what God has appointed." Christendom is not unique in accommodating the notion that worldly and otherworldly power are integrally related. How, precisely, are they related? Aye, there's the rub. Paul's most explicit statement on the nature of political power is quoted by Thomas Cranmer on behalf of Henry VIII in his brief against papal primacy, and Jacques-Bénigne Bossuet, spiritual advisor to Louis XIV, invokes it in formally articulating the theory of the divine right of kings. Luther cites it in setting forth his "Two Kingdoms" doctrine concerning temporal authority. Royalists and revolutionaries vigorously parsed the terms of this text as the American colonists fought for independence from Great Britain. The claim that civil authority "does not bear the sword in vain" (13:4) has figured in Christian discussions of just war theory and capital punishment from the time of Thomas Aquinas to the present. This perspective on state power is shared by 1 Peter (2:13–17) but not by the author of Revelation (13:1–18).

This is not a call for the establishment of a Christian theocracy, a possibility Paul could scarcely have imagined at a time when Roman rule showed no sign of ending. The fairness of Roman tax policies is a pressing issue in the late 50s. Advising the Romans to pay "taxes to whom taxes are due," Paul exhibits some of the artful ambiguity found in Jesus' response on the same question (Mark 12:17 RV: "Render unto Caesar the things that are Caesar's, and unto God the things that are God's"), an ambiguity later exploited by many Mennonites and other tax protestors. Paul's impulse is to give the powers that be the benefit of the doubt, thinking it wise for them to avoid attracting unnecessary attention by appearing to shirk their civic duties. The second-century *Acts of Paul* depicts the apostle's martyrdom at the hands of Nero, the man who sits on the throne when he tells the Roman Christians to honor the emperor.

Even when they are not subjected to external pressures, Paul recognizes that solidarity will be necessary if the Christian community in Rome is to remain intact. Toward this end, he relays instructions in Rom. 14:1–15:13 that are similar to those he gives to the Corinthians (1 Corinthians 8–10). The scruples of members Paul labels "the weak," who abstain from meat and wine and celebrate special holy days, annoy or embarrass "the strong," who regard such observances as self-righteous or superstitious. The weak may be Jewish believers, while the strong are probably Gentiles. Anti-Jewish prejudice in the ancient Mediterranean often focused on these very practices, and their common confession that "Christ is risen" did not immediately eliminate the mutual antipathy that had for centuries characterized Jew–Gentile relations. Paul's counsel reflects heightened tensions within the group when Jewish believers returned to Rome after the death of Claudius. Paul urges them to bear with one another and not pass judgment on matters where persons of good faith can have legitimate disagreements. His prayer for them thus brings together the theological exposition that dominates the first several chapters with the moral exhortation that follows it: "May the God of steadfastness and encouragement grant you to live in harmony with one another, in accordance with Christ Jesus, so that together you may with one voice glorify the God and Father of our Lord Jesus Christ" (Rom. 15:5–6).

# 1 Corinthians

No source reveals as much about the day-to-day realities, the hopes and fears, or the beliefs and behaviors of first-century Christians than Paul's "first" letter to the Corinthians. The canonical text known as 1 Corinthians mentions an even earlier letter from Paul (5:9–13), one of many that have not survived. None of the letters from the Corinthians themselves have survived, notwithstanding the presence for many centuries in the canon of the Armenian church of a text purporting to be a request for Paul's opinion on a variety of disputed teachings, appended to a pseudonymous work known as *3 Corinthians*. Piecing the situation together on the basis of Paul's extant correspondence sheds enough light to put the lie to one popular notion, namely, that the early church enjoyed an idyllic period of peace, love, and harmony and only much later fell into dissension, heresy, and debauchery.

Corinth was a bustling seaport situated on an isthmus connecting the Greek mainland with the Peloponnesus. It was destroyed in

146 BCE and then rebuilt less than a century before Paul's arrival. Ethnically, religiously, and socioeconomically diverse, its residents were known for their skill in bronze- and leather-working as well as for other, more prurient trades. Stories relayed by Strabo of a thousand sacred prostitutes at the temple of the city's patron deity Aphrodite may be exaggerated, and a reputation for licentiousness that made it literally synonymous with fornication (*korinthazomai*) for many Greek speakers may not be totally deserved. Nevertheless, the range of issues addressed by Paul suggests that some of his readers required remedial moral instruction.

Acts 18 complements the general picture of the church's origins gained from the letter. Paul spends a year and a half in Corinth after founding the church there in the late 40s with Timothy and Silas. Disagreements that arise in the wake of his departure for other missionary fields provide the occasion for a series of letters in which the Corinthians ask for guidance and Paul replies with his answers. In deciding to appeal to their leader, they discover they have an additional problem: they have aligned themselves with different leaders. Chloe, Paul's informant, has brought this factionalism to his attention. In an 1831 essay on the divisions at Corinth, F. C. Baur reconstructed the "hidden" history of early Christianity as reducible to a war of attrition between Paul's law-free gospel popular among Gentiles and Peter's law-observant Jewish Christianity, with détente not coming until the second century in the form of "early Catholicism." Baur and his "Tübingen School" believed this "compromise" was a negative development and that Acts attempted to conceal the messier realities of the first century. This reconstruction betrayed the heavy influence of G. W. F. Hegel's thesis/antithesis/synthesis dialectic, and the fact that the fault lines in Corinth and elsewhere fall in far more complicated patterns than Baur imagined has not kept it from becoming one of the most influential theories in the history of New Testament scholarship.

After a thanksgiving that anticipates many of the themes that he will take up later (1:4–7), Paul urges the Corinthians to end their divisions and explains that relying on "human wisdom" will put them at odds with "the power of God and the wisdom of God" (1:24). This wisdom is encapsulated for Paul in the slogan "Christ crucified," a message that, as he recognizes, appears as "a stumbling block to Jews and foolishness to Gentiles" (1:23). Rather than adjust his gospel to the predilections of his target audiences, he reminds his readers that they must maintain this counter-cultural ethos as they settle their disputes with one another and make their way in wider Greek society.

But before he goes about applying the "Christ crucified" principle to the questions they have posed, he feels compelled to address a few matters they have neglected to mention. Most urgent is a case of incest among their members. They are boasting of their Spirit-endowed wisdom, and yet they tolerate this moral turpitude "that is not found even among the pagans" (5:1–2, 6). More troubling still is the possibility that they are not boasting despite this permissiveness but on account of it, embracing a "realized eschatology" that they feel releases them from bourgeois standards of morality that no longer apply to those living the life of angels (Thiselton 1978: 510–26). Other interpreters believe Paul is chastising his readers for adopting ethical sensibilities informed by pagan philosophies inimical to the gospel. In either case, when Paul addresses the Corinthians as "saints"/"sanctified" (1:2), implying that they are to be "set apart" in their calling, this is surely not what he has in mind. Later critics slander the Christians by accusing them of incest (Athenagoras, *Leg.* 3; Minucius Felix, *Oct.* 9), and Paul may fear that the Corinthians are helping to prove those rumors true. Paul is additionally displeased that they do not have basic decision-making procedures in place that would aid in maintaining community discipline, which would further enable them to avoid airing their dirty laundry by suing one another in the civil courts (6:1–8).

Paul finally takes up the questions they have asked in chapter seven. Again, the subject is sexuality: "It is well for a man not to touch a woman" (7:1). Unless one realizes that ancient documents lacked punctuation, this statement may leave the impression that Paul holds a thoroughly negative view of sexual relations. His subsequent comments, however, indicate that this is one prevalent view held by some of the Corinthians who are on the ascetic end of the spectrum from the libertines who, for example, see no problem in visiting prostitutes (6:15–20). Paul says that it is preferable to remain celibate since unmarried Christians may more fully devote themselves to God's service, but for those who cannot live up to what come to be called "counsels of perfection" in connection with monasticism, he concedes "it is better to marry than to be aflame with passion" (7:9; Chaucer's Wife of Bath cites Paul's advice in contemplating her sixth marriage). Throughout his answer, Paul steers back and forth between points on which he has a "command of the Lord" and those on which he is offering his own opinion (7:10, 12, 25). While he does not offer a robust endorsement of marriage, he certainly regards it as preferable to fornication or divorce. As a practical principle, he advises, "Let each of you remain in the condition in which you were called" (7:20–24). Whether his position on the issues he addresses here would have been markedly different had he not believed they were in some sense living in the "end-times" (7:26, 29–31) is impossible to ascertain.

Fleshly matters of a different sort occupy the next three chapters: Is it permissible for Christians to consume meat that has been sacrificed to pagan idols? Those who say no reason that consuming such food brings one into an intimate and inappropriate communion with the honored deity. Those who say yes reason that "all of us possess knowledge" that there is only one God and that any purported communion is illusory inasmuch as there exists no deity to honor through sacrifice (8:1–6). On the theological principle, Paul agrees with the latter, though he will later acknowledge that "demons" are involved in the worship associated with these rites (10:20). But he exhorts them to abstain anyway, sacrificing their "liberty" lest it "somehow become a stumbling block" to the "weak believers" (8:9–11). Above all, Paul wants these "enlightened" believers to remain cognizant of the effect even of their own licit behavior on others in the assembly (Dawes 1996). What at first appears as a digression in 1 Corinthians 9 comes into clearer focus as an object lesson. Just as Paul voluntarily forfeits his apostolic prerogatives for the benefit of his followers, so also should they be willing to give up the "right" to eat meat—not in order to imitate Paul but, ultimately, to imitate Christ (9:1–18; 11:1). He furthermore warns them not to overestimate their own wisdom or ability to resist temptation with reference to the story of the golden calf in Exodus (1 Cor. 10:1–13). If the Israelites, who had witnessed God's miraculous power in delivering them from Egypt, could so quickly fall into grave spiritual error, Paul hints that the Corinthians should perhaps err on the side of caution when it comes to even perfunctory participation in pagan rituals, however spiritually "gifted" they may be. Augustine and other ancient and medieval writers follow Paul's example in reading the Exodus narratives typologically, as prefiguring later events in the New Testament and the history of the church.

From these extramural affairs, Paul turns his attention to conduct inside the assembly. Should a woman pray or prophesy "with her head unveiled" (11:2–16)? Without any clear word from above, Paul attempts to settle the dispute by arguing from Scripture and tradition. He has fewer qualms in criticizing their comportment when they gather at the house of a member on the first day of the week to commemorate Jesus' final meal before his death (11:17–34; Murphy-O'Connor 2002: 178–85). He quotes Jesus' "words of institution" as he received it from the primitive church in a form that closely resembles the narrative found in Luke. Different ecclesiastical bodies practice this ritual with varying degrees of frequency, referring to it as Communion, the Lord's Supper, or the Eucharist. Paul is upset that the Corinthians have turned the occasion into a party that, rather than promoting the unity in diversity that he celebrates in the following chapter, accentuates the divisions separating members of different socioeconomic classes (Theissen 1982: 69–119). Admittedly, their improprieties do not compare with the orgiastic abominations of the Borborite or Phibionite services in the second century reported by Epiphanius (*Pan.* 25–26). The consequences that Paul says will follow from consuming "the body and blood of the Lord . . . without discerning the body" or "in an unworthy manner" nevertheless indicates the gravity of their failings. Longstanding theological debates about the significance of the sacrament focus on this text, one of the very few where Paul quotes Jesus. Is it a purely symbolic commemoration at the moment of consecration? Are the elements transformed into the actual body and blood of Jesus (the "Real Presence") by means of transubstantiation? Is there a sacramental union of the bread and wine with the body and blood of Christ, a process called consubstantiation by Lutherans, in which Christ's body and blood are present "in, with, and under" the forms of bread and wine?

In addition to the class divisions, the Corinthians are divided over the relative value they accord to the various spiritual gifts they display, such as miracle-working, prophecy, and healing (12:1–31). It is difficult to discern the precise sorts of phenomena that were occurring at such a distance, but the effect on communal relations is palpable. Paul stresses the need to remember that they are all members of one body of Christ by virtue of their baptism in one spirit (12:12–13). Love constitutes the proper mode in which these gifts should be exercised, a lesson he teaches in his "hymn" in chapter thirteen that has become a staple of American wedding ceremonies ("Love is patient; love is kind . . . it bears all things, hopes all things, endures all things"). Along with faith and hope, love is one of the three theological virtues, gifts infused by the Holy Spirit (as distinct from the cardinal virtues of prudence, justice, temperance, and fortitude).

If the space he devotes to it is an indicator, speaking in tongues is the most polarizing spiritual gift (14:1–40). Glossolalia appears to have taken two forms in the New Testament: known human languages spoken by individuals with no prior knowledge of them (Acts 2), and "tongues of angels" corresponding to no known language. When it is not done "decently and in order," that is, without someone able to interpret a language that no one understands, Paul argues that tongues should be avoided inasmuch as they fail to edify the body of believers. His most noteworthy comment comes at the end of his disquisition on speech in the assembly (14:33–36). Where he merely qualified the conditions under which women might prophesy in 1 Cor. 11:2–16, here he states that "women should be silent in the churches." How might one account for these seemingly inconsistent instructions? Perhaps Paul is a misogynist or unwilling to follow the radical message of inclusiveness he preaches elsewhere (Gal. 3:28–29) to its natural conclusion. It may be an insertion into a later manuscript by a writer seeking to squelch women's participation in the teaching ministry of the church, as 1 Tim. 2:11–15 has been interpreted, and thus not reflective of Paul's own views at all. Or it may be that the different instructions envision different circumstances that are opaque to modern readers and that a particular problem in Corinth causes Paul to invoke the protocols of the traditional synagogue. Whatever the solution, this passage has earned Paul a reputation as "the eternal enemy of Woman," in the phrase of George Bernard Shaw.

Paul began the letter summarizing his gospel as "Christ crucified" (1:23). He concludes it by adding belief in the bodily resurrection of Jesus as a non-negotiable condition of Christian faith (15:1–57). "If there is no resurrection of the dead, then Christ has not been raised," he declares, "and if Christ has not been raised then . . . your faith has been in vain" (15:13–14, 17). The Corinthians apparently accept the claim that Jesus rose from the dead, but some are denying the corollary that there will be a general resurrection of all the faithful at the end of time. This view, he says, overlooks the fact that Jesus' resurrection is but the "first fruits" of the glorious fate that awaits his followers. As evidence of their own confusion, he wonders why some of them participate in an otherwise undocumented practice of vicarious baptism "on behalf of the dead" if they did not expect a general resurrection (15:29; Mormons cite this enigmatic verse in support of proxy baptism, for which extensive genealogical records are indispensable for believers who wish to come to the aid of their ancestors). Paul's attempt to describe the nature of the resurrected body can be difficult to follow even for readers familiar with Hellenistic Jewish ideas about "soul" and "spirit." He rejects the notion that body and soul are utterly separate or discontinuous. Their ethical shortcomings are in part a result of confusion on this point. To be sure, the individual's resurrection body will be radically, spiritually transformed, but it will be a "body" (*sōma*) nonetheless. This transformation represents the only hope of overcoming death, "the last enemy that shall be destroyed" (15:26 KJV). Quoting the prophet Hosea (13:14), Paul asks in 1 Cor. 15:55, "O death, where is thy sting? O grave, where is thy victory?" Alexander Pope ("The Dying Christian to His Soul"), G. F. Handel (in the libretto of *Messiah*), and J. K. Rowling (on the tombstone of Harry Potter's parents) are among those whose works allude to these lines from the KJV declaring God's ultimate victory.

# 2 Corinthians

Were one to write a novel focusing on the relationship between Paul and his followers in Achaia, 1 and 2 Corinthians provide a wealth of source material. The plot of such a novel could take any number of possible turns due to the many vague references in 2 Corinthians that require no explanation for the parties involved in the events that have transpired since 1 Corinthians was delivered ca. 51 CE. At least one more letter from Paul has arrived, one written "out of much distress and anguish of heart and with many tears" after a second, "painful visit" to Corinth (2:1–4). As in Galatia, rival teachers have sown seeds of doubt concerning Paul's worthiness as a minister of the gospel (2 Cor. 10–12). The audience may have witnessed a showdown between Paul and these so-called "super-apostles" that left them unimpressed with their founder (10:8–11; 11:5–6). His goal in 2 Corinthians is to remind his readers that the "ministry of reconciliation" (5:18) he exercises is not, in this present age, a ministry characterized by power and glory. Rather, his afflictions are the sign and seal of authentic apostleship. And if they endure the trials and tribulations that come in this vale of tears, they too will be prepared "for an eternal weight of glory beyond all measure" (4:17).

Piecing Paul's message together is complicated by the literary puzzles presented by the canonical form of 2 Corinthians. A majority of scholars look at 2 Corinthians and conclude that it is a composite of anywhere from two to six separate letters. These "partition" theories detect "seams" in the text where Paul's argument appears to shift abruptly and unnaturally. For example, why does Paul introduce his plan to take up a collection for the saints in Jerusalem in 2 Cor. 9:1 after spending the preceding chapter discussing the same topic? Why does his tone suddenly change from hopeful and encouraging to biting and sarcastic at 2 Cor. 10:1? Why does he interrupt his invitation to "open [their] hearts" (6:13; 7:2) to urge them not to be "unequally yoked together with unbelievers" (KJV) in 2 Cor. 6:14–7:1? The most common answer is that these disjunctions are the result of imperfect editing by the person(s) who brought various fragments together into their present form. Yet this scholarly consensus does not quite tie up all the loose ends: If 2 Corinthians has been cut-and-pasted together, how and when did this editing take place? Why did no one notice it before the modern period? Are all fragments from the hand of Paul, or has any non-Pauline material found its way into the final product, as many suspect with 2 Cor. 6:14–7:1? Has Paul's "tearful letter" not survived, or is it embedded within the text of 2 Corinthians? Is it possible that rhetorical analyses identifying the letter as a specimen of forensic rhetoric or as an extended apologia account for the literary "problems," which have perhaps been overstated (Stegman 2005: 50–55)?

Any reading of 2 Corinthians based on a particular partition theory is necessarily a precarious enterprise. While reserving judgment on the question, it is possible to examine Paul's major concerns as they appear—in reverse order—in three major portions of the text: chapters 10–13, 8–9, and 1–7.

*Chapters 10–13.* Numerous comments testify to the stormy relationship Paul has had with his Corinthian correspondents. The length and urgency of his comments in 2 Cor. 10–13 suggest that matters have worsened in response to insinuations about Paul made by outsiders. No other passage from any of Paul's letters reveals so much about what his opponents thought of him (Sumney 1999: 102–30). He lacks gravitas and cuts a much less imposing figure in person than in his letters. "His letters are weighty and strong," someone says, "but his bodily presence is weak, and his speech contemptible" (10:1, 10, 16). His lack of training as a public speaker may have been accentuated through comparison with the "super-apostles," rival teachers who arrived in Corinth during his absence (11:5–6; 12:11). His boasting is thus perplexing and off-putting to some members of the community (2 Cor. 10:8). Paul's response—more boasting (10:15; 11:10, 16–18, 21, 30; 12:1, 5–6, 9)!—may not have endeared him to everyone. Among the experiences he mentions is a mystical experience when he was "caught up to the third heaven" (12:2–4), a comment that becomes the starting point for the third-century *Apocalypse of Paul*, which in turn influences Dante in writing the *Inferno*. Questions about Paul's integrity and the legitimacy of his ministry have also arisen. Itinerant preachers customarily presented letters of recommendation upon arriving at a new locale, and Paul earlier addresses murmurs about his failure to conform to this practice: "Surely we do not need, as some do, letters of recommendation to you or from you, do we? You yourselves are our letter, written on our hearts, to be known and read by all" (3:1–2). He thus rejects the notion that he has somehow overstepped his authority (10:14; 13:10).

Paul does not stop at defending himself against criticism that he is weak. He instead goes on the offensive, claiming that it is his experience of weakness and suffering that qualifies him as an apostle. Floggings, stonings, imprisonment, insults, starvation, shipwreck—these and many other hardships he has endured (11:23–29). Tantalized by his enigmatic reference to a "thorn in the flesh" in 2 Cor. 12:7, scholars have speculated that Paul was afflicted by everything from migraines, epilepsy, a speech impediment, demonic possession, repressed homosexual desires, and a nagging wife, to astigmatism, bipolar disorder, the evil eye, persistent hiccups, sciatica, and gout. Attempts by Paul's modern critics to attribute elements of his teaching or personality they find objectionable to this "thorn" frequently produce unintentionally humorous results. It may be wisest to understand this "messenger of Satan" in context as a rival teacher who has made life difficult for him, one of the "deceitful workers" in 2 Cor. 11:13–14, where he comments, "Even Satan disguises himself as an angel of light." Whatever it is, Paul cites it as a reason for boasting insofar as it demonstrates his weakness, and whenever he is weak, he says, he is actually strong (11:30; 12:5, 10; 13:9). He quotes the risen Jesus— "My grace is sufficient for you, for power is made perfect in weakness" (12:9)—as if to counter the idea that this is wishful thinking on his part. The repeated mention of "affliction" along with "consolation" in the letter's opening (1:3–8) makes it plain that this theme is no after-thought.

*Chapters 8–9.* Among the charges addressed by Paul is the insinu-ation that he is insufficiently Jewish (11:22–23). His discussion of the offering in chapters 8–9 responds to this attack from a different angle. Paul had agreed to remember the poor in Jerusalem (Gal. 2:10; cf. 1 Cor. 16:1–3). Whereas the churches in the Diaspora were promi-nently Gentile, in Jerusalem they were Jewish. The collection is thus more than a goodwill gesture on behalf of an impoverished commu-nity; it is a token of solidarity between Jews and Gentiles whereby Gentiles acknowledge Jews as their "elder brothers in the faith of Abraham" (to borrow the phrase of John Paul II) and Jews welcome Gentile believers as their spiritual equals. His opponents may sus-pect him of a scam designed to line his pockets, and his latter-day critics often look at it as a "polite bribe" paid to James for tolerating Paul's law-free gospel in his outreach to non-Jews (Orlando 2015: 125). Paul regards the collection as an eschatological prelude to the fulfillment of biblical prophecies describing the nations flocking to Mount Zion bearing gifts for Israel (Isa. 60:1–7). In using theologically charged language throughout this passage, it is clear that Paul thinks of the collection as more than just a monetary transfer. He repeat-edly uses *charis*, "grace," though English translations obscure this emphasis by employing a range of synonyms in several verses where it occurs (8:4, 6, 7, 9; 9:8). When he tells the Corinthians that "God loves a cheerful giver" (9:7), he is reminding them that they must act in the same spirit typified by Jesus—who "though he was rich" become poor for their sake (8:9)—if their contribution is to have its maximum effect.

*Chapters 1–7.* The collection is critical to the success of the "ministry of reconciliation" to which Paul has dedicated his life (5:18). If chapters 10–13 constitute a defense of his personal worthiness as a minister, and chapters 8–9 lay out some of the tangible means by which reconciliation will be achieved, chapters 1–7 articulate Paul's theology of this ministry. While the term "minister" (3:6; 6:4; 11:5, 23) may sound familiar to modern ears, the job description was not obvi-ous to ancient readers. Neither was it self-evident to Paul, who hardly had twenty years of precedents—much less twenty centuries—with which to make sense of his calling. A minister is a servant (*diakonos*) who acts on behalf of someone or something else. In 2 Cor. 2:14–6:10 one finds Paul's account of that "something else."

Paul states that his qualifications as a "minister of a new covenant" come from God, not from any human agency. No ordinary letter written in ink would suffice, he says, since "the letter kills, but the Spirit gives life" (3:6; a similar antithesis is found in Rom. 2:29; 7:6). Origen, Augustine, and other patristic authors invoke Paul's letter-spirit dichotomy in support of the allegorical exegesis that would become a hallmark of medieval interpretation. This comment initially applies to the letters of recommendation produced by his rivals, but here Paul makes "the letter" stand for the law bequeathed to Israel at Sinai, the "old covenant" which he proceeds to contrast with the new covenant. The Letter to the Hebrews is the only book in the New Testament that explores the "new covenant" theme at greater length than Paul does here. Many interpreters believe that these texts encourage a form of supersessionism that denigrates Judaism and misrepresents the Hebrew Bible as proclaiming a wrathful God as distinct from the loving God of the New Testament. Yet Paul the Pharisee stops far short of the unequivocal anti-Judaism one finds in such works as the second-century *Epistle of Barnabas* (4.6–8), which asserts that the covenant belonging to the Jews is broken and that it is utter foolishness to believe that the new covenant is "both theirs and ours" (Longenecker 2007: 26–44).

Paul's exposition of Exod. 34:29–35 resembles rabbinic midrash in method if not in substance (Stockhausen 1989). When Moses descended from the mountain with the Ten Commandments, his face glowed so brightly that the people could not bear to look on it, though it would eventually fade. (Michelangelo's horned *Moses* and other iconographic depictions are based on translations that render the ambiguous Hebrew word for "rays of light" as "horns.") The veil Moses wore, according to Paul, is still in place: "Indeed, to this very day, when they hear the reading of the old covenant, that same veil is still there, since only in Christ is it set aside" (3:14–16). Those who read Moses "unveiled," that is, "in Christ," are vouchsafed a view of God so direct that they are "being transformed into the same image from one degree of glory to another" (3:18).

In contrasting the "ministry of death" with the "ministry of the Spirit" (3:7–8), Paul does not mean to say that those aligned with the latter will escape hardship. They will be abused and persecuted in every way, as they are "always carrying in the body the death of Jesus, so that the life of Jesus may also be made visible" in their bodies (4:7–12). But the gospel entails not only a re-enactment of the cross; it also enables those in Christ to participate in a "new creation": "everything old has passed away; see, everything has become new" (5:17). The overcoming of social and ethnic boundaries is thus a part of the all-encompassing "renovation" process by which "God in Christ was reconciling the world to himself" (5:19)—a powerful response to anyone who may doubt the magnitude of Paul's ministry and the importance of cooperating in it.

# Galatians

---

**OUTLINE**

---

Little is known about Paul's time with the churches of Galatia, yet he has undeniably formed a strong bond with the Christians of central Anatolia to whom he sends this letter. They would have plucked out their very eyes for him, he says (4:15). Bypassing the thanksgiving with which he customarily opens his letters, Paul assumes an air of authority in addressing what he perceives to be a grave threat to their souls. He is alarmed that they have embraced "a different gospel" from the one he delivered to them and pronounces an anathema on anyone who preaches it (1:6–9). Paul's purpose in this letter is to delineate the shortcomings of this alternative teaching and replace it with a proper understanding of the working of God's grace.

That the misunderstanding Paul seeks to correct did not arise organically is suggested by the way he addresses it. Galatians 1:10–2:21 contains more autobiographical data than any of Paul's other letters. From this account of his ministry, which is difficult at points to coordinate with the narrative of Acts, one learns of his turn from persecutor to proselytizer on a special mission from God to proclaim the good news among the Gentiles. His converts include the Galatians, who were flourishing in their new faith until rival teachers arrived to "bewitch" or "confuse" them (3:1; 5:10). It appears that these teachers are Jewish-Christian missionaries who contend that Paul has led them astray by relaxing the demands of the Torah, in particular by doing away with the requirement of circumcision and by dismissing the dietary laws of kashrut as nugatory. For this reason, they are often referred to as

"Judaizers." Modern readers may wonder why anyone would consider Torah observance obligatory for Christians. As Paul's spirited apologia suggests, the notion that worship of the Jewish God made manifest in a Jewish messiah as prophesied in the Jewish Scriptures requires the observation of Jewish law had begun to take hold in Galatia.

To say that Paul does not take kindly to this questioning of his apostolic authority is an understatement. Do they mean to compel Gentile believers to undergo circumcision as necessary for salvation? "I wish those who unsettle you would castrate themselves," he responds (5:12; cf. 6:12–15). Do they consider it unclean to dine with non-Jews? Even Peter practiced open table fellowship in Antioch before losing his nerve when "certain people" from "the circumcision faction" in Jerusalem showed up (2:12; Reformed and Orthodox theologians have often cited this incident in arguments against Catholic claims for the papacy based on the primacy of Peter). But in his prickly self-defense in the face of doubts about his integrity, Paul does not settle for lobbing sarcastic counter-accusations of hypocrisy. Rather, he marshals textual evidence from the Hebrew Scriptures in support of a subtle theological argument that intersects on key points with his exposition in the Letter to the Romans.

His main thesis is that Jews and Gentiles alike are "justified" or made righteous "not by the works of the law but through faith in Jesus Christ," and that "if justification comes through the law, then Christ died for nothing" (2:15–16, 20; cf. 3:24). Martin Luther loved Galatians like he loved his wife—"it is my Katie von Bora," he says in one of his table talks—because it so forcefully articulated the doctrine of justification by faith, and it is clear from his 1531 lectures that he saw Paul's conflict with the Judaizers over faith and works reprised in his own struggle with the Roman Catholic Church. Far from seeing this idea as a betrayal of Jewish law or departure from tradition, Paul argues that it is the inescapable logic of the biblical witness. He quotes Gen. 15:6—Abraham "believed God, and it was reckoned to him as righteousness"—and points out that the law was not given to the Moses until 430 years later (3:6, 17). If it was possible to be declared righteous before the promulgation of the Torah, then it is possible to be justified apart from "works of the law." The mechanism is the same as it has always been, namely, faith (*pistis*). When Paul says that the Scriptures foresaw that God would justify the Gentiles by faith, he can thus assert that his message and missionary modus operandi do not constitute a grievous departure from tradition (3:8).

According to Paul, the law was instituted as a provisional measure "so that what was promised through faith in Jesus Christ might be given to those who believe," but this "disciplinarian" or "guardian" no longer fills the same role now that Christ has come (3:23–26). Many scholars believe the key phrase used here and in Romans by Paul, *pistis Christou*, should be translated "the faith of Christ" rather than the more common (at least since the Reformation) "faith in Christ." At stake in this debate over grammar is the matter of whether it is: (1) the individual's belief in Jesus and the atoning efficacy of his death that results in the promise of salvation; or (2) the faith(fulness) displayed by Jesus toward God and his people that obtains it, though these two options are not mutually exclusive in theological terms (Hays 1997: 35–60).

Faith affects not only the vertical relationship between the believer and God but also relations on the horizontal plane. Distinctions of race, class, and gender are relativized by the operation of grace through faith: "There is no longer Jew or Greek, there is no longer slave or free, there is no longer male and female; for all of you are one in Christ Jesus" (Gal. 3:28). Here Paul appears to turn on its head an ancient rabbinic benediction in which Jewish men thank God that they were not born a Gentile, a slave, or a woman (*b. Men.* 43b). In modern times, this verse has been taken up as a mantra by various egalitarian movements. Catherine Booth, co-founder of the Salvation Army, cited it in support of women's participation in ordained ministry, and in the Anglican Church it is used as a reading on the Feast of William Wilberforce, in honor of the tireless campaigner against the British slave trade (Moxnes 2014: 133–56). Interpreters disagree about Paul's intended message, in part because these distinctions have so obviously persisted: is it about salvation—implying that in God's eyes, after Christians have put on a new self in baptism, they are equal—or is it about reforming the social order—that everyone already enjoys equal status in God's eyes, and that through this renewal this equality should be made manifest?

If their willingness to undergo circumcision is any indication, the Galatians' faults certainly do not include fear of commitment. Paul worries that, under the mistaken impression that such "works of the law"—ceremonial duties stipulated in the Law of Moses that function as badges of Jewish ethnic identity—will garner them salvation, they are disastrously submitting to a "yoke of slavery" (5:1). To illustrate his point, Paul returns to Genesis to make an argument that is distinctive to Galatians (4:21–31). He turns the two sons of Abraham, Ishmael and Isaac, and their two mothers, Hagar and Sarah, into an allegory of two covenants, one instituted at Sinai and in effect in "the present Jerusalem" and the other corresponding to "the Jerusalem above." Hagar represents slavery while Sarah represents freedom. Those "under the law" belong to the former, and the "children of the promise"—those united with Jesus by faith—belong to the latter. Paul's abstruse rhetoric has inadvertently made it easier to caricature Judaism as a bankrupt and legalistic form of "works righteousness," as does Marcion, Paul's second-century "champion" who believed that the God of the Old Testament and the God of the New Testament were two opposing deities. Paul does not consider the law problematic unless one regards it as necessary for salvation, thus rejecting Christ as the sole basis for redemption. For this reason, scholars often describe the Second Temple Judaism with which Paul would have been familiar as "covenantal nomism," wherein obedience to the commandments is understood as a privilege granted to God's chosen people, but not a means of "earning" salvation.

"For freedom Christ has set us free" (5:1), Paul declares in one of the most oft-quoted lines of the letter, spending the final two chapters warning them not to use this freedom for self-indulgence. Their moral life should be a spirit-filled response to the gift of salvation made available on the cross. His wish is that they are able to say with him, "It is no longer I who live, but it is Christ who lives in me" (2:20).

# Ephesians

Ephesus, situated on the western coast of modern-day Turkey, was one of the largest cities in the Roman Empire and among the most important in the history of early Christianity. According to Acts, Paul ministered there for three years. The first collection of Paul's letters may have been brought together in the city, which also receives a "letter" from Christ in Rev. 2:1–7 and from Ignatius of Antioch early in the second century. Some early traditions also report that John lived there for a time with the mother of Jesus (Trebilco 2004).

But was the Letter to the Ephesians originally addressed to Ephesus? Some of the earliest manuscripts lack the words "in Ephesus" in the salutation, which reads, thus, "to the saints who are also faithful in Christ Jesus." Early patristic writers are familiar with versions of the letter that lack an Ephesian address. Marcion in the mid-second century identified Ephesians with the letter to Laodicea mentioned in Col. 4:16. The author and audience appear not to have met in person, though they are acquainted through other sources (Eph. 1:15; 3:2). Details of local affairs in Ephesus are conspicuous by their absence—not what one might expect in light of Acts 20, which depicts the relationship between Paul and the Ephesian believers as a tender one that developed over an extended period. Together with the generalized nature of the contents and the omission of personal greetings to named individuals like those seen in other Pauline letters, this leads many scholars to conclude that, like 1 Peter, it may have originated as a circular letter sent to several churches in western Asia Minor.

Whether they reside in Ephesus proper or elsewhere in the region, the audience consists of Gentiles, formerly "aliens from the commonwealth of Israel, and strangers to the covenants of promise" (2:11–12; 3:1; 4:17). Signs of Jew–Gentile friction, so prominent in Acts and Romans, are absent, however, as Christ has broken down the "dividing wall" and "reconcile[d] both groups to God in one body through the cross, thus putting to death that hostility through it," thus making the Gentile believers "members of the household of God" (2:14–20). This emphasis on the role of the uncircumcised in God's eternal plan (3:5–6) would resonate with non-Jews unsettled by the idea that their inclusion in the people of God might have been an afterthought. To the contrary, they are among those chosen "before the foundation of the world to be holy and blameless" (1:4), a text frequently cited by John Calvin in support of the doctrine of predestination. Allusions throughout the letter to baptism may function as reminders for recent Gentile converts still discovering the full significance of their decision to lead a new life (1:13; 4:5, 30; 5:8, 26; it has been suggested that it is more fitting to read Ephesians as a baptismal homily than as a letter). Paul's exposition highlights the workings of God's grace that would have special relevance for his Gentile readers:

> God, who is rich in mercy . . . even when we were dead through our trespasses, made us alive together with Christ . . . For by grace you have been saved through faith, and this is not your own doing; it is the gift of God.
>
> (2:5, 8)

Martin Luther finds in these lines a powerful expression of the doctrine of justification by faith. Whatever their prior religious commitments, Paul is facilitating their initiation into "the mystery of Christ," a mystery hidden for eons until its revelation in the church (3:4, 8–9).

Notwithstanding these thematic parallels with other letters, many scholars have questioned its claims to Pauline authorship. The florid literary style of Ephesians, they argue, differs from that of the undisputed letters in featuring lengthy, grammatically complex sentences and in using terminology and metaphors not found elsewhere in Paul's corpus. Proponents of Pauline authorship regard this as a subjective determination, countering that the vocabulary of Ephesians is no more idiosyncratic that that of Galatians. Settling this matter depends in part upon one's understanding of the relationship between Ephesians and Colossians. By some estimates, Ephesians contains thematic or linguistic parallels to nearly half of the contents of Colossians. These connections concern such matters as the divine mystery (Eph. 3:2–3; Col. 1:25–26), the putting off of the old nature and putting on the new (Eph. 4:22–32; Col. 3:5–12), condemnations of vice (Eph. 5:3–6; Col. 3:5–9), singing hymns (Eph. 5:19–20; Col. 3:16–17), household codes (Eph. 5:21–6:9; Col. 3:18–4:1), and mention of his courier, Tychicus (Eph. 6:21–22; Col. 4:7–8), among many others appearing in the same sequence in both letters. For most scholars, this proves that the author of Ephesians is familiar with and dependent on Colossians. But what is the most natural corollary from this premise? Is it that Paul is the author of both? That Paul is the author of neither? Or that Paul is the author of Colossians but not of Ephesians, the author of which decided to produce a "Pauline" letter based on a letter accepted as authentic?

Perceived theological differences further complicate the question (Muddiman 2001: 17–20). As in Colossians, Christ is the "head" that supports the body, that is, the church (Eph. 4:15–16; 5:23), while in 1 Cor. 12:12, 27 the church is itself the body of Christ. Whereas Ephesians describes salvation as a present reality (2:5–6), Paul speaks of it in the future tense (Rom. 5:9–10; 13:13; 1 Cor. 5:5; 1 Thess. 5:9). Some scholars feel that the first distinction is overly subtle and that the second one overlooks the way in which the undisputed letters describe salvation variously as a past, ongoing, and future reality (Rom. 5:1–2; 8:24; Phil. 2:12). Similarly, when Ephesians speaks of the universal church in the singular, it is thought to conflict with the dominant notion of the church in Paul's letters as a local community. Yet Jesus, in Matt. 16:18–20 and 18:15–20 can speak of the church in both aspects. While the prevailing view is that a follower of Paul or a Pauline "school" has attempted to summarize the apostle's teachings some years after his death by drawing on his other writings, debate about these matters has not ceased.

The body of the letter can be divided into two halves. In the first half (1:3–3:21), the author describes in the indicative what God has accomplished at the cosmic level and in the lives of individuals. The second half of Ephesians (4:1–6:20) is written in the imperative, laying out instructions on how to walk as children of the light. This section includes a call to unity within the church often quoted by participants in the ecumenical movement:

> There is one body and one Spirit, just as you were called to the one hope of your calling, one Lord, one faith, one baptism, one God and Father of all, who is above all and through all and in all.
>
> (4:4–6)

Much of this instruction is paraenetic in nature, filled with uncontroversial ethical admonitions in the form of virtue and vice lists. Most prominent is the "household code" in 5:21–6:8, which broadly resembles other such lists of duties attending the husband–wife, parent–child, and master–slave relationships. Comparison with the parallel passage in Col. 3:18–4:1 reveals differences that reflect the special foci of the author. The most striking difference is the expanded meditation on marriage. The command to the wife to submit to the husband is unremarkable. But the description of the husband as the "head" of the wife as an analogy for Christ's role as head of the church is novel. Husbands are to love their wives "just as Christ loved the church and gave himself up for her" (5:25). The emphasis on the sacrificial nature of conjugal love and the allusion to Gen. 2:24 ("the two shall become one flesh") contribute to the popularity of this passage as a reading in wedding ceremonies. The extent to which one should understand Eph. 5:21 ("Be subject to one another out of reverence for Christ") as qualifying the rest of the instructions that follow has been a point of contention in discussions about gender equality.

Finally, the process of leading a life "worthy of the calling to which [they] have been called" (4:1) involves each individual in a struggle that plays out in settings that transcend the household and the local congregation. They must don "the whole armor of God" because their fight is "not against enemies of blood and flesh, but against the rulers, against the authorities, against the cosmic powers of this present darkness, against the spiritual forces of evil in the heavenly places"

(6:10–17). Their equipment includes the "belt of truth," "breastplate of righteousness," "shield of faith," "helmet of salvation," and "sword of the Spirit." This martial imagery has inspired hymnodists such as Charles Wesley ("Soldiers of Christ, Arise, and put your armor on") and allegorists from Prudentius (in his *Psychomachia*) to Edmund Spenser (in *The Faerie Queene*), as well as, in some Christian circles, furnished the elements of a popular Halloween costume for children. It is also a key text undergirding theologies of spiritual warfare in Pentecostalism, especially among African Christians, and its exhortation to resist "the wiles of the devil" is echoed in the Catholic prayer to St. Michael the Archangel.

# Philippians

---

**OUTLINE**

---

Christianity first makes landfall in Europe at Philippi, a leading Macedonian city named for the father of Alexander the Great that had been incorporated as a Roman colony a few generations before Paul's arrival. According to Acts 16, Paul had been summoned in a vision to cross over from Asia. Decades later, Polycarp (*Phil.* 3.2) indicates that Paul had written multiple letters to Philippi, though this is the only one that has survived. Like Ephesians, Colossians, and Philemon, it is written from prison, perhaps in Ephesus, Caesarea, or Rome.

Although they are not a wealthy community, the Philippians have contributed generously to Paul's mission (Phil. 4:10–20; cf. 2 Cor. 8:1–6). A primary purpose of the letter is to thank them for the gifts they have sent, which helps to account for the pervasive tone of joy and gratitude. Paul also wants to reassure any readers with misgivings about their associations with a teacher—to whom they have donated considerable funds—who is constantly running afoul of the authorities. He is especially anxious to make the point that his imprisonment does not hinder the spread of the good news. Their friendship has been forged in a shared experience of suffering for the sake of the gospel, and this letter is intended to overcome the pain of separation that prevents them from comforting one another (1:8, 27, 30; 2:12, 19; 4:10). Many scholars believe that Philippians in its present form has been compiled using excerpts from two or three separate letters due to abrupt shifts in tone or subject, but the emphasis on joy amidst suffering throughout the text militates against this theory. Furthermore, praising one's friends by contrasting them with enemies, as one sees in contested passages such as Phil. 3:2 ("Beware of the dogs . . . "), was a common rhetorical strategy (Fitzgerald 1996: 141–60).

What form of persecution the Philippians are experiencing is unclear (1:28–30). Although there is little evidence for a large Jewish presence in the city, warnings about "those who mutilate the flesh" and Paul's boasting about his impeccable Hebrew pedigree may reflect Jewish opposition (3:2–6). Partly due to the large-scale resettlement of retired Roman soldiers, the official imperial cult was firmly entrenched, which may indicate Gentile pressures as well. At the very least, they may be feeling the tension inherent in their dual status as Roman citizens—an honor granted to residents of Philippi by August Caesar—and as citizens of the commonwealth (*politeuma*) of heaven (3:20). The letter's most memorable lines underscore Paul's irenic tone in the face of trying circumstances he and his readers are facing. Contemplating the very real possibility of his own imminent death in jail, he reflects that "to live is Christ, and to die is gain" (1:21). He prays that the Philippians may be blessed with "the peace of God, which passeth all understanding" (4:7 KJV), and concludes with supreme confidence: "I can do all things through [Christ] who strengthens me" (4:13).

It appears that harassment from without has taken a toll on internal relations, as Paul repeatedly urges the Philippian community to be "of one mind" (2:2; 4:2). Paul supports this call to unity by quoting from what most scholars believe to be an early Christian hymn in Phil. 2:6–11. This passage exhibits the rhythm, parallelism, and strophic structure one sees in much Greek poetry. More to the point is its content rather than its form. Paul exhorts the Philippians to pattern themselves after Jesus:

> [w]ho, though he was in the form of God,
> did not regard equality with God
> as something to be exploited,
> but emptied himself,
> taking the form of a slave,

> being born in human likeness.
> And being found in human form,
> he humbled himself
> and became obedient to the point of death—
> > even death on a cross.
> Therefore God also highly exalted him
> and gave him the name
> that is above every name,
> so that at the name of Jesus
> every knee should bend,
> in heaven and on earth and under the earth,
> and every tongue should confess
> that Jesus Christ is Lord,
> to the glory of God the Father.

The structure and message of this "Christ hymn," with its "V-shaped" trajectory charting Jesus's descent into human mortality and subsequent ascent to glory, fits well with Paul's concerns elsewhere in the letter, often in paradoxical form. Just as Christ's death results in his exaltation, for Paul "dying is gain" (1:21). Paul also eschews any bragging rights based on his lineage in exchange for knowledge of Christ because he comes to regard those advantages as "rubbish" (3:4–9). The interjection "even death on a cross" at the halfway point has the rhetorical effect of an exclamation mark. It is easy to imagine Paul inserting such a parenthetical remark inasmuch as the crucifixion was a great scandal for Jews and Gentiles alike, and Paul never flinches when citing it as the reason for the exaltation of Christ described in the second half of the hymn.

Even more prevalent is the motif of imitation. The hymn is introduced with a call to emulate Christ. The body explicates this pattern as self-denial. When Paul presents himself as a model, it is on these same terms (3:17). He states that he will "remain in the flesh" for the Philippians in spite of his own desires because it is more needful for them (1:21–26). Timothy is also commended to the Philippians because he does not pursue his own interests, like Epaphroditus, who risked his life for Christ and who will cause the church to rejoice when they see him (2:19–22, 25–30). Knowing Christ is defined in terms of sharing his suffering and "becoming like him in his death," after which the believer may hope to "attain the resurrection from the dead" (3:10–11). The pattern enacted by Jesus of self-denial and glorification by God may thus be replicated in the life of the believer.

One phrase from the Christ hymn played a role in the Trinitarian controversies addressed at the ecumenical councils of Nicaea in 325 and Chalcedon in 451. Jesus did not consider equality with God as "a thing to be grasped" (RSV) or "something to be exploited" (NRSV). The Greek word used, *harpagmos*, allows for either translation. If one reads it with the connotation of "clinging," then the view of Athanasius makes sense: Jesus already possessed divine status, but did not insist on keeping or taking advantage of it, instead divesting himself of his divine nature in a process of "emptying" (*kenosis*). In this view, it follows that Jesus enjoyed preexistence as a heavenly being before becoming human. If one reads it with the connotation of "seizing," then the hymn appears to describe Jesus as refusing to reach after something he does not already possess. In this view, the position of Arius and others that Jesus was not coequal, coeternal, or consubstantial with God the Father comes into clearer focus. Athanasius prevailed in this battle for orthodoxy, but debate over the implications of early Christological formulas was by no means settled (Martin and Dodd 1998). "Death of God" theologians of the 1960s saw the trajectory of the hymn as an affirmation of their view that God had divested himself so completely as to relinquish any transcendent existence.

# Colossians

Located in the Lycus Valley of western Anatolia, Colossae was just a stone's throw from the much larger city of Laodicea. Acts records nothing about Colossae, the Letter to the Colossians indicates that Epaphras and not Paul was the founder of the church there (1:7; 2:1; 4:12–13), and Tacitus (*Ann.* 14.27) mentions an earthquake that appears to have destroyed the city in the early 60s. Together with Ephesians, Philippians, and Philemon, Colossians is labeled one of the Captivity Letters, so called on account of the author's reference to his imprisonment at the time of writing (4:3).

Citing differences with the undisputed letters, many scholars believe that Paul's Letter to the Colossians was neither written by Paul nor sent to Colossae. They point to distinctive vocabulary and discern theological shifts away from characteristic Pauline positions. For example, Jesus' role in the creation of the world (1:15–18) is emphasized more heavily than his role in the end of all things, eschatological realities are described as in some sense already present (2:12–13; 3:1), and the church is conceived in cosmic terms rather than as a local assembly, with Christ referred to as "the head of the body, the church" (1:18; 2:19). Defenders of Pauline authorship note that the vocabulary of Colossians is no more peculiar than that of Philippians and that the quotation of hymns and the possible use of a scribe may further skew any statistics pertaining to its literary style. They further observe that Jesus functions as "Alpha" as well as "Omega" in the undisputed letters (1 Cor. 8:6; 2 Cor. 4:4) and that the church assumes supra-local as well as more mundane dimensions in both the disputed and undisputed letters (1 Cor. 15:9; Gal 1:13; Col. 4:15–16; 1 Tim. 3:15).

If Colossians is a pseudonymous writing, it is thought either that one of Paul's associates wrote it on his behalf shortly after his death, or that devotees of the apostle composed it long afterwards in order to apply his authoritative voice to a new situation, drawing names and details from the authentic Letter to Philemon—eight named individuals appear in both Philemon and Colossians—so as to lend it biographical verisimilitude. Colossae's demise in the earthquake would, in this scenario, conveniently remove anyone who might question its genuineness. For defenders of Pauline authorship, this latter theory is too clever by half insofar as the "borrowing" of a cast of characters from a private letter is not the most obvious strategy for convincing a broader readership of its authenticity.

In either scenario, little can be said about the audience apart from what is implied in the author's instructions to them. While ancient sources suggest that Colossae had a sizeable Jewish population, the congregation addressed here is likely Gentile in composition (1:27; 2:13).

The author also assumes that they have regular contact with the Christians in Laodicea, with whom he instructs them to exchange letters he has written (4:16; a brief epistle "to the Laodiceans," consisting of fragments drawn mostly from Galatians and Philippians, circulated under Paul's name in the fourth century). This instruction may suggest that the two groups are dealing with similar issues.

And what are those issues? The primary impetus is the worry that the readers will be led astray "through philosophy and empty deceit" (2:4, 8, 16–23). The author does not appear to mean an established school of moral philosophy like Platonism or the first-century Stoicism of Epictetus, who was born in nearby Hierapolis. Speculation abounds as to the precise character of these dangerous teachings (Francis and Meeks 1975). Is it one of the indigenous Phrygian cults? Is it one of the mystery cults imported from further east associated with such deities as Attis, Cybele, and Mithras? Is it a nascent form of the Gnosticism that will appear more fully formed in the second century? Is it a syncretistic form of Hellenistic Judaism, with mystical tendencies involving "worship of angels" and "dwelling on visions" (2:18)? Mention of "festivals," "new moons," and "sabbaths," along with the reassurance that they need not be troubled by anyone who might condemn them in matters of food and drink may be evidence of some Jewish source for the Colossian heresy, yet one might expect some engagement with texts from the Hebrew Bible as one sees in Galatians were it simply a matter of "Judaizers" insisting on full Gentile adherence to the Torah (2:11–14). The strictures the author dismisses (2:21: "Do not handle, Do not taste, Do not touch") might be related to a wide range of ascetic sensibilities that, when combined with the ritual taboos and calendrical observances, were dismissed by many writers as superstitious and harmful to the soul, having only "an appearance of wisdom in promoting self-imposed piety, humility, and severe treatment of the body, but . . . of no value in checking self-indulgence" (2:23). Their baptism and rising with Christ have prepared them to put on a new self quite apart from these habits of mind and body.

The theological foundation for the author's rebuttal of these teachings is found in the stately hymn he quotes in Col. 1:15–20 (Martin 1964). Whatever they may have heard concerning "elemental spirits (*stoicheia*) of the universe" (2:8, 20)—Are these angels and demons? Are they the building blocks of the physical universe (earth, air, fire, water)?—they are to know that nothing is more elemental than Christ, who is:

> [t]he image of the invisible God, the firstborn of all creation; for in him all things in heaven and on earth were created, whether thrones or dominions or rulers or powers—all things have been created through him and for him. He himself is before all things, and in him all things hold together . . . For in him all the fullness of God was pleased to dwell, and through him God was pleased to reconcile himself [to] all things, whether on earth or in heaven, by making peace through the blood of his cross.

Here one finds expressed a "high" Christology, emphasizing Jesus' divine qualities, that has few parallels in the New Testament. It recalls but also goes beyond biblical descriptions of Wisdom personified as an agent in creation (Prov. 3:19; 8:22; Wis. 7:26). In the various propositions and prepositions the hymn contains, interpreters have found much on which to disagree. Arius and Athanasius both invoked it in their disputes over the nature of Christ in the fourth century. Seizing on the final verse, read in tandem with Col. 3:11 ("Christ is all and in all"), the hymn has also fueled debate from the time of Origen to the present about the reconciliation of which the author writes and whether it warrants a universalist view of salvation.

Lest one conclude that Colossians is preoccupied with abstract theological ruminations and esoteric practices no longer transparent to modern readers, the letter also includes ethical guidelines for the most quotidian of affairs: life in the home. Like similar lists found in Jewish and Greco-Roman sources as well as in the New Testament (e.g., 1 Pet. 2:13–3:7), the "household code" in Col. 3:18–4:1 details the reciprocity owed by individuals to other family members. Here the focus is on relations between husbands and wives, fathers and children, and masters and slaves. A similar household code is found in the Letter to the Ephesians, which many scholars take to be a deutero-pauline composition that borrows from Colossians and thus represents the earliest surviving interpretation of that letter. Many interpreters feel the "bourgeois" contents of these codes to be in tension with the eschatologically charged, counter-cultural ethos of Paul as articulated in the authentic letters, especially the radically egalitarian declaration in Gal. 3:28–29 that "there is no longer Jew or Greek . . . slave or free . . . male and female." If so, then Colossians exhibits an internal tension, as it states only a few verses earlier that the readers have clothed themselves "with a new self," and "in that renewal there is no longer Greek and Jew, circumcised and uncircumcised, barbarian, Scythian, slave and free" (3:9–11). This juxtaposition is a reminder of the challenges faced by Paul and his followers as they strove to "set [their] minds on things that are above" (3:2–3) while remaining embedded in social structures here below.

# 1–2 Thessalonians

---

**OUTLINE**

| | |
|---|---|
| 1 Thess. 1:1–10 | Salutation and Thanksgiving |
| 2:1–3:13 | Paul's relations with the Thessalonians |
| 4:1–12 | Moral exhortations |
| 4:13–5:11 | Instructions about the end-times |
| 5:12–22 | Moral maxims |
| 5:23–28 | Closing benediction |
| | |
| 2 Thess. 1:1–12 | Salutation and Thanksgiving |
| 2:1–17 | Correction of eschatological misunderstandings |
| 3:1–18 | Warnings against idleness |

---

Thessalonica was a major Macedonian port city situated on the Egnatian Way, the main road connecting Rome to the eastern empire. According to Acts 17:1–9, Paul founds the church there with Silas ca. 49 CE before harassment at the hands of local Jews forces them to leave town. He desires to return since his initial stay was cut short, but circumstances have kept him away (1 Thess. 2:17–18). In the meantime, he writes this first letter—widely regarded as the oldest document in the New Testament—to encourage the Thessalonians and strengthen their fledgling faith in trying times. They are Gentiles who have "turned to God from idols, to serve a living and true God" (1:9). Paul praises them from the outset for their "work of faith and labor of love and steadfastness of hope" (1:2–4). He will repeat these compliments about their faith and love (1:8; 3:6; 4:9–10), but worries that their hope is waning.

Paul demonstrates his pastoral skill in tailoring his instructions to fit his audience. As recent converts with minimal catechizing—Paul nowhere quotes the Scriptures, perhaps because they were insufficiently familiar with it—they are prone to draw the wrong conclusions from their experience. Paul is patient with them rather than caustic and demanding. His approach is like that of Hellenistic philosophers who display frank speech but know how to soften their tone when the situation calls for it (Malherbe 1987: 61–94). Here he uses emotive language, reminiscing about their time together and reminding them that he was "gentle as a [wet] nurse" among them and also likening himself to a father and an orphaned child (1:4–2:16; 3:1–10). Presenting the Thessalonians with models to emulate (1:6; 2:14; 3:1–4) and digesting ethical principles into pithy maxims (5:12–22) are two other rhetorical devices on display that one also finds among the philosophers of the time such as Epictetus and Plutarch.

The fragility of their situation is a function of two factors. First, they have undergone persecution at the hands of their non-Christian neighbors (1:6–7; 2:14–17). The Thessalonians have become "imitators of the churches of God in Christ Jesus that are in Judea, for [they] suffered the same things from [their] own compatriots as they did from the Jews" (2:14). A level of anxiety normally accompanies religious conversion even when it is not compounded by mistreatment by one's peers. Any ostracism may have been motivated by their detachment from the worship of Greek and Egyptian deities in a city that was also deeply invested in the imperial cult, or class-based animus against a group consisting of manual laborers (Ascough 2000: 314–15). Some scholars find it improbable that Jews persecuted Christians and out of character for Paul the Jew to then describe "the Jews" in vv. 15–16 as having "killed both the Lord Jesus and the prophets," conjecturing that the entire passage is a later non-Pauline insertion. Apart from the fact that all ancient manuscripts contain these verses, this view ignores the way Paul emphasizes the solidarity of his Gentile converts with the Christians of Judea, not only contributing financial support but now also sharing in their sufferings (cf. 2 Cor. 8:1–6). Paul's advice is to live quietly, mind their own affairs, "behave properly toward outsiders and be dependent on no one," and not to repay evil for evil (4:11–12; 5:15).

Second, the Thessalonians are in danger of losing hope due to the death of community members since Paul's departure. Paul's primary aim in writing this letter is to correct their misunderstandings about the end-times and thereby to allay their fears about the ultimate fate of their brothers and sisters in Christ (4:13). Their worry is that those who have died before Jesus' Second Coming (*parousia*) will miss out on the full manifestation of God's kingdom. Expectation of Christ's imminent return was widespread in the early church (Heb. 10:25; Jas. 5:7–9; 1 Pet. 4:7), though Paul's own comments on the question are ambiguous, sometimes intimating that he anticipates being alive (1 Cor. 15:51–52) and sometimes that he expects to be among the dead who will be raised when it occurs (1 Cor. 6:14; 2 Cor. 4:14; Phil. 1:20). Many scholars concur with Albert Schweitzer's claim that "the whole history of Christianity down to the present day . . . is based on the delay of the Parousia," while others note that unequivocal evidence for any crisis created by the failure of Jesus to return visibly and establish God's kingdom is sparse (Schweitzer 1961: 360).

Paul's language and view of history is heavily indebted to the Jewish apocalypticism that is also reflected in Jesus' discourse in Matt. 24: 29–35, making it all the more difficult to elucidate his ideas about how the eschaton will unfold with any precision. Does he expect it to play out literally as described in 1 Thess. 4:14–17, with Christ descending from the heavens, a trumpet sounding, and the faithful meeting him in the clouds? Any attempt to pin Paul down, of course, runs counter to his subsequent advice to the Thessalonians. He assures them that the dead are not without hope because they will be raised just as Christ rose from the grave. But no one knows when the end will arrive. It will come "like a thief in the night" (5:1), presumably emphasizing the element of surprise since thieves do not sound trumpets when they enter a house. He further mixes his metaphors by comparing the Lord's advent to the labor pains of a pregnant woman. Speculating about "the times and the seasons" (5:1) will only serve to increase their anxiety. About Jesus' triumphal return there can be no doubt because he has already vanquished death, even if the timetable for his return remains a mystery. The important thing, he says, is that "awake or asleep," they belong to Christ and that they live morally sober lives "worthy of God, who calls you into his own kingdom and glory" (5:4–10; cf. 2:12). Paul's eschatological thinking thus influences but does not determine his ethical instruction.

Nothing in 1 Thessalonians has had a larger impact on contemporary culture than Paul's eschatological musings, specifically his description in 4:16–17 of what is commonly referred to as "the Rapture." This term is used in certain strands of premillenialist Christianity to describe a moment when the faithful are "caught up" in the sky to meet

Jesus at the Second Coming. Dispensationalist theology focusing on the Rapture reached a wide audience with the publication of the 1909 Scofield Reference Bible, which includes extensive footnotes that attempt to coordinate the scenario sketched out in 1 Thessalonians with various biblical prophecies and the apocalyptic scenarios envisioned in the Book of Revelation. Obsession with such an esoteric notion did not prevent Hal Lindsey's *The Late Great Planet Earth* from becoming one of the most popular books of the 1970s or the *Left Behind* series of Christian thrillers by Tim LaHaye and Jerry Jenkins (1995–2007) from selling nearly 100 million copies.

Of course, the earliest stage in the reception history of 1 Thessalonians falls just before the writing of 2 Thessalonians. A slight majority of scholars believe that "Paul" is a pseudonym used by the author of 2 Thessalonians. Of the disputed letters, however, it is the most widely accepted as authentic. Its style is no different from 1 Thessalonians. In fact, many scholars think that the similarities are so great not because they are from the same hand but because the author of one is consciously imitating the other. A more substantial factor objection is the perceived difference in the eschatological orientations of the two letters. Whereas 1 Thessalonians suggests that Jesus will return without warning, 2 Thessalonians lays out a series of events that will occur before the Day of the Lord arrives. This timetable is described in 2 Thess. 2:1–12 in cryptic language as a cosmic drama involving Jesus, Satan, "the lawless one" (sometimes identified as the antichrist), and a "restrainer." Given that Second Temple Jewish apocalyptic writings have little trouble holding both views in creative tension—Jesus himself in Matthew 24 tells his disciples of several signs that will precede the eschaton yet also maintains that it will arrive suddenly, "like a thief," at an unknown hour (24:1–8, 36–44)—it may be that the literary inconsistency is in the eye of the beholder rather than inherent in the texts.

Questions about pseudonymity, however, are not the peculiar concern of later interpreters. "As to the coming of the Lord Jesus Christ," writes the author, the Thessalonians are not to be alarmed by any letter "as though from us" purporting that "the day of the Lord is already here" (2 Thess. 2:1–2). Is Paul speaking hypothetically, or have letters in his name begun to circulate? Is a pseudonymous author attempting to deflect suspicions about the reliability of 2 Thessalonians? Was 2 Thessalonians written prior to 1 Thessalonians? Is 2 Thessalonians intended to correct or supplant 1 Thessalonians, especially on eschatological matters, brazenly insisting on its own genuineness (3:17)? Should 2 Thessalonians be considered authentic and 1 Thessalonians spurious?

Perhaps a more prosaic explanation is in order: What if the Thessalonians have misconstrued some of Paul's exotic language in his first letter pertaining to the Day of the Lord (1 Thess. 4:13–5:11)? It would not be the first instance of miscommunication between Paul and his addressees (cf. 1 Cor. 5:9–11). The audience is already on edge, and Paul's comment that the end would come "like a thief in the night"—unsurprisingly, in retrospect—has done nothing to relieve their anxiety. It appears that the abuse and ostracism mentioned in 1 Thessalonians has intensified (2 Thess. 1:4–8; 3:3). In the escalation of their distress, they may be under the impression that the hour of their deliverance is at hand, a concept commonly found in apocalyptic literature produced in settings of persecution. Just as they misunderstood the nature of the Parousia earlier, they now may be under different illusions about the Second Coming. In this situation, Paul's earlier admonition not to "fall asleep as others do, but . . . keep awake" (1 Thess. 5:6) may have been understood not as a figurative call to moral vigilance but literally as a directive to discern the signs of the times. For some of their number, this may have become an obsession distracting them from their regular duties, hence the injunction against idleness (3:6–13; in later centuries, many millenarian "doomsday cults" such as the Children of God and the Order of the Solar Temple have "rationally" concluded that there is little point in continuing to work or hold onto one's possessions if the world is soon to end). The instruction that "anyone unwilling to work should not eat" (3:10) has become the letter's most frequently quoted verse, appearing in such disparate sources as Saint Francis of Assisi's First Rule, John Smith's journals at Jamestown, and propaganda posters during the Bolshevik Revolution, after which it is enshrined by Joseph Stalin in the 1936 Constitution of the Soviet Union (Bartlett 2012: 36–56).

In his response, Paul offers reassurance that God is just and will come to their aid against their enemies and comfort them in their tribulation (1:6; 2:16–17; 3:3, 16). The Day of the Lord will be of such magnitude that there will be no doubt of its arrival. Finally, he also reminds them that they must not "be weary in doing what is right" in the interim between the "already" of Jesus' death and resurrection and the "not yet" of his glorious return (3:13).

# 1–2 Timothy and Titus

The Pastoral Epistles—1–2 Timothy and Titus—are unique among the letters of Paul in that they are addressed to individuals rather than to groups, as even the Letter to Philemon is addressed to others who meet at the church in his house. So called since the nineteenth century on account of their pervasive concern for "pastoral" affairs, these letters are ostensibly addressed to two of Paul's most trusted co-workers. Timothy is a young man, the son of a Jewish mother and a Greek father (Acts 16:1–3; Phil. 2:19–24; 2 Tim. 1:5). He is named as the co-sender of several Pauline letters (2 Corinthians, Philippians, Colossians, 1–2 Thessalonians, Philemon). Titus is a Gentile convert who has rendered special service to Paul in his collection for the needy Christians in Jerusalem, where he also became embroiled in debates about the necessity of circumcision for

non-Jews (2 Cor. 8:6; Gal. 2:1–3). There is no independent corrobo-
ration of the claim made in the fifth-century *Acts of Titus* that he was
descended from the legendary King Minos of Crete.

Most scholars, however, do not interpret these letters as though
they were written to the historical Timothy and Titus. The identity of
the author and the audience(s) of the Pastoral Epistles are more vigorously disputed than for any other Pauline letter. There are two main
ways of reading them. The dominant approach is to treat the three
letters as parts of a single pseudonymous composition written long
after Paul's death, perhaps as late at 130 CE, for the purpose of giving
instruction regarding the structure and internal relations of the local
church community, so that the audience may know "how one ought
to behave in the household of God" (1 Tim. 3:15). Waning expectations of Jesus' return from heaven to inaugurate his kingdom on
earth and the consequent need for the church to manage its affairs
in the world call out for authoritative teaching. The genre of this fic-
tional correspondence is understood to be an early form of "church
orders" like those seen in the second century and in such writings
as the *Didache* and the *Didascalia Apostolorum* (MacDonald 1988:
203–24). In this approach, "Timothy" and "Titus" are not the real
recipients but are instead part of a literary conceit in which a wider
audience that respects "Paul" may eavesdrop on him as he holds forth
on controversial questions that, not coincidentally, happen to be facing the community in the present. In this construal, the function of
2 Timothy, which evinces little interest in "church order," is to present
Paul's final "testament," with the aged apostle offering himself as an
example and imparting words of wisdom and encouragement to his
protégé as he nears the end of his life.

Several factors commend this approach: (1) the Pastoral Epistles
are not widely quoted by the earliest non-biblical authors and are missing from Marcion's second-century Pauline corpus, the *Apostolikon*;
(2) Acts does not portray missionary activity carried out by Paul in
the time or place implied in the letters; (3) relative to other letters, the
Pastoral Epistles contain a high proportion of words found nowhere
else in the New Testament. Of the terms Paul uses elsewhere, many
seem to have meanings not typically attached to those terms in his
other letters. "Faith," for example, is sometimes characterized less
as an existential commitment to the person of Christ than assent to

a "deposit" of specific theological propositions (1 Tim. 4:1; 6:20). "Law" is something that may be used "lawfully" (1 Tim. 1:8). "Savior" is applied to God in addition to Jesus (1 Tim. 2:3; Titus 1:3; 3:4); (4) the Pastoral Epistles are preoccupied with organizational and administrative matters—e.g., qualifications for bishops, deacons, and elders (1 Tim. 3:1–13; Titus 1:5–9), payment of teachers (1 Tim. 5:17–19), and requirements for enrollment on a list of "real widows" (5:3–16)—to an extent not seen in the rest of Paul's correspondence. The household codes (1 Tim. 6:1–2; Titus 2:1–10) likewise sound a hierarchical, "bourgeois" note that many scholars find jarring when juxtaposed with the egalitarian, eschatological, counter-cultural ethos of the Pauline letters; and (5) the Pastoral Epistles exhibits a polemical edge in its efforts to combat false teaching and inculcate sound doctrine that appears to fit with the heightened concerns about heresy found in second-century literature (1 Tim. 1:3–8; 4:1–2; 6:3–5, 20; 2 Tim. 2:14–18; Titus 1:10–16; 3:9–11). An incipient form of Gnosticism has been proposed as the particular teaching the author opposes (cf. 1 Tim. 6:20: "what is falsely called knowledge [*gnosis*]").

At the other end of the spectrum are those scholars who believe that Paul himself or, at Paul's behest, a close associate wrote the Pastoral Epistles as separate letters to Timothy and Titus addressing distinct situations in their respective roles as his surrogates. Some defenders of Pauline authorship propose that these letters most closely resemble those belonging to the epistolary genre *mandata principis*, "commandments of the ruler" (Johnson 2001; note the frequency of the "commands/charges" to Timothy in 1 Tim. 1:3, 5, 18; 4:11; 5:7; 6:14). Letters in this genre are sent by a superior to a representative to delineate the responsibilities of the representative in a new assignment. Their function is not entirely unlike that of the oath of office taken at a presidential inauguration. The audience of such letters includes the newly appointed delegate, who receives the endorsement of the superior, and also the community to which he has been assigned, who then have some mechanism for holding the delegate accountable for the conscientious performance of his duties.

Defenders of Pauline authorship further respond: (1) echoes of the Pastoral Letters can be heard prior to Marcion, in the writings of the Apostolic Fathers; (2) Acts does not provide a complete account of Paul's ministry, which could have included a release from his

Roman confinement and further missionary travels back in the eastern Mediterranean as envisioned by the Pastoral Epistles before a second trial (cf. 2 Tim. 4:16); (3) differences in language and style are to be expected when writing on different topics, perhaps with the aid of a scribe, to close confidants rather than to a group; (4) concerns about "church order" and "division of labor" in the church are not absent from the Pauline letters (1 Cor. 12:28; Phil. 1:1). Moreover, if the conception of the church as something more otherworldly and exalted than a local assembly of Christ-believers is thought to mark texts like Ephesians and Colossians as post-Pauline productions, then the author's wrangling with the nitty-gritty problems of communal life perhaps points back in the opposite direction; (5) the polemical tendencies of the Pastoral Epistles are perhaps different in degree from the undisputed letters but not really in kind. The vague terms in which the false teachings are described, at least, do not warrant definite determinations that they could only have originated long after Paul's time.

The stated purpose of 1 Timothy is to exhort Timothy, in his role as Paul's envoy in Ephesus, to counter the influence of teachers who "occupy themselves with myths and endless genealogies that promote speculations" rather than the *oikonomia theou*, a difficult phrase variously translated as "divine training," "God's plan," and "God's stewardship" (1:3–4). It is linguistically and thematically linked with the restatement of the author's aims in 1 Tim. 3:14–15 to remind Timothy and his charges of the proper management of affairs in the household of God (*oikos theou*).

Timothy's task entails the handing on of "sound doctrine" (1:11; 6:3). The "liars" he is to oppose forbid marriage and demand abstinence from certain foods, leading many scholars to characterize them as proto-Gnostic. In response to such hyper-ascetic attitudes about the material world, Paul affirms the goodness of God's creation (1 Tim. 4:1–5). Because ideas have consequences, sound teaching is closely related to sound moral behavior in Greco-Roman and Hellenistic Jewish philosophical traditions such that a defect in one area will inevitably register as a defect in the other. The inclusion of virtue and vice lists (1:9–10; 6:4–11) provides the audience with an inventory by which to gauge their moral progress. Positive and negative role models likewise present them with concrete examples to follow. Paul himself— once the foremost of sinners—constitutes the most striking example of the power of God's transformative grace (1:12–17). Timothy in turn is to set an example for the congregation (4:12).

Indications that the author is concerned about the demeanor of women in the church can be seen in the most controversial passage in the Pastoral Epistles (1 Tim. 2:8–15). Women are to dress modestly—an unremarkable accommodation to prevailing cultural norms—and also to "learn in silence with full submission." "I permit no woman to teach or to have authority over a man," the author writes. Debate about the scope of this prohibition—Does it apply to all women or only wives? Does it apply to all contexts or only to public worship settings? Does it depend on the subsequent theological rationale involving Adam and Eve and the claim that women "will be saved through childbearing"?—begins in the ancient church and intensifies dramatically in the modern period. Elizabeth Cady Stanton, in *The Women's Bible* (1898), speaks for many of both sexes when she rejects this teaching as "the unilluminated utterance of Paul, the man, biased by prejudice," casting it as a retreat from more progressive notions of gender equity embraced by Jesus. Behind this text and in the extended discussion of widows (5:3–16) some see evidence for an order of female itinerant preachers like Thecla, who appears in the second-century *Acts of Paul*, from whose clutches the proto-orthodox author of 1 Timothy seeks to reclaim and "rehabilitate" Paul (Bassler 1984). It has been further suggested that this author has also inserted the similar instruction on women's silence into the text of 1 Cor. 14:33–36.

To maintain order in the face of potentially crippling divisions over this and other issues, the author seeks to solidify the hierarchy of bishops and deacons in 1 Tim. 3:1–13. Timothy is to make sure that these leadership posts are filled by the most qualified men (and perhaps women, if *gynaikes* in 1 Tim. 3:11 denotes deaconesses like Phoebe in Rom. 16:1 rather than the deacons' wives). They are to oversee such affairs as the disposition of the church's finite resources in caring for the widows in their midst (5:3–16). Prudence and moral probity are the chief qualities desired in a leader. For this reason, the Pastoral Epistles have been derided as inculcating a "good manners Christianity" that is overly concerned to be "well thought of by outsiders" (3:7). "Outsiders" may not have regarded the church in the desired light, according to the apocryphal *Acts of Timothy*. In this fifth-century work, Timothy is clubbed to death by Ephesian rioters upset by his criticism of their pagan festivities, a fate that almost befalls Paul in the same city in Acts 19.

The Letter to Titus is more similar in form and content to 1 Timothy than to 2 Timothy. Paul has left Titus in Crete to "put in order what remained to be done" in the church there, namely, to appoint elders (1:5–9). Like Timothy in Ephesus, Titus is contending with opposing teachers who are "teaching for sordid gain what it is not right to teach" (1:10–11). These opponents, who are peddling "Jewish myths" (1:14), are distracting the community with "stupid controversies, genealogies, dissensions, and quarrels about the law" (3:9). The author denounces the propensity of these "idle talkers and deceivers" for fruitless philosophical debate, perhaps even making ironic allusion in Titus 1:12 to a well-known logical riddle, the Liar Paradox, when he quotes a Cretan prophet asserting that all Cretans are liars. (Is he lying or telling the truth?)

Whether it issues from purely Jewish sources or from a nascent form of Gnosticism found more fully developed in the second century, the overly ascetic thrust of these teachings draws a terse response: "To the pure all things are pure" (1:15). This response may have been too succinct, as patristic writers would later complain of it being employed by heretics for libertine purposes. Jerome quotes it in discussing his uneasy conscience over his enjoyment of pagan literature, but D. H. Lawrence and Aldous Huxley have no such qualms, misquoting it satirically as "To the Puritan, all things are impure."

The complaint that these teachers are "upsetting whole families" helps to explain the emphasis in the requirements listed for elders on the moral qualities of the man as head of household. The subtle differences between Titus 1:5–9 and 1 Tim. 3:1–13 merit attention for what they may reflect about the different social realities underlying the respective letters. Likewise, the household code in Titus 2:1–10 serves to illustrate a crucial aspect of the gospel: that the salvation vouchsafed by God is experienced not simply when the soul reaches its final home in heaven but, rather, transforms lives in the here and now, at home and in society at large (3:1–7). "For the grace of God has appeared, bringing salvation to all," the author writes:

> [t]raining us to renounce impiety and worldly passions, and in the present age to live lives that are self-controlled, upright, and godly, while

we wait for the blessed hope and the manifestation of the glory of our
great God and Savior, Jesus Christ.

(2:11–13)

Of the three Pastoral Epistles, many scholars consider 2 Timothy
to be the one with the strongest case for Pauline authorship. When
2 Timothy is written, Paul is in prison and senses that death may
be near (1:8; 4:6). He meditates on his life's work in the course of
offering additional encouragement to Timothy, who continues to
face daunting challenges in the discharge of his pastoral duties (1:7;
2:1, 14–15). "Share in suffering like a good soldier of Christ Jesus"
(2 Tim. 2:3), he exhorts Timothy. The "soldier of Christ" (*miles
Christi*) motif has been applied figuratively to the medieval code of
chivalry as one sees in the Arthurian legends and to the monastic
vocation by Bernard of Clairvaux and Francis of Assisi, as well as,
more literally, to the Knights Templars and other participants in the
Crusades. "Onward, Christian Soldiers" and "Stand Up, Stand Up
for Jesus" are just two of many popular hymns that similarly depict
the Christian life in martial terms as a battle against sin and hardship.

As in farewell discourses such as the Jewish *Testaments of the
Twelve Patriarchs* and personal paraenetic letters like 1 Thessalonians,
here the author dispenses ethical advice by holding up both negative
examples to avoid (1:15; 2:16–18; 3:1–9; 4:14) and positive models to
emulate (1:5, 16–18; 4:11). The Hebrew Bible is a storehouse of such
lessons in virtue and vice. "All scripture," he proclaims, "is inspired
by God and is useful for teaching, for reproof, for correction and for
training in righteousness" (3:16; doctrines of biblical inspiration hinge
on how one understands the adjective *theopneustos*, "God-breathed,"
which appears almost nowhere else in Greek literature). In 2 Timothy,
Paul himself is the most immediate paradigm for Timothy to observe
(2:9–10; 3:10–11): "I have fought the good fight, I have finished the
race, I have kept the faith" (4:7–8). It is not only to Paul, "but also to
all who have longed for his appearing" that the Lord will give "the
crown of righteousness."

# Philemon

Had it not been written by Paul, the brief Letter to Philemon likely would not have been included in the canon. It is a semi-private note written from prison, addressed not only to Philemon, a man of abundant means, but also to members of the church that meets at his house. If he has used his wealth to support Paul's ministry (vv. 4, 7), this may account for the letter's deferential tone. Yet Philemon owes Paul a debt, too—"[his] own self," probably an allusion to the former's conversion to Christianity by the latter.

Reminders of the ties that bind them in Christian friendship are scattered throughout the letter, but it is not a casual missive to an acquaintance or to make travel arrangements for an impending visit. It serves a dual purpose: to ask a favor and to vouch for Onesimus. The precise nature of Paul's request, however, is opaque, as are the circumstances prompting him to intercede on Onesimus's behalf. Most interpreters believe that Onesimus is a slave who has become "separated" from Philemon (vv. 15–16). "Separation" in this reading is a euphemism for escape—a grave offense under Roman law—or else flight to Paul who, as a friend of his master (*amicus domini*), might mediate in a dispute that has resulted in estrangement. However Onesimus ends up in Paul's company, it seems that he has, like his master, become a Christian in the meantime.

Any attempt at understanding Paul's message in this letter entails an attempt at anticipating the reaction(s) of the recipient(s). Paul hopes that Philemon will remain his "partner" (v. 17). Is Paul asking Philemon to grant Onesimus freedom, perhaps so that he can be released for service as part of Paul's missionary team (vv. 11, 20; cf. Col. 4:9)? In Roman society, Paul would have a legal obligation to return Onesimus, and he would thus be asking Philemon to forfeit not only this legal protection but a substantial monetary investment as well, which would in turn affect his ability to act as a financial supporter of Paul. Philemon would not need reminding that Christianity was regarded by Romans as socially destabilizing in part because they suspected that embracing the faith went hand in hand with freeing one's slaves. Is this why Paul is so coy, explicitly stating that he is not commanding Philemon to obey instructions that he never spells out (vv. 8–9, 14)? Other slave-holding members of the house church would pick up on this subtext, as would any other slaves connected to Philemon's household. One can imagine a range of reactions to the hypothetical manumission of a runaway slave who becomes a Christian, from resentment at bad behavior being rewarded to a wave of copycat "conversions."

What if Paul is merely asking Philemon not to punish Onesimus for some misdeed but stopping short of calling for his emancipation? Many interpreters note that it is not at all unnatural to read v. 16 as Paul proposing that Philemon treat Onesimus "no longer *as if* [or, *like*] he were a slave [even though he remains one] but better than a slave . . . as a dear brother." Hard as it is for modern readers to fathom, it was not self-evident that slavery was inherently evil. Virtually everyone in the ancient world saw it as an inevitable part of the natural order of things. Is Paul simply asking Philemon to treat Onesimus with respect on Sundays as an equal "in the Lord," paying no attention to the glaring difference in their socioeconomic levels the rest of the week? Members of contemporary faith communities attest that such a notion is hardly a preposterous one, albeit not when one party is legally permitted to humiliate, extract sexual favors from, and inflict grievous bodily harm on the other party. It has been suggested that Paul foresees the awkwardness of any conceivable course of action and fails to articulate a specific directive because he cannot decide how best to proceed (Barclay 1991).

Perhaps this is where the other audience members mentioned in the salutation enter the picture. The use of the plural pronoun "you" in vv. 22–25 ("you guys" or "y'all" in English) indicates that Paul expects them to be privy to the letter's contents, whether it is to join in a process of discernment or to hold Philemon accountable for the decision he makes. That the letter has survived may be a sign that Philemon complied with Paul's request, whatever it may have been. That the bishop of Ephesus mentioned by Ignatius (*Eph.* 1.3) around the turn of the century may be the selfsame Onesimus who, furthermore, oversees the first official collection of Paul's letters out of gratitude, is a tantalizing yet unprovable hypothesis.

This letter attracts little attention in the pre-modern period. Its reception in later times is often a matter of not-so-benign neglect. Slave owners in the antebellum South, not surprisingly, invoked Philemon in defending their "property rights." That Paul has an apparent opportunity to condemn slavery in unambiguous terms, but fails to do so, is a sin of omission that many African Americans find hard to forgive (Callahan 2004).

# Hebrews

---

**OUTLINE**

| | |
|---|---|
| 1:1–2:18 | The superiority of Christ and his Salvation |
| 3:1–4:13 | Jesus and Moses compared; the example of the wilderness generation |
| 4:14–5:10 | Jesus the Great High Priest |
| 5:11–6:20 | Christian maturity: warnings and encouragement |
| 7:1–28 | Jesus and Melchizedek |
| 8:1–10:18 | The New Covenant: sin and the sacrifice of Jesus |
| 10:19–11:40 | By faith: drawing near to God and to one another |
| 12:1–29 | Training for the Kingdom of God |
| 13:1–25 | Closing exhortations, greetings, and benediction |

---

After the Letter to Philemon, the King James Bible and many other editions of the New Testament contain "The Letter of Paul the Apostle to the Hebrews." Many would characterize it after the fashion of Voltaire when he wryly observed that the Holy Roman Empire was neither holy, nor Roman, nor an empire—this is not a letter, it was not written by Paul, and it was not intended for "Hebrews." How should one assess such a claim about these basic issues?

(1) Is it a letter? It concludes like a letter, with personal greetings and messages, but it opens in a decidedly non-epistolary manner and resembles a sermon or an essay. The author refers to it as a "word of exhortation" (13:22). There are enough specific allusions to the situation of a particular audience (e.g., 5:11–12; 10:24–25, 32–34; 12:4; 13:7, 22–24) to justify reading it as a letter, albeit an atypical one.

(2) Is it by Paul? Doubts arise as soon as Paul's name is attached to it in the second century. Tertullian, for example, thought it was by Barnabas. The fourth-century consensus that it belonged in the Pauline corpus facilitated its acceptance into the canon. During the Reformation, Luther, who thought it was by Apollos, denied Pauline

authorship on the basis of its teachings on repentance and was tempted to omit it from his 1522 translation of the New Testament. The image of Jesus as high priest (2:17; 7:1–28), the emphasis on sanctification (2:11; 10:10) over justification, and on Jesus' exaltation to "the right hand of God" (1:3–4; 10:12–13) over resurrection, and the inattention to the status of Gentiles distinguish the concerns of Hebrews from those of Paul. No modern scholar regards it as Pauline, if only for the simple reason that it nowhere claims to be written by Paul. Little can be said about the anonymous author apart from the clues contained in his (see the gender of the participle in 11:32) letter: he is a believer in Jesus as the Messiah who has read the Jewish Scriptures and writes about them in elegant Greek.

(3) Is it intended for "Hebrews?" In the first century, Jews were not typically referred to as "Hebrews," a title that may not have been found in the earliest copies of the document. Furthermore, it would be odd to describe the alternative to progress in faith as falling away "from the living God" (3:12) if it was addressed to a Jewish readership. But the author's heavy reliance on the Jewish Scriptures, interpreted in quintessentially Jewish ways, leads most scholars to posit a Jewish or mixed audience, probably located in Rome, some time in the last quarter of the first century. Although Hebrews deals with the tabernacle of the Pentateuch and not the temple in Jerusalem, other scholars believe that the temple's destruction would have seemed like providential proof of the author's argument about the obsolescence of the sacrificial system established under Moses and that text's silence on this point is thus evidence of a date prior to 70 CE.

Wherever they are and whenever they are reading it, Hebrews is addressed to a group of Christians whose faith, the author fears, is flagging. They have experienced some sort of persecution (10:32–24; 13:3, 13) and as a result, they may be considering a return to a more familiar religious environment. At the very least, they have lost their spiritual momentum and have ceased pressing forward, "toward perfection" (6:1). The author is writing to explain that "the new and living way" (10:20) opened by Jesus, by which they have access to "the throne of grace" (4:16), leads in only one direction. The new covenant inaugurated by Jesus, about which Hebrews says more than any other book in the canon, does not contradict the old covenant but, rather, brings it to fulfillment and therefore calls for their fidelity lest they "neglect so great a salvation" (2:4).

The letter opens by directing the readers' attention to the past while simultaneously sounding a note of eschatological urgency. "Long ago God spoke to our ancestors in many and various ways," the author begins, adding, "but in these last days he has spoken to us by a Son" (Heb. 1:1–2). Not all modes of divine speech—be it the Law, the Prophets, or the other writings cited for what they reveal about God's dealings with humanity (Gen. 14:18–20; Num. 14:1–12; Ps. 2; 95; 110; Jer. 31:31–34)—possess the same character or function. That the son by whom God speaks has appeared at a relatively late moment in salvation history does not imply that the message he conveys is in any way secondary or superfluous. The author will make a series of comparisons between Jesus and previous messengers, such as the angels (1:5–14) and Moses (3:1–6), always concluding that everything about Jesus is "better." These predecessors nonetheless played a crucial, if ancillary role; indeed, the *a fortiori* argument that runs through the entire letter presupposes that they are trustworthy, as far as they go (2:1–3; 9:13–14; 10:28–29; 12:9, 25). The stakes are now much higher than in the past, and so the audience must be even more attentive to the good news of Jesus. The author does not want them to be "among those who shrink back and so are lost, but among those who have faith and so are saved" (10:39).

In the Christological controversies of the period before the Council of Chalcedon in 451 CE, Heb. 1:3 was among the most frequently discussed passages (Greer 1973). Athanasius, Basil, and others who viewed the Son as fully divine and coequal with the Father, were more likely to quote the description of Jesus as "the exact imprint of God's very being." Arius, Ulfilas, and other theologians opposed this doctrine of the *homoousion*, which found its way into the Nicene Creed, preferring to cite other texts that seem to imply that the Son was a created being, subordinate to the Father (2:8–9; 5:7–8; 10:7–9). Whether or not the author thinks Jesus had a beginning, he is emphatic that he has no end. He is a priest "forever" (5:6; 6:20; 7:17, 21), interceding in heaven at God's right hand. Only in the role of "merciful and faithful high priest," by becoming human and experiencing death, could he atone for the sins of the people (2:9, 14–17).

Collapsing space and time, in Heb. 3:7–4:11 the author places his audience in the same existential situation as the Exodus generation. Just as the Israelites failed to enter the Promised Land after their wanderings, so too do they risk exclusion from God's future "rest" if they are disobedient. Every day is the "Today" of which the Holy Spirit speaks in Scripture. And it is the word of God, "sharper than any two-edged sword . . . able to judge the thoughts and intentions of the heart," that will discern whether they are among the faithful (4:12–13). No sooner does he issue this sobering reminder of a final reckoning than he encourages them with a description of Jesus as a priest who is able to sympathize with weakness because he has been tested "in every respect . . . yet without sin" (4:15). Here, as elsewhere in the letter, the author pursues a rhetorical strategy whereby he employs language which evokes dread in the starkest of terms—even Jesus experiences "godly fear" (5:7 KJV)—yet argues that his readers have grounds for unparalleled boldness. Yes, he will intone in Heb. 10:31, "It is a fearful thing to fall into the hands of the living God," but he would likely agree with D. H. Lawrence, of all people, who would add "it is a much more fearful thing to fall out of them" ("The Hands of God").

The author comes closer to his central concern when he highlights their spiritual lethargy in Heb. 5:11–6:2. It is the failure of his readers to progress beyond "the basic elements" when they ought already to be teachers that troubles him. A soul at rest tends to stay at rest, to adapt Newton's first law. For Christians, standing still is tantamount to turning back. In the letter's most nettlesome passage, the author states that "it is impossible to restore again to repentance those who have once been enlightened" and then fallen away (6:4–6; Bateman 2007). Second-century Montanists cited it in support of their belief that remission of grave post-baptismal sin was not possible. Novatianists believed it ruled out the readmission of Christians who recanted their faith during the Decian persecution of 249–250 CE. It has figured prominently in debates about the Calvinist doctrine of the "perseverance of the saints" and the popular Baptist slogan that a Christian is "once saved, always saved." Here and in Heb. 10:26, the author most likely has intentional apostasy in mind. As heirs to the promise made to Abraham by which God demonstrated "the unchangeable character of his purpose," it is imperative that they remain true to their baptismal vow (6:13–18).

For modern readers, perhaps the most peculiar aspect of the author's exposition is his comparison of Jesus and Melchizedek, a mysterious figure whose presence in the Bible is limited to a brief cameo in Genesis 14, where he blesses Abraham, and a reference in Psalm 110 (7:1–28; Horton 1976). The Dead Sea Scrolls and Jewish pseudepigraphical texts (11QMelch; *2 Enoch* 69–74) describe his miraculous birth and ascribe to him various divine or angelic attributes. Rabbinic and targumic writings (*b. Ned.* 32b) identify him as Noah's son Shem and speculate that he instructed Abraham in the Torah long before Moses. Much later, the Book of Mormon (Alma 3.17–18) states that his home, Salem, was an evil city that Melchizedek was able to save through his preaching of repentance. He appears nowhere else in the New Testament. Here his function is to explain how Jesus can be a priest—again, a Christological affirmation that is unique to Hebrews—when he is not descended from Levi (7:13–14). Jesus' priesthood "according to the order of Melchizedek" is superior to the levitical priesthood, attained as it is "through the power of an indestructible life" (7:16). Furthermore, according to Hebrews, the necessity of repeating the sin offerings on a regular basis implies that the sacerdotal system laid out in the Torah was never intended to operate in perpetuity (Heb. 7:11; 9:6, 25–26). Jesus' sacrifice, by contrast, was "once for all." He is therefore singularly and eternally qualified to intercede with God on behalf of the people and secure their salvation. Hebrews helpfully identifies this as his "main point" (8:1–2).

This point is spelled out concisely in Heb. 8:6: "Jesus has now obtained a more excellent ministry, and to that degree he is the mediator of a better covenant, which has been enacted through better promises." As if to counter the charge that Christian claims imply that God is capricious or, still worse, unfaithful to past promises made to Israel, in Heb. 8:8–13 the author cites Jer. 31:31–34, one of the longest biblical quotations in the New Testament, to demonstrate that God had intended to do a new thing all along. Sacrifices performed in the tabernacle on the Day of Atonement (Yom Kippur) further reveal their provisional and derivative character (9:1–28). Because the law had "a shadow of the good things to come" but "not the true form," its sacrifices were unable to alleviate the problem of sin (10:1). In this and similar dichotomies (earthly/heavenly; visible/invisible: 8:1–5; 9:11, 23–24; 11:1–3), many scholars detect the influence of Platonic dualism of the sort found in the

Jewish writings of Philo and later in the Christian theologian Origen, both from Alexandria. Hebrews converts these metaphysical categories into eschatological categories after the manner of Jewish apocalyptic writings such as *2 Baruch* and *4 Ezra*, with various institutions of the old covenant foreshadowing those of the new. Does this perspective constitute a form of supersessionism? Resolution of the hermeneutical challenges these texts pose influence Jewish–Christian relations from antiquity to the present, with greater poignancy in the aftermath of the Holocaust (Kim 2006).

Persecution has caused some members to wonder if their allegiance to Jesus is worth the price. The author commends them for their faith in "something better and more lasting" (10:34), illustrated by their willingness to suffer the plundering of their possessions. They are not the first to endure this fate, neither will they be the last. Beginning with its famous definition of faith—"the assurance of things hoped for, the conviction of things not seen"—chapter eleven then commemorates their spiritual forebears who "died in faith without having received the promises, but from a distance . . . saw and greeted them" (11:13). These heroes of Jewish history, a veritable "who's who" of ancient Israel, did not abandon their sojourn because they desired "a better country" (11:16). John Bunyan and other Christian writers have drawn inspiration from this narrative in describing the life of faith as a journey with its destination in heaven. The fate of the patriarchs and matriarchs depends on the "success" of the audience: insofar as God has "provided something better so that they would not, apart from us, be made perfect" (11:40), quitting the race now will spell defeat for everyone. The "cloud of witnesses" cheering on the audience as they "run the race," then, is by no means a crowd of disinterested spectators (12:1). If the audience experiences resistance, they can comfort themselves by recalling that it was no less so for Jesus (12:1–2). In their readiness to endure abuse they may emulate "the pioneer and perfecter of our faith," who is "the same yesterday and today and forever" (12:2; 13:8, 13–15).

# James

James, an Anglicized form of the Hebrew Jacob, is a popular name in the early church. Two of the twelve apostles bear this name (Matt. 10:2–4), but it is James "the brother of the Lord" (Mark 6:3; Gal. 1:19), later called James the Just, who assumes a larger role in the New Testament. Along with Peter and John, he is a "pillar" of the church in Jerusalem (Gal. 2:9; Eusebius, *Hist. eccl.* 2.23.4) who presides over the apostolic conference described in Acts 15 and is martyred in 62 CE (Josephus, *Ant.* 20.200). It is this James who appears in the letter's opening greeting "the twelve tribes in the Dispersion." Those who see this identification as reliable highlight its Palestinian provenance (implied in 1:1) and its many striking parallels with Jesus' teachings that appear to rely on oral traditions rather than on the written gospels (e.g., Jas. 1:4/Matt. 5:48; Jas. 1:5–6, 17/Matt. 7:7–8, 12; Jas. 1:22/Matt. 7:24–26; Jas. 4:4/Luke 16:13; Jas. 5:17/Luke 4:25). Those who see the letter as a pseudonymous writing point to its fluent Greek style, its supposed preoccupation with Pauline teachings about justification by faith apart from the law, and its limited influence on early patristic literature. If it is by James, the letter may be one of the earliest writings in the canon. If it is pseudonymous, it is written some time later in the first century.

The author evinces thoroughly Jewish sensibilities in his remarks about the law (1:25; 2:8–13) and easy familiarity with figures from the Hebrew Scriptures such as Abraham, Rahab, and Elijah (Foster 2014). He addresses a group of Jewish Christians who meet in a "synagogue" (2:2). There are no signs of the Jew–Gentile tensions seen in Paul's letters, though second-century Jewish-Christian groups such as the Ebionites will recruit James to their side in disputes about Torah observance, arguing that Paul's "law-free" gospel runs counter to the teachings of Jesus. A number of interpreters contend that James barely qualifies as Christian literature, making only two passing references to Jesus (1:1; 1:2; "Lord" in 5:7–11, 14–15, and elsewhere may have Jesus as its referent). For Luther, *was Christum treibet* ("what shows thee the Christ") was the criterion for determining which writings authentically express the heart of the gospel, regardless of their authorship. By this measure, in Luther's mind, James fell short.

While the recipients of the letter likely share a Jewish background, its message is immediately relevant to a general Christian audience. No specific crisis appears to have precipitated its composition. These factors, together with the absence of any obvious controlling thesis or overarching structure, lead many scholars to classify it as an example of Wisdom literature (cf. Jas. 1:5; 3:13–17). Jewish Wisdom writings such as Proverbs, Ecclesiastes, and Sirach address common problems of human experience rather than dwell on the peculiar concerns of Israel. In this respect, they share the outlook of Greco-Roman moralists like Plutarch and Epictetus, focusing on everyday challenges and the timeless virtues and vices humans exhibit in meeting them. Temptation, endurance, hypocrisy, envy, undeserved suffering, proper and improper speech—James deals with these and other topics commonly found in Wisdom literature. At the same time, the author condemns mistreatment of the poor by the rich (2:1–7; 5:1–6), demands special care for widows and orphans (1:27), calls his readers to conversion (4:1–10), and engages in other forms of critique characteristic of the Hebrew prophets. Throughout the letter, one hears the authoritative voice of the sage, be it James or someone borrowing his mantle.

If there is a dominant theme, it has to do with the relationship between what one professes and how one lives (3:14; 4:17; 5:12). "Be doers of the word, and not merely hearers," or else one's "religion" is worthless, James warns his readers (1:22, 27). It is in light of this theme that one should understand the discussion of faith and works in Jas. 2:14–26. Luther and many other readers believe that James' declaration that "faith without works is dead" (2:17, 20, 26) is directed at Paul and is contrary to the principle of *sola fide* ("faith alone," though the only occurrence of the phrase "faith alone" in the New Testament—Jas. 2:24—is preceded by the word "not"). Without hearing the tone of the speakers' voices in vv. 18–20 or even knowing how to punctuate the back and forth of the diatribe, it is difficult to know exactly who is speaking which precise words and thus to determine whether James is contradicting Paul (McKnight 1990).

To settle the matter, it is critical to note that James and Paul are speaking about different senses of "faith" and "works" and also focus on different moments in the story of Abraham to illustrate their respective arguments. Whereas Paul in his comments on justification (Rom. 3:28; Gal. 2:16) understands faith as radical trust in God's fidelity, James assert that any "faith" taking the form of mere intellectual assent to a proposition is inadequate. "Even the demons believe—and shudder," he explains (2:19). The "works of the law" mentioned by Paul, furthermore, include ceremonial obligations that distinguish Jews from Gentiles such as circumcision and Sabbath observance, while James has in mind good deeds such as feeding and clothing the needy (2:14–16). Such deeds do not merit the salvation available only by God's grace but, rather, express the individual's faith and bring it to maturity. Faith and works reinforce one another in the life of the believer. Comparison of their treatments of Abraham illustrate these subtle differences. Both quote Gen. 15:6 (Rom. 4:3; Gal. 3:6; Jas. 2:23), where Abraham "believes" and puts his trust in the God who has promised to make of him a great nation against all odds. James additionally refers to the story in Gen. 22:1–19 in which Abraham is tested by God and demonstrates his faithfulness through his willingness to sacrifice Isaac. The two writers highlight different stages in the individual's response to God's call, with Paul focusing on the faith that brings one into relationship with God and James clarifying what organically proceeds from that faith, perhaps by way of correcting a misapplication of Pauline teaching. Paul's own letters indicate that he sometimes had to confront misunderstandings and distortions of his views.

As the author's warnings about the power of the tongue make clear, words as well as deeds may reveal the depth of one's faith (3:1–12). Conflicts and disputes in the community are a function of deeper defects and thus reveal the orientation of its members to God and to "the world" (4:1–2). "Do you not know," the author asks in Jas. 4:4, "that friendship with the world is enmity with God?"— an awkward question that the proud and the rich are especially apt to avoid (2:5; 4:13–5:6). To those who are subject to the depredations of the rich, the author holds up Job "as an example of suffering and patience" (5:9–11). Many readers of the canonical book of Job observe that its protagonist's blistering speeches are not exactly those of a patient man and wonder if the author instead has in mind the pseudepigraphical *Testament of Job*. The "patience of Job" functions as a virtue particularly suited to "the coming of the Lord" on the day of judgment (5:8–9; cf. 2:13; 4:12).

Until that time, members should support one another in prayer. In particular, the instruction to the sick to "call for the elders (*presbyteroi*) of the church and have them pray over them, annointing them with oil in the name of the Lord" (5:14) was interpreted by the Council of Trent as authorizing what came to be known as the sacrament of extreme unction. As a final example of the ways in which the "effectual fervent prayer of a righteous man availeth much" (5:16 KJV), the author reminds his readers that their care for one another can achieve spiritual as well as physical results: "whoever brings back a sinner from wandering will save the sinner's soul from death and will cover a multitude of sins" (5:20).

# 1–2 Peter

As "Prince of the Apostles," the "rock" on which Jesus promised to build his church (Matt. 16:18), and patron saint of fisherman, the figure of Peter inspired several writings in early Christianity (Bond and Hurtado 2015). There is a *Gospel of Peter*, two *Apocalypses of Peter*, letters from Peter to James and Phillip, and an *Acts of Peter* containing the Quo Vadis legend, which culminates with Peter's return to Rome where he is crucified upside down by Nero. A majority of scholars believe that 1–2 Peter belong with these other pseudepigraphical writings of the second century and later, arguing that the fluid Greek prose is not that of an unsophisticated Aramaic-speaking fisherman and that the persecution mentioned in 1 Peter (1:6–7; 3:9; 4:12–29; 5:9) occurs during the reign of Domitian or later, a few decades after Peter's death. Defenders of Petrine authorship of 1 Peter contend that Silvanus (5:12) is not simply Peter's messenger but also his scribe, thus accounting for the literary qualities that other scholars deem anomalous. References to persecutions, moreover, are so vague that they might have occurred almost anywhere at any time in the first century. The date of composition obviously hinges on the question of authorship. If it is by Peter, then it is written in the early 60s. If not, it is written near the end of the century, when it is quoted in *1 Clement.*

Writing from "Babylon"—as in the Book of Revelation, probably code for Rome—the author addresses "the exiles of the Dispersion" in the provinces of Pontus, Galatia, Cappadocia, Asia, and Bythinia. Despite the reference to the Diaspora and frequent allusions to Scripture in its Septuagint form, the audience consists of Gentile Christians. They have "already spent enough time in doing what the Gentiles like to do" but now have been "ransomed from the futile ways inherited from [their] ancestors" (1:18; 4:3–4). "Once you were not a people," he writes to them in 1 Pet. 2:10, echoing Hosea (2:2–3), "but now you are God's people," applying to Christians terminology once reserved for Israel.

On the basis of "new birth" imagery and references to purification by water, it has been suggested that 1 Peter originated as a liturgical composition for the occasion of their baptism (1:3, 22–23; 2:2; 3:21). While most interpreters do not classify the letter as a baptismal homily, it is recognized that it addresses circumstances related to their profession of faith in Christ (4:14–16). The audience is experiencing alienation and some form of duress from the broader culture. Details are lacking, and it has been further suggested that the first section (up to 4:11) was written when the threat of persecution was only potential while the latter section was written when actual persecution had commenced (4:12; 5:9–10). Any such persecution may have entailed slander, insults, and other types of harassment, or a more serious "fiery ordeal."

The purpose of 1 Peter is to offer encouragement and advice to these Christians in their trials and tribulations. They should not be surprised when they are mistreated and should rejoice insofar as they are participating in the sufferings of Jesus (2:21; 4:1, 13). "The end of all things is near" (4:7), when God will come as judge and his glory will be revealed (1:7, 13; 2:12; 5:1). At that time, the author says, "the God of all grace . . . will himself restore, support, strengthen, and establish you" (5:10). In the meantime, they are to have courage and anticipate the challenges they will meet: "Always be ready to make your defense to anyone who demands from you an accounting for the hope that is in you; yet do it with gentleness and reverence" (3:15–16). Their pursuit of holiness (1:13–15; 3:9) will yield fruit in their relationships—be it in the role of husband, wife, or slave, as outlined in the "household code" (2:18–3:7), or as ordinary citizen striving to honor the emperor while fearing God (2:13–17)—and will make them fit to be "built into a spiritual house, to be a holy priesthood, to offer spiritual sacrifices acceptable to God through Jesus Christ" (2:4–5). Protestant theologians support the notion of the "priesthood of all believers" whereby all Christians enjoy unmediated access to God by citing the author's declaration in 1 Pet. 2:9 that his audience is "a royal priesthood." Catholic theologians respond that this does not preclude the existence of a specially ordained priesthood exercised by "elders" (*presbyteroi*) charged with "tending the flock" in imitation of Jesus, "the chief shepherd" (5:1–4; cf. 2:25).

The most obscure passage in 1 Peter hints at the sweeping extent of Jesus's own shepherding of souls (Elliott 2000: 706–10). Christ suffered "once for all" and "made a proclamation to the spirits in prison, who in former times did not obey" (3:18–20). Who are these "spirits," where is the "prison," and why did Jesus preach to them? Often this text is read together with 1 Pet. 4:6, where the gospel is proclaimed "even to the dead so that, though they had been judged in the flesh as everyone is judged, they might live in the spirit as God does." Do these texts refer to the saints in limbo who died before the advent of Christ, for their salvation? Early Christian traditions speculate that, in the words of the Apostle's Creed, Jesus "descended into hell" on Holy Saturday for this purpose. Does it instead refer to fallen angels imprisoned in a subterranean pit until the day of judgment, as one finds in Jewish apocalyptic texts such as *1 Enoch* 10? Many scholars prefer the latter option, but from the vivid narrative of the fourth-century *Gospel of Nicodemus* describing the "Harrowing of Hell" (*Descensus ad Inferos*) to Dante's *Inferno* and beyond, the former has proven more popular.

But the reception history of 1 Peter begins even earlier, with the author of 2 Peter telling his readers that this is "the second letter" he has written them (3:1). Differences in style and vocabulary, noted by Origen and other early patristic writers, are only one of many factors cited by scholars who argue that the two letters cannot have the same author. The audience, identified simply as "those who have received a faith as precious as ours" (1:1), are expected to be familiar with "our beloved brother Paul" and "all his letters," which are prone to misinterpretation, like "the other scriptures" (3:15–16; much to the chagrin of modern scholars, the author does not say which letters or how many). That Paul's letters are accorded quasi-scriptural status reflects a context perhaps as late as half a century or more after their deaths in the mid-60s. Additionally, the author's clear reliance on the Letter of Jude in 2 Pet. 2:1–3:7 suggests a later dating, though Jude's date of composition is itself contested. Defenders of Petrine authorship note that the use of a scribe would account for some of these elements.

Paul and Jude appear to belong to an earlier generation than the author, who urges his readers to "remember the words spoken in the past by the holy prophets, and the commandment of the Lord and Savior spoken through your apostles" (3:2). This characterization of the apostles as forging for later generations an indispensable link to the origins of the Christian movement has led many scholars to view 2 Peter as an example of "early Catholicism," a label that often carries a derogatory connotation (e.g., Käsemann 1964). For those who apply it to 2 Peter, it implies an ossified "deposit" of faith one "receives" (1:1) in the form of dogmatic teaching typified by the nascent orthodoxy of the second century, rather than a mode of existence one lives out in a spiritually dynamic manner, a faith that moreover is not an individualized "matter of one's own interpretation" (1:20). Historical-literary determinations about the authorship of 2 Peter, which a large majority of scholars regard as pseudonymous, are technically separate from assessments of its theological value, though the "division of labor" between the two tasks often breaks down in practice, as one sees in other intracanonical comparisons (e.g., John versus the Synoptic Gospels and Paul versus James).

The author of 2 Peter seeks to achieve three related purposes. First, he wants his readers to "become participants of the divine nature" and gain "entry into the eternal kingdom of our Lord and Savior Jesus Christ" by leading upright lives (1:4, 11; 3:11). This is not a new teaching, he says (1:12; 3:1). By continuing to remind them of things they already know, he exhibits the standard traits of paraenetic moral discourse. In 2 Peter, this rhetorical strategy is combined with features of the testamentary genre in which a respected patriarch imparts advice before his death. Acts 20:17–35 and 2 Timothy represent other examples of the genre. Many interpreters believe that the mention of his imminent "departure" (1:13–14) is an after-the-fact allusion to Peter's martyrdom intended to strengthen the moral exhortation the letter contains.

Second, the author wants to warn his readers about the danger of false teachers (2:1–22; 3:3–6, 14–17). These warnings expand on the material shared with Jude. One learns very little about the heresy these teachers are propagating or anything else about them apart from their character. Lust and greed are their primary motivations (2:2–3, 6–7, 13–14, 18–20; 3:3), a point he illustrates by comparing them to the residents of Sodom and Gomorrah. Some scholars associate this charge of libertinism with second-century Gnostic sects.

Third, in the face of an apparent delay, the author seeks to reassure his readers that Jesus will indeed return and that there will be a final judgment (3:1–16). "Scoffers" are calling divine providence into question, sarcastically asking, "Where is this promise of his coming? For ever since our ancestors died, all things continue as they were from the beginning of creation" (3:4). One may perhaps surmise that the "destructive opinions" and "bombastic nonsense" of the false teachers concern this very question (2:1, 18). With no direct access to their side of the conversation, the degree to which the audience is actually embarrassed or disillusioned by any such "delay" is uncertain (Talbert 1966). Even apart from Jesus's sayings seeming to indicate that he would soon return after his death (e.g., Matt. 10:23; 16:28), such works as Plutarch's "On the Delays of the Divine Vengeance" and Jewish Wisdom writings such as Ecclesiastes demonstrate that the timing of God's justice has presented humans with a perennial theological conundrum. Paraphrasing Ps. 90:4, the author reminds his readers in 2 Pet. 3:8 that "with the Lord one day is like a thousand years, and a thousand years are like one day," a conception of time likewise found in the Qur'an (22.47; this verse also plays a role in many attempts to reconcile the Genesis account of creation with evolutionary theory). Any perceived tardiness is not a sign of divine neglect. To the contrary, he tells them, "the Lord is not slow about his promise . . . but is patient with you, not wanting any to perish, but all to come to repentance" (3:9; cf. 3:15).

Apocalyptic writings from the Second Temple period as well as early rabbinic texts entertain the same notion (*1 Enoch* 60.4–6; *b. Sanh.* 97b). The author of 2 Peter tells his readers that their holiness may thus hasten the coming of the Day of the Lord, which will not just be the end of the world in a fiery conflagration, but a glorious beginning of "new heavens and a new earth, where righteousness is at home" (3:11–13).

# 1–2–3 John

"Johannine" is an adjective used in reference to early Christian traditions connected to the figure of John. But which John? The Baptist? The son of Zebedee and disciple of Jesus (Matt. 4:21)? The author of Revelation? The John for whom the Fourth Gospel is named? And are any of these figures to be identified with one another or with "the Beloved Disciple" (John 13:23) or the unnamed "Elder" of 2–3 John? Most scholars believe that the Fourth Gospel and the Johannine Letters belong to a different orbit from that of Revelation and that they invoke the authority of the same John, namely, the apostle known as the Beloved Disciple. Theological and literary similarities between the Gospel and the Letters abound—e.g., the sensory language and incarnational motifs of their respective prologues (John 1:1–18; 1 John 1:1–4), the use of "light" and "dark" imagery (John 8:12; 12:46; 1 John 1:5–7; 2:9–11), the emphasis on "truth" and "love" (John 3:16; 14:15; 15:10; 1 John 4:7–21; 2 John 6; 3 John 3–4, 8), "us" versus "them" ethical dualism (John 15:18–25; 17:6–26; 1 John 2:15–17), and the reference to a "new commandment" (John 13: 34–35; 1 John 2:7–8; 2 John 6). The prevailing view is nevertheless that they were written by different members of the same Johannine circle or "school," perhaps a decade apart late in the first century.

The form of 1 John is not at all like a letter, but its theological exposition and moral exhortation are clearly prompted by the circumstances of a specific community. In this sense, then, the Johannine Letters are as a group the least "general" of the General Epistles. Like Hebrews, 1 John is more like a homily, replete with touching appeals to emotion, snatches of poetic beauty, and strongly worded admonitions. These elements are also found in John. Whereas the tension felt there is between Jesus and his disciples on the one hand and "the Jews" on the other, here it is internalized. The author has little to say about outsiders. Any split with the synagogue is now a thing of the past. His concern is with those who have caused a bitter schism in the community: "They went out from us, but they did not belong to us; for if they had belonged to us, they would have remained with us" (2:19). These defectors are "liars" who "walk in darkness" and do not love their former "brothers" (1:6; 2:4, 9–11; 4:20–21). "They are from the world," he says, but "we are from God" (4:5). God and "the world" are set at odds, in the dualism of 1 John, the latter being aligned with the "unholy trinity" of "the lust of the flesh, and the lust of the eyes, and the pride of life" (2:16 KJV).

Christological disputes appear to have caused the dissension that elicits this harsh invective. The author says that the defections are a harbinger of the "antichrist" (2:18). The antichrist is popularly associated with the "man of lawlessness" in 2 Thess. 2:3–4 and especially the "beast" of Revelation (11:7; 13:11–18), but it is only in the Johannine Letters that this figure is so named. Who is the antichrist? Not any of the candidates who are put forward with each generation, such as Nero, Napoleon, or Hitler. In 1 John it designates a spirit that does not confess "that Jesus Christ has come in the flesh" (4:2–3; cf. 2:22–23; 2 John 7). It may be that the abstract language of the Fourth Gospel has given rise to competing interpretations of its portrait of Jesus, as would occur in the second century when both the Gnostics and their opponents cited it in support of their conflicting teachings. The emphasis in the author's argument on "the flesh" indicates that his opponents may grant that Jesus is in some sense divine but deny his humanity. Scholars speculate that they may embrace a form of Docetism—from the Greek word meaning "to seem or appear"—and thus imply that Jesus did not truly become a human being or severely downplay its significance. Inasmuch as the real, physical, atoning sacrifice of Jesus is the clearest token of God's love, denying that "the blood of Jesus . . . cleanses us from all sin" has as its ethical corollary the refusal to "love one another" (1:7; 2:2; 4:10–12). "Whoever does not love does not know God," the author states, pithily explaining the basis for this claim in the letter's best known saying, "for God is love" (4:8, 17).

The close relationship between God, Jesus, and "the Spirit" seen throughout the letter (3:24; 4:1–3, 13) becomes even closer at 1 John 5:7–8 in some late manuscripts, which add the statement, "There are three that testify in heaven, the Father, the Word, and the Holy Spirit, and these three are one." This text, known as the Johannine Comma, appears in no ancient Greek manuscripts. It is the most explicit "biblical" articulation of the doctrine of the Trinity, though other passages readily lend themselves to Trinitarian exegesis (Matt. 28:19; 2 Cor. 13:14). Notwithstanding the suspect status of this particular text, the author seeks to reinforce a proper understanding of the nature of God, Christ, and the Spirit as essential to his readers' hopes of eternal life (5:13). Toward this end, in the concluding verses (5:16–20), he also reiterates his earlier warnings with respect to "mortal sins" that some identify with blasphemy against the Holy Spirit (Matt. 12:31–32) and later theologians will develop into a taxonomy of "seven deadly sins."

In their extreme brevity, 2 and 3 John are perhaps the most enigmatic books in the New Testament and are also the most similar to typical Hellenistic letters. Both frustrate the reader when the author says he has much to communicate but would rather wait until they can meet face to face (2 John 12; 3 John 13), leaving one to wonder whether the most crucial points are left unsaid. Since "she" is subsequently addressed with plural pronouns, the "elect lady" in the opening of 2 John is likely a reference to a group within the larger community addressed in 1 John. The Elder calls "deceivers" the antichrist, describing them in terms that echo the heresy 1 John attaches to that label (2 John 7). The elect lady is not to welcome these deceivers because to do so would be to cooperate with evil.

Hardly anything can be known about the individuals named in 3 John. It is affectionately addressed to Gaius, who "walks in the truth" (1–4). He is urged to offer hospitality to itinerant Christian missionaries, unlike a certain Diotrephes (5–10). Does the Elder's dispute with Diotrephes concern doctrine, as it does with the "deceivers" in 2 John? Is it matter of personalities or politics? These questions remain a mystery. The letter is meant to serve as a recommendation for Demetrius (11–12), who may be arriving with this and other missives for the wider community—perhaps 1 and 2 John—from the Elder. It is also a reminder of the importance of hospitality in the early spread of the Christian message and the challenges its adherents faced in defining the boundaries of fellowship (1 John 1:6–7; cf. John 13:20).

# Jude

The only Jude mentioned in the New Testament with a brother named James (Jude 1) is the one included among "the brothers of the Lord" in Mark 6:3. The fact that Jude, like James and Jesus, was one of the most common names among first-century Jews makes it difficult to distinguish this Jude from others, such as the one surnamed Iscariot (Luke 6:16; John 14:22) and the one invoked in later times as the patron saint of desperate causes. Most scholars believe that the salutation here is intended to signify the brother of James "the brother of the Lord" in Jerusalem (Gal. 1:19) and thus a relative of Jesus. So little is known about any of these Judes that it is impossible to prove or disprove the attribution. Likewise, little can be said with certainty about the date of this brief letter. It must be earlier than 2 Peter, which appears to quote it, and later than the Jewish pseudepigraphical texts to which it alludes, but it is difficult to be more precise than placing it some time in the latter half of the first century.

Jude's audience, "those who are called" (v. 1), is no less obscure. The author writes to them in fluent Greek but appears to rely on the Hebrew text of the Bible instead of the Septuagint. In addition, he assumes that they will be familiar with texts that were popular among Jews in Palestine. They also know of "the predictions of the apostles" (vv. 17–18). Had the author made clear which apostles he had in mind or how many, one might determine whether this indicates that they were convened by companions of Jesus or came into existence when "the apostles" were already a recognized group.

The author's stated purpose brings their situation into clearer focus. He exhorts them "to contend for the faith that was once for all entrusted to the saints" because "certain intruders" are "pervert[ing] the grace of our God into licentiousness and deny[ing] our only Master and Lord, Jesus Christ" (vv. 3–4). This description recalls the antinomianism rejected by Paul in Rom. 6:1, where he asks rhetorically, "Should we continue in sin in order that grace may abound?"—"by no means!" is his answer. Their flouting of moral and social norms is described as "blemishes on [their] love-feasts" (v. 12) in terms that bring to mind Paul's censure of the Corinthians' behavior at communal meals (1 Cor. 11:17–34). In what precise sense these false teachers are denying Jesus is not said. Here the author presupposes that defective doctrine and bad morals are integrally related without spelling out the theological shortcomings of his opponents, a characteristic one commonly finds in philosophical and religious polemic in the Hellenistic period. In Jude, the false teachers are said to "defile the flesh," reject authority, blaspheme, complain, boast, and cause divisions.

Of special note is the dense intertextuality Jude exhibits. In its twenty-five verses, there are allusions to several canonical and extracanonical writings. There is reference to: (1) Jewish traditions that understand Gen. 6:1–4 as a description of fallen angels; (2) the story of Sodom and Gomorrah in Gen. 19, highlighting the element of "unnatural lust" that figures in later definitions of sodomy; (3) a dispute between the archangel Michael and the devil in the *Assumption of Moses*; (4) the biblical accounts of Cain, Balaam, and Korah (Gen. 4; Num. 16; 22–24); (5) the apocalyptic vision of *1 Enoch*, seeming to accord it authority in a manner that caused many patristic writers to question Jude's own canonical status; and (6) "predictions of the apostles" similar in content to biblical warnings about deceivers in the end-times (Matt. 24:3–12; 1 Tim. 4:1–3). The original context of these allusions repays close re-reading for what they reveal about Jude's reasoning. After each citation, the author explains that the earlier incidents prefigure the events transpiring in their midst in a mode of exegesis resembling the *pesher* technique seen in the Dead Sea Scrolls. Whereas most of the letter focuses on these negative examples, it closes with the positive admonition to "have mercy on some who are wavering; save others by snatching them out of the fire; and have mercy on still others with fear" (vv. 22–23).

# 4

## THE LITERATURE OF THE NEW TESTAMENT

### Apocalyptic literature

It is a truth universally acknowledged that Revelation is the most bizarre, most difficult to interpret, and thus the most commonly misunderstood book in the New Testament. Its colorful reception history amply attests to the appeal it has had around the globe and across many centuries. Like a candle, it sheds light but can also consume the reader who comes too close to it for too long. A recognition that the Book of Revelation is not totally unique aids readers in making sense of it.

The last book in the New Testament belongs to a literary genre that takes its name from the first word in Revelation, *apokalypsis* ("unveiling" or "disclosure"), whence comes its alternate title, the Apocalypse. Beginning ca. 200 BCE, several Jewish texts take this form in whole or in part, such as *1–2 Enoch*, the *Apocalypse of Zephaniah*, and *2–3 Baruch*, as well as portions of the canonical books of Ezekiel, Daniel, and Zechariah. Christian authors follow suit, ascribing apocalyptic writings to Peter, Paul, James, and others. Jesus' final discourse in the Synoptic Gospels and various portions of Paul's letters also contain apocalyptic elements. An oft-quoted definition of the genre describes it in this manner (Collins 1979: 9):

> A genre of revelatory literature with a narrative framework, in which a revelation is mediated by an otherworldly being to a human recipient, disclosing a transcendent reality which is both temporal, insofar as it envisages eschatological salvation, and spatial insofar as it involves another, supernatural world.

The content of such works is often conveyed via fantastic imagery and complex symbolism involving numbers and animals. Inasmuch as they feature assurances of God's sovereignty, apocalyptic works deal with themes related to the problem of theodicy and often arise out of groups experiencing real or perceived persecution.

Perhaps the most common misconception about apocalyptic literature is that it deals exclusively with events that will precede the Parousia and the end of the world. To be sure, the themes and motifs of apocalypticism overlap with those of other eschatologically oriented works. But just as the phenomenon of prophecy in the ancient world is concerned with the past and present in addition to the future, apocalyptic literature imagines events in a world under the watchful eye of a God "who is and who was and who is to come" (Rev. 1:4, 8; 4:8). In addition to an overview of its literary features, some of the particular ways in which these general concerns manifest themselves are considered below in the analysis of Revelation.

## SUGGESTIONS FOR FURTHER READING

On the literary genre and the broader phenomenon of apocalypticism, see C. Rowland, *The Open Heaven: A Study of Apocalyptic in Judaism and Christianity* (New York: Crossroad, 1982); and J. J. Collins, *The Apocalyptic Imagination* (New York: Crossroad, 1987). Excellent commentaries on the text of Revelation include G. B. Caird, *The Revelation of St. John* (London: A. & C. Black, 1966); and D. E. Aune's three-volume *Revelation* (Dallas, TX: Word, 1997–1998). A much briefer but very reliable guide is that of B. M. Metzger, *Breaking the Code: Understanding the Book of Revelation* (Nashville, TN: Abingdon, 1993). An engaging tour of Revelation's reception history is provided by A. W. Wainwright, *Mysterious Apocalypse* (Nashville, TN: Abingdon, 1993).

# Revelation

**OUTLINE**

Anyone familiar with the reception history of Revelation approaches the book with great trepidation. What the original audience thought of it is hard to fathom beyond the fact that they deemed it worthy of saving, copying, and sharing with others. Many patristic authors were hesitant to accept it into the canon on account of its habitual use and abuse by such prophetic movements as the Montanists, who believed that the New Jerusalem of Rev. 21:1–4 would soon descend to earth at a small town in Phrygia. Others who do not protest its inclusion in the canon are nonetheless bewildered by it and keep their distance. Even John Calvin, who wrote commentaries on nearly every other book in the Bible, declined to take on the task of explicating the Apocalypse.

How does one make sense of the complicated numerology—the thousand years, the four horsemen, the two witnesses, the four creatures, the twelve heavenly gates, the twenty-four elders, the forty-two months, the thousand years, and the 144,000 on Mount Zion, not to mention the seven lampstands, seals, trumpets, plagues, bowls, and angels, or the "mark of the beast," 666? Little wonder Isaac Newton was mesmerized by the Apocalypse. And what of the animals and various hybrids—lions, lambs, leopards, bears, oxen, eagles, dragons, locusts, scorpions, horses, and birds? To be sure, it helps to read it alongside other apocalyptic texts, but even this genre classification does not tell the whole story. The author refers to it as a "prophecy" (1:3; 22:18–19), hints that it should be read aloud, and includes material from other genres such as letters (2:1–3:22) and hymns (e.g., 5:12–13; 7:12; 11:15–18). Political cartoons provide a helpful analogy. Newcomers to the United States may be confused by drawings of donkeys and elephants or references on the business page to bears and bulls, but longtime residents readily understand their meaning. Up to a point, this is how the symbolism of Revelation functions. The original audience did not find it to be as esoteric as do readers from a different time or place. But it would be a mistake to assume that John is simply giving voice to unremarkable attitudes and expectations. No one else in the first-century church produced anything quite like Revelation. It may be that, in some respects, he shocked his original audience as much as he shocks the modern reader.

Revelation's mysteries begin with its author. From an early date, the author, who refers to himself as John (1:1, 4, 9; 22:8), has been identified as the apostle of that name. Already in the third century, Dionysius of Alexandria noted stylistic differences between Revelation and the Fourth Gospel and concluded that the author was someone else named John, namely, John the Elder mentioned by Papias (Eusebius, *Hist. eccl.* 3.39.4). In spite of many parallels with the gospel—e.g., the image of Jesus as a lamb (Rev. 5:6–9), "I am" statements on the lips of Jesus (Rev. 1:8, 17–18; 2:23), an emphasis on "witness" (Rev. 1:5; 3:14; 20:4)—many modern scholars agree with Dionysius even if little else is known about the Elder other than that he resided in Ephesus. If he is the author, then the author departs from the custom of using a pseudonym and ascribing his work to a revered figure from the ancient past. His rough Greek style resembles that of a non-native speaker. Together with his familiarity with the temple, the pervasively biblical imagery he employs suggests that the author is a Jewish-Christian, perhaps from Palestine. By one count, well over half of the verses in Revelation make allusion to the Hebrew Bible without ever quoting it verbatim.

When, where, and to whom is he writing? The clearest indication comes in Rev. 1:9, where he tells his audience that he is their brother who shares with them "the persecution and the kingdom and the patient endurance." He has been exiled to Patmos, a tiny island that is today a four-hour boat ride from Ephesus on the western coast of Turkey, "because of the word of God and the testimony of Jesus." The persecution reflected in this opening is sometimes connected to the events in mid-60s Rome, when Nero scapegoats the Christians for the great fire. In this reading, Revelation is dated ca. 68–69 CE, the turbulent "Year of the Four Emperors" when Nero is deposed and Judea is under siege by Roman armies. But that persecution had little effect on the Roman province of Asia, the location of the seven churches addressed in Rev. 2:1–3:22. It is thought that Christians in this region constitute John's intended audience.

Ancient and modern interpreters alike prefer to date Revelation to the mid-90s, near the end of the reign of the emperor Domitian (81–96 CE). Conscientious objectors to Domitian's demand that he be acknowledged as *dominus et deus noster* ("our Lord and God") were in danger of being charged with political subversion due to the character of the imperial cult that did not countenance "separation of church and state." Those who refused to honor the Roman gods were often accused of atheism and subjected to various forms of discrimination. The Roman historian Suetonius describes Domitian as depraved, and while he may exaggerate the emperor's atrocities, various sources indicate that Christians had been periodically ostracized and harassed in the eastern provinces a decade or two earlier. Systematic, empire-wide persecution is not documented until much later than Domitian's reign. John's own banishment and the martyrdom of a believer named Antipas (2:13), however, give the audience cause for worry that greater oppression is among the things that "must soon take place" (1:1). John therefore writes to provide encouragement, warning, and consolation for Christians who have not yet joined the ranks of those "slaughtered for the word of God" but who may face an imminent "hour of trial that is coming" (1:3; 2:10; 3:10; 6:9).

This way of approaching the Apocalypse is not the only one that has been taken over the centuries. It is related in some ways to one form of the so-called "preterist" approach that sees most of the book's symbols and prophecies "of what must soon take place" (1:1) as having their referents in the author's own time or shortly thereafter while also recognizing that the final chapters may look ahead to events anticipated at the Second Coming and the end of the world. For example, in this approach, "Babylon" is code for Rome, and John's visions reflect various circumstances in the empire that is the source of pain for his fellow Christians and that he hopes to see humbled.

"Historicist" approaches, by contrast, see Revelation as offering a broad sweep of the history of the church in the period leading up to John's time and of the centuries that have followed it up to the present. Joachim of Fiore, a thirteenth-century monk, is the key figure in the emergence of this interpretive paradigm. His view that the third age of salvation history—after the first two periods that began with the appearances of Abraham (the Age of the Father) and Jesus (the Age of the Son)—was to commence in 1260 with an outpouring of the Holy Spirit is just one of many historical-theological schemas for organizing history with Revelation as a guide. Protestant Reformers identifying the pope as the antichrist and other interpreters who seek to fit, e.g., the rise of Islam or specific natural disasters into a timeline that corresponds to the "plot" of Revelation fall into the historicist camp.

"Futurist" approaches, so called because they treat the descriptions from the fourth chapter to the end of the book as literal or figurative prophecies of events that will not transpire until the time immediately preceding the end of history, are perhaps the best known in the modern world. Movements that believe the Second Coming to be imminent and that the present order of things will soon be radically, supernaturally transformed may be classified as futurist in their orientation. Millerites, Jehovah's Witnesses, and many other millenarian movements that emerge in the mid-nineteenth century adhere to this approach, as do, more disastrously, such sects as the Branch Davidians and the participants in the Münster Rebellion of 1534–35.

Finally, "idealist" approaches to Revelation eschew any attempt to coordinate its symbolism with specific historical circumstances, whether past or future, and instead emphasize the timeless character of the spiritual struggle between good and evil. For the idealist approach, it is misguided to look for fulfillments of putative prophecies, of which the details are much less important than a message that is equally relevant to all Christians at all times and places.

There are myriad variations of these interpretive approaches, many of which assume different ways of resolving the vexed question of Revelation's structure. It has been suggested that it is organized according to principles derived from Jewish or Christian liturgy, Greek tragedy, or the book of Daniel, to name only a few theories. The most obvious structural attribute is a series of sevens—seven letters, seven seals, seven trumpets, seven plagues, seven bowls poured out— but one set does not always end neatly before another begins, and within each set of seven one often sees still more going on such that the relationship between part to whole is obscure. Does Revelation have a single continuous plot that moves forward from start to finish? Alternately, does each cycle recapitulate a single "story" from a different angle and under a different aspect? And talk of "structure" seems to presuppose a conscious design on John's part. How much artifice is involved in the composition? Revelation is framed as a vision, after all. Whatever one makes of John's claim of heavenly communications, it may well be that an ecstatic experience of some sort or a dream best explains the phantasmagoric quality of the account that meets the reader upon opening the book.

However much the Apocalypse may repeat itself, it undeniably moves toward a climax. The following overview attempts to chart this trajectory. More than with any other book in the New Testament, to "explain" Revelation is to break its spell. In order to experience it as John intended, nothing can really substitute for hearing it read aloud, in its entirety. One hopes that the brief commentary offered here will not incur the penalty stipulated for anyone who "takes away from the words of the book of this prophecy" (22:19).

## THE SEVEN LETTERS TO THE SEVEN CHURCHES

John introduces his account of the "revelation of Jesus Christ" with a sense of urgency: "the time is near" (1:1–3). This opening is reminiscent of the opening of Mark's gospel in its ambiguity. Is Jesus the source or the subject of the "revelation?" It would seem he is the former, since John writes that "God gave him" this revelation in the form of a vision "in the spirit on the Lord's day" on Patmos. But no sooner does he address his audience in the form of an epistolary greeting like those found in Paul's letters than the lines begin to blur. Is it

Jesus or is it God who says, "I am the Alpha and the Omega," or both at different times (1:8, 11, 17; 21:6; 22:13; cf. Isa. 44:6)? The voice comes from "one like a Son of Man" with a two-edged sword coming out of his mouth (1:12–17). It reassures John ("do not be afraid") and then dictates the letters to the seven churches that are represented by seven lampstands.

Ephesus, Smyrna, Pergamum, Thyatira, Sardis, Philadelphia, and Laodicea each receive a brief "spirit letter" from Christ via John (2:1–3:22). It is thought that Revelation was delivered to the churches in these cities situated in close proximity along the same Roman road in western Asia Minor. Each letter indicates a familiarity with the local circumstances of the community addressed and includes a special message (Hemer 1986). For example, the Ephesians are credited with resisting the false teachings of the Nicolaitans, but are cautioned not to grow weary in bearing witness in one of the empire's largest cities that was home to the Temple of Artemis. Smyrna seems to be in danger of imminent persecution, perhaps at the hands of slanderous individuals "who say they are Jews and are not, but are a synagogue of Satan" (2:9). Pergamum, "where Satan lives" (2:13), was the site of a massive altar to Zeus, which may be connected to the reference to food sacrificed to idols. Thyatira is contending with a prophetess John calls Jezebel (2:20). Because the Laodiceans "are neither cold nor hot . . . [but] lukewarm," Christ says he will spit them out, perhaps an allusion to its location between the hot springs of nearby Hierapolis and the cold mountain water of Colossae. By convicting the Laodiceans of complacency, the author gives an indication that persecution is not the only threat facing the Christians of Asia Minor. At the end of each letter there is the exhortation, "Let anyone who has an ear listen to what the Spirit is saying to the churches."

## THE LAMB AND THE THRONE

A new section begins with a door opening in heaven and John being invited into the heavenly throne room where he sees twenty-four elders and four living creatures (4:1–5:14). The winged appearance of the creatures and their song ("Holy, Holy, Holy") strongly recall the scene of Isaiah in the temple (Isa. 6:2–3) and are later echoed in the Sanctus of the Latin Mass and in a popular hymn. The figure seated on

the main throne, usually identified as God, holds a scroll with seven
seals that no one is able to open, until "the Lion of the tribe of Judah"
appears. (Rastafarians believe that Haile Selassie, the emperor who
placed the lion on the Ethiopian flag, was the reincarnation of Jesus.)

When John turns to see the lion, he sees a lamb instead (5:6).
Stranger still, it is paradoxically "standing as if it had been slaughtered," in a striking juxtaposition of power and weakness. The image
may be related to the lamb that was sacrificed at Passover or to the
Suffering Servant "like a lamb that is led to the slaughter" (Isa. 53:7,
the same text puzzled over by the Ethiopian eunuch in Acts 8:32–33).
This is the most common image used for Jesus in Revelation. The
elders sing his praises accompanied by hosts of angels, because by
his blood he has ransomed "saints from every tribe and language and
people and nation" (Rev. 5:9), thus anticipating the universal victory
celebrated at the end of the book.

## THE SEVEN SEALS AND THE SEVEN TRUMPETS

The lamb begins to open the seals on the scroll, the first four of which
bring forth horses with riders (6:1–8). They are white, red, black, and
pale. These Four Horsemen of the Apocalypse, a favorite subject of
artists such as Albrecht Dürer, represent conquest, warfare, famine,
and death, conditions that will coincide with God's judgment. The
fifth seal reveals the souls of martyrs crying out to God to avenge their
blood. An earthquake occurs with the opening of the sixth seal, after
which there is a hiatus before the seventh seal is broken (7:1–17).
In this interim, John observes a multitude of 144,000 souls, 12,000
from each of the twelve tribes of Israel, along with an innumerable
throng praising God and the lamb. He does not explain if they are past
martyrs or a vision of future martyrs who "[will?] have come out of
the great ordeal" (7:14). When the seventh seal is finally opened, there
is a dramatic silence in heaven for half an hour in preparation for the
next series of signs. (God's silence is explored in Ingmar Bergman's
classic 1957 film *The Seventh Seal*.)

Seven angels blow seven trumpets, unleashing all manner of meteorological and environmental havoc, in addition to
human misery in the form of torture and death on a colossal scale
(8:6–10:21; the interlude between the sixth and seventh trumpets

in Rev. 10:1–7 inspired Olivier Messiaen's *Quartet for the End of Time*, first performed in 1941 in the German camp where the French composer was imprisoned). Lest John think his testimony is finished, an angel commissions him to "prophesy again about many peoples and nations and languages and kings" (10:11). A preliminary task is to measure "the temple of God" (11:1–3). Here as elsewhere in Revelation, the distinction between earthly and heavenly settings is not clear cut. Worship and warfare above often run parallel to worship and warfare below.

Who are the "two witnesses" and what is the significance of the 1,260 days they will prophesy? The imagery suggests an association with Joshua and Zerubbabel (Zech. 4:14), and the time period coincides with the period described in Daniel (9:27; 12:7), but John does not explain what these biblical figures have to do with the plight of his audience. When their work is finished, they are killed by the beast from the bottomless pit, who will return to sow mayhem in the following chapters. Even with more upheaval on the horizon, the seventh trumpet sounds and heavenly worship resumes in words that Handel will incorporate into his *Messiah* sixteen centuries later (11:15–18).

## THE DRAGON, THE BEAST(S), AND THE 144,000

With this song echoing in John's ears, another portent appears in the heavens (12:1–6). The pregnant woman clothed with the sun and a crown of twelve stars has been associated with Israel, the church, Eve, and the serpent in Gen. 3:15–16, and various figures from Greco-Roman and ancient Near Eastern myths. Given that she births a son "who is to rule all the nations with a rod of iron," she has also been identified with Mary the mother of Jesus. The dragon who threatens her, identified as Satan (12:9), then engages in battle with Michael and the angels (12:7–16). Although the angels are victorious, the enemy is still not finished. Two beasts rise out of the sea and worship the dragon (13:1–18). The beast with ten horns and seven heads symbolizes the Roman Empire and the worship it blasphemously demands of its subjects. As agents of the dragon, they are "allowed to make war on the saints" (13:7). A second beast with two horns appears and performs great signs, deceives the people, and makes it so that all must have its mark on their hand or forehead. Most scholars relate this to the divine honors ascribed to the emperor on Roman coinage.

"The number of the beast" is one of the most infamous riddles in the Bible (13:18). What does 666 signify? It is popularly associated with the antichrist, though that figure is only named in the Johannine letters and is described differently (1 John 2:18, 22; 4:3; 2 John 7). Ingenious attempts at deciphering it have drawn on the ancient practice of gematria and other numerological systems, with mixed results. (Ancient manuscripts that give the number as 616 complicate matters.) The most plausible answer is that it is a veiled reference to Nero, who was rumored to have come back from the dead to cause more strife. There is no shortage of other candidates who have been put forward: Muhammad, the papacy, Martin Luther, Napoleon, Rasputin, Adolf Hitler, Ronald Reagan, Mikhail Gorbachev—the list goes on and on. A central character in Tolstoy's *War and Peace* "discovers," after several attempts, that his own name adds up to 666, and one of the most chilling scenes in film history occurs in the 1976 thriller *The Omen*, when the parents of a child find a birthmark on their child in the shape of those infernal digits.

Juxtaposed to the followers of the beast are the 144,000 singing and standing on Mount Zion with the lamb and the lamb's name on their foreheads (14:1–4). They are described as virgins, presumably in accordance with rhetorical conventions equating idolatry with sexual immorality. An angel declares, "Fallen is Babylon," a prophecy that will come to fulfillment by the book's end (14:8; 18:1–3). Another angel spells out the consequences to follow for the beast's followers. They will drink the wine of God's wrath and be tormented with fire. To execute God's vengeance, "one like the Son of Man" arrives with a sickle in hand to reap the harvest of grapes and throws the vintage "into the great wine press of the wrath of God" which is "trodden outside the city." The blood that flows from it stretches for two hundred miles (14:14–20). This arresting image of Jesus at the head of an army and with his robe dipped in blood (cf. 19:11–16) is somewhat less popular than that of the meek and mild rabbi who counsels his disciples to turn the other cheek when wronged. Julia Ward Howe shows that it is not without its appeal when she borrows from Revelation 14 for the opening lines of her abolitionist "Battle Hymn of the Republic."

## THE SEVEN BOWLS OF WRATH, THE WHORE OF BABYLON, AND THE VICTORY OF CHRIST

The next portent introduces a section that is replete with Exodus imagery (Rev. 15:1–16:21). After those who have overcome the beast sing the Song of Moses and of the Lamb as a harbinger of judgment, seven angels pour out the seven bowls of God's wrath that bring on seven plagues. The liturgical elements of this passage sit uneasily with the description of wholesale destruction, a reminder that John wants his readers to realize that there is no place for neutral bystanders in the cosmic struggle he is depicting. What sounds like worship from one perspective, sounds like malevolence from another. It is impossible to experience both perspectives simultaneously.

Assembled at Armageddon, the two sides are ready for the last battle (16:16; 17:1–19:21). The Whore of Babylon riding on a scarlet beast with seven heads and ten horns who is "drunk with the blood of the saints" represents Rome and its seven hills, "the great city that rules over the kings of the earth" (17:6, 9–12, 18). Angels and other heavenly voices narrate the course of the conflict in verse form (18:1–19:8; Handel borrows 19:6 KJV for his chorus: "Hallelujah: for the Lord God Omnipotent reigneth"). At the end of the battle, the "King of kings and Lord of lords" dispatches the two beasts to the lake of fire (19:11–20).

## THE MILLENNIUM, THE FINAL JUDGMENT, AND THE NEW JERUSALEM

The concluding chapters of Revelation document the consummation toward which the entire book—indeed, from John's vantage point, all of history—has been moving inexorably from the beginning. Satan is thrown into a bottomless pit for a thousand years and those who were martyred for their testimony to Jesus reign for a thousand years (20:1–6). This thousand-year reign is usually referred to as the millennium. Visions of a messianic age in which the forces of evil are vanquished at the end of time can be found in various Jewish texts from the Second Temple period (e.g., *4 Ezra* 7:28; *2 Baruch* 29–30). Christian interpreters have devised various systems to make sense of this description. Premillennialists believe Revelation teaches that

Christ will return before the beginning of the thousand-year period. Implicit in this view is the theological conviction that the corruption of the world is so deep that nothing short of God's intervention can turn things in the right direction. Postmillennialists maintain that Jesus will return after a thousand-year period in which the people of God gradually usher in the kingdom of God through an intentional effort at ethical reformation. This view is more optimistic about human nature and its capacity for escaping the power of sin in realizing its goals. Amillennialists regard the thousand years as purely symbolic in nature. After the millennium, John says that Satan is released to cause mischief but only for a short while, until the last judgment commences (20:7–14).

With the appearance of a new heaven and a new earth, the story moves toward its denouement. The rapturous vision of the New Jerusalem descending from heaven "like a bride adorned for her husband" picks up the theme of the Lamb's marriage supper from earlier (21:1–2; cf. 19:7–9) and recalls similar imagery from the Hebrew Bible (Isa. 61:10; Song of Songs). Fulbert of Chartres drew inspiration from this text in composing "Chorus Nova Jerusalem," one of the most popular hymns of the Middle Ages. At the end of a detailed description of the heavenly city, John notices that it has no temple, "for its temple is the Lord God the Almighty and the Lamb," and it has no need of the sun, "for the glory of God is its light, and its lamp is the Lamb" (21:22–23; cf. 22:5). In the midst of the city are flowing rivers and the tree of life—clear allusions to the Eden story from the first book of the Bible at the end of its last book, even if John was unaware that his words would bring the canon to a close (22:1–5).

In the final lines, John relays the repeated message he has received from Jesus: "See I am coming soon" (22:7, 12, 20). This provides encouragement to the audience that has been called on again and again to endure through extreme difficulty and distress (e.g., 1:9; 2:1–3, 25; 13:10; 14:12). If they are able to endure, they will join Jesus as "conquerors" (2:7, 11; 3:5; 5:5; 12:11; 15:2; 17:4; 21:7). An analogy that has been used to describe the early Christian view of history is especially apt for Revelation (Cullman 1964: 84). Just as the Allied victory in World War II was effectively clinched with the successful D-Day invasion of June 1944, but was not finally sealed until VE-Day nearly a year later, so also is there an "already" implicit in the Christian proclamation along with a "not yet." Although history did not immediately come to an end, Jesus' victory over the power of death in the resurrection struck the decisive blow that guarantees victory. John hopes that this message of hope enables his audience to endure when circumstances—even as awful as those described in his book—threaten to overwhelm their faith.

# 5

## KEY CONCEPTS

Most modern readers of the New Testament do not read it in the original Greek. Fortunately, there are many solid English translations available. Even when it is translated, however, the meaning of many terms is not self-evident or easily communicated by a single English equivalent. In addition, the terminology employed by scholars can seem like a foreign language to the non-specialist. This chapter provides brief explanations of sixty terms, names, and concepts frequently encountered in the New Testament and in the secondary literature devoted to it.

\*\*\*

### APOCALYPSE

Apocalypse is a literary genre that takes its name from the first word of the Book of Revelation, *apokalypsis* ("unveiling" or "disclosure"). Several Jewish and Christian examples of the genre appear from ca. 200 BCE to ca. 200 CE such as *1–2 Enoch*, *4 Ezra*, the *Treatise of Shem*, the *Questions of Bartholomew*, and the *Apocalypse of Peter*. Whereas

Revelation is the most prominent example, other canonical texts contain extended passages replete with apocalyptic themes and motifs (e.g., Daniel 7–12; Mark 13; 2 Thess. 2). These themes and motifs include special messages revealed by angelic messengers or interpreters, fantastic imagery and symbolism involving numbers and animals, stark dualisms of time (this age versus the age to come) and space (this world versus the heavenly world), cosmic transformation, and assurances of God's sovereignty in the face of widespread evil. Such writings often arise from and are popular in situations of real or perceived persecution, and consequently function to provide consolation to their audiences. "Apocalyptic" can thus denote a world view or social movement as well as a literary genre. Apocalypticism is typically related to but not exclusively defined by eschatological speculation about the end of the world. The degree to which the teachings of Jesus and Paul exemplify this world view is hotly debated, with one famous scholar (E. Käsemann) declaring that "apocalyptic is the mother of all Christian theology." (See also Eschatology.)

## APOCRYPHA

The books included in the Apocrypha, sometimes referred to as the Deuterocanonical books, are considered canonical in Roman Catholicism and Orthodox Christianity but not in Protestantism or Judaism. They include seven full texts (Tobit, Judith, Wisdom of Solomon, Ecclesiasticus [Ben Sira], Baruch, 1–2 Maccabees) as well as additional material that appears in the Septuagint versions of several canonical texts such as Daniel and Jeremiah (e.g., Bel and the Dragon, Susanna, Psalm 151). They provide valuable information about Jewish history and society in the so-called "intertestamental" period. None are clearly and unambiguously quoted by New Testament writers, though it appears that early Christians may have considered them canonical insofar as they regarded the Septuagint as authoritative. The books of the Apocrypha are not to be confused with non-canonical Christian writings produced beginning in the second century that are often referred to as "apocryphal," such as the *Gospel according to the Hebrews*, the *Protevangelium of James*, and the *Acts of Peter*.

## CANON

The Christian canon consists of those books the church regards as authoritative. Because they were Jewish, Jesus' earliest followers naturally assumed that the Hebrew Scriptures should possess this status. Over time, additional writings that expressed the church's conviction that Jesus was the Messiah were deemed valid for use in communal worship and as a basis for formulating doctrine. Lists of authoritative Christian writings appear as early as the late-second century, a period when some groups wanted to expand the canon and others wanted to constrict it. The list of twenty-seven books unanimously accorded canonical status today first appears in a Festal Letter written in 367 CE by the north African bishop Athanasius.

## CHRISTOLOGY

Who is Jesus and what is the nature of his significance? Christology is a branch of theology that seeks to answer this question. Biblical scholars normally use it to designate the particular ways in which the New Testament authors themselves appear to answer it, referring to various Christologies (e.g., Markan, Lukan, Johannine, Pauline) associated with different texts. Christological analyses often focus on the titles applied to Jesus (e.g., Son of Man, Son of God, Savior), his relationship to humans and to God, or how he viewed his own identity and mission.

## CIRCUMCISION

The sign of the covenant between the God of Israel and his chosen people according to Gen. 17:9–27, circumcision involves the removal of the foreskin, customarily eight days after birth. Israelites were not unique in adopting this practice, though it becomes more distinctive during the Hellenistic period, when it is frequently regarded as a sine qua non of Jewish identity. In the New Testament, it plays a major role in the "Jerusalem conference" in Acts 15 convened to discuss the grounds on which Gentiles should be admitted into the messianic community. Its value in relation to faith in Jesus is also a point of contention between Paul and his adversaries in Galatians.

## COVENANT

A covenant (Heb. *berith*; Grk. *diathēkē*) is an agreement or treaty between two parties. In the Bible, it denotes the special relationship between God and Israel. Yahweh establishes covenants with a number of individuals (e.g., Noah, Abraham, Moses), which may take the form of unconditional promises made by God (Gen. 9:13; 17:4–14) or may be framed as contingent on the satisfaction of certain terms related to the law (Exod. 19:3–6). Paul relays early church tradition in 1 Cor. 11:23–26 that quotes Jesus as speaking of a "new covenant" at the Last Supper (cf. Luke 22:20). Paul elsewhere speaks of being called as a minister of a new covenant that he contrasts with written laws (2 Cor. 3:6). Hebrews likewise describes Jesus as inaugurating a new covenant, quoting Jer. 31:31–34. The role such texts played in the eventual separation of Christianity from Judaism as a separate religion is a matter of great debate among scholars.

## DEUTEROPAULINE

This term is applied to books that are attributed to Paul but that, according to a majority of scholars, were not written by him: Ephesians, Colossians, 2 Thessalonians, 1–2 Timothy, Titus. Scholars that label these letters "deuteropauline" believe that, despite apparent differences in theology, they were likely written by devoted followers of the apostle eager to perpetuate his teachings for new situations in the years following his death. (See also Pseudonymity.)

## DIASPORA

From the Greek word meaning "scattering," this term refers to the dispersion of Jews outside their homeland in Palestine, either through voluntary emigration or forcible deportation to other areas of the Mediterranean and ancient Near East. The Assyrian conquest of Israel in 722 BCE is the first major impetus for Jewish dispersion. Those dispersed at this time appear to have become so thoroughly assimilated that they disappear from Jewish history. The Babylonian Exile following the destruction of the temple in 586 BCE is better documented in biblical sources. By the time of Jesus, most Jews live in the Greek-speaking

Diaspora, and it is partly on account of this demographic reality that early Christian missionaries like Paul, a Diaspora Jew, have their most enduring successes outside the homeland. (See also Hellenism.)

## ESCHATOLOGY

Eschatological teachings found in the Bible focus on "last" (Grk. *eschatos*) things. Traditional Christian doctrine identifies four "last things": death, judgment, hell, and heaven. These motifs are present in much early Christian eschatology, especially in references to the kingdom of God or the "day of the Lord" when a new era of peace and prosperity will dawn. As most New Testament scholars approach the subject, however, eschatology involves a broader understanding of what is to transpire at the transition from the present age to the age that is to come, whether that transition is soon to arrive or in the more distant future. With respect to the Fourth Gospel and some other texts, scholars also speak of "realized eschatology," that is, the notion that the eschaton has already arrived in the person of Jesus and in the active presence of the Holy Spirit in the church. Most scholars believe Jesus saw his mission in thoroughly eschatological terms, though some depict him as a teacher of wisdom who eschewed speculation about the end. The degree to which Jesus' and Paul's ethical teachings are dependent upon their thinking about the end is hotly debated. Apocalypticism and eschatology are often closely related, but the former is not necessarily an expression of the latter.

## ESSENES

Josephus mentions the Essenes as one of the main Jewish sects in first-century Palestine. They lived in semi-isolation at Qumran, a settlement near the Dead Sea. It is widely thought that the Dead Sea Scrolls, discovered in 1947, comprised the library of this community. Their discovery greatly enhanced scholars' appreciation of the diverse political and religious context of ancient Judaism. The ascetic and apocalyptic motifs found in these writings have parallels with some strands of early Christian thought, though the degree to which Essene ideas directly influence New Testament writers is disputed.

## EXEGESIS

Exegesis is the systematic process by which an interpreter comes to an informed understanding of a text. As its etymology (Grk. *exēgeomai*, "to lead out") suggests, the aim is to draw from the text the meaning that the author intended to convey to the original readers. As such, it is usually contrasted with eisegesis, the habit of arbitrarily or anachronistically reading meaning "into" a text. There is no precise, step-by-step method that is applied to any and every biblical text. Different genres demand varied approaches. Nevertheless, close attention to the linguistic, literary, structural, and historical aspects forms the foundation for any further interpretation of a given text, which may focus on theological, sociological, rhetorical, political, or some other dimension of that text. (See also Hermeneutics.)

## FAITH

The Letter to the Hebrews (11:1) famously defines faith as "the assurance of things hoped for, the conviction of things not seen." While this should not be considered a dictionary definition, it underscores two separate but related aspects of *pistis/pistuein* as it is used in the New Testament. It can refer to simple assent to a statement or notion without tangible evidence of its truth, as when one "believes in God" (cf. Heb. 11:6; Jas. 2:19). More commonly, it denotes a posture of trust or reliance. The object of trust is often unstated. Faith is implicitly directed toward God. Paul writes that God justifies "the one who has faith in Jesus" (Rom. 3:26; Gal. 2:16). In recent years, many scholars have argued that the operative phrase in this formulation (*pistis christou*) should be rendered "faith of Christ" rather than "faith in Christ," with the implication that Paul is calling on his readers not to treat Jesus as they do God but to emulate Jesus' trust in God. This debate has a literary-grammatical component but also an obvious historical-theological corollary, calling into question as it does certain Reformation-era readings of Paul and other New Testament texts, such as the Letter of James. Luther and others read Jas. 2:26 ("faith without works is dead") as a contradiction of Paul's doctrine of justification by faith, though it is important to note that Paul never uses the phrase "faith alone." Given Paul's own linkage of faith and "works" or obedience in describing justification (e.g., Rom. 5:18–19;

6:16–17; 16:26: "the obedience of faith"), it may be best to view them as two aspects of a unitary virtue.

## FORM CRITICISM

New Testament form critics focus their attention on the individual literary units of which the gospels are composed. The gospels contain many of the same stories, which have been compared to pearls on a string as they are often arranged in different orders. Form critics analyze these units and classify them as various "forms," such as miracle stories, parables, pronouncements, and controversies, and seek to reconstruct the probable preliterary form in which they circulated as oral tradition. Tracing the developmental process by which these stories and sayings came to be incorporated in written gospels involves identifying the "setting in life" (Ger. *Sitz im Leben*) in the ministry of Jesus or the context of the early church in which they took literary shape and served a specific function. For example, stories about Jesus jousting with the Pharisees would have been particularly relevant after the destruction of the temple in 70 CE when conflict between the church and this Jewish sect becomes especially acute, or communal worship and celebration of the Eucharist would have been a natural occasion for remembering the Last Supper. A subsidiary aim of form criticism is to assess the historical reliability of sayings attributed to Jesus, though the application of various criteria sometimes results in speculative results. (See also Oral tradition.)

## GLOSSOLALIA

The phenomenon of speaking in tongues, or glossolalia, takes two forms in the New Testament: (1) at the Pentecost gathering described in Acts 2, Peter and the other apostles speak under the influence of the Holy Spirit and are understood by the assembled pilgrims in their own languages. This is usually understood to mean that they are miraculously speaking human languages they were previously unable to speak; and (2) in Paul's letters (1 Cor. 14), it takes the form of ecstatic speech that does not appear to correspond to any known human language. It may be understood as an angelic language (1 Cor. 13:1) that requires interpretation, one of the other "spiritual gifts."

## GNOSTICISM

In the study of early Christianity, this term is applied broadly to religious systems that emphasize the importance of esoteric knowledge (*gnosis*) in understanding the nature of God, humanity, the cosmos, and salvation. It is strongly dualistic, tending to subordinate the material realm to the spiritual realm and attributing the creation of the former to lesser deities. "Gnostics" likely did not refer to themselves by this term but are so called by early Church Fathers like Irenaeus, who strenuously opposed them and whose writings are often the only record of what they taught—until, that is, the discovery of several Coptic texts such as the *Apocryphon of John*, the *Gospel of Thomas*, the *Dialogue of the Savior*, and *Eugnostos the Blessed* at Nag Hammadi in 1945. Teachings that appear in a more developed form in the second century may be present already when the New Testament is being written.

## GOSPEL

*Euangelion* is the Greek term normally translated as "gospel" or "good news." In the preaching of Jesus, it denotes the auspicious activity of God, and Jesus himself becomes a part of the content of this "good news" in the preaching of the early church. Later in the first century, "gospel" becomes the name of a literary genre that focuses on the life, death, and resurrection of Jesus. The gospel genre has been described as a "passion narrative with an extended introduction" (Kähler 1964). In addition to the four canonical gospels—Matthew, Mark, Luke, and John—beginning in the second century, there are several apocryphal gospels appearing under the name of such figures as Thomas, Peter, Mary, and Philip.

## GRACE

God's special favor shown to humans is described in the New Testament as a gift (Grk. *charis*). Paul emphasizes this grace bestowed through Jesus for the salvation of sinners (Rom. 3:24; 4:16; 2 Cor. 6:1; Gal. 2:17–21).

## HAGGADAH /HALAKAH

Haggadah refers generally to rabbinic narratives that interpret or expand upon the non-legal content of the Hebrew Bible. It is usually paired or contrasted with halakah, which refers to the body of legal rulings promulgated by the early rabbis, codified in the Talmud and based on their interpretations of the legal portions of the Hebrew Bible.

## HELLENISM

Alexander the Great's military conquest of much of the Mediterranean and ancient Near East, including Palestine in 333 BCE, was accompanied by the wide dissemination of Greek cultural influences and institutions. Hellenism heavily influenced Jewish culture and religion in the subsequent centuries, especially but not exclusively in the Diaspora where Greek became the common language used by Jews and Gentiles alike. The Septuagint is one of the most important products of Hellenistic Judaism. It is usually this version of the Scriptures quoted by the Greek-speaking authors of the New Testament.

## HERMENEUTICS

Hermeneutics is the "science" of interpretation. Its aim has been described as elucidating the meaning of "meaning"—where it resides (with the author? inside the autonomous text? with the reader?), how it is generated, and by what means it can or should be uncovered. Sometimes the practice of hermeneutics approaches a text with the aim of discerning and distinguishing between "what the text meant" to its first readers and "what a text means" in the here and now. Hermeneutical theory in recent decades has increasingly emphasized the recognition that all interpretation takes place within a specific context and in accordance with various ideological assumptions.

## HOLY SPIRIT

In the New Testament (e.g., John 14; Acts 2), God's spirit or presence that dwells in Jesus and, later, in the Christian community is referred to as the Holy Spirit. The spirit (*pneuma*) is connected to such activities as baptism, prophecy, speaking in tongues, and leading a moral life. In Christian theology, the Holy Spirit is identified as the third person of the Trinity, partly on the basis of such texts as Matt. 28:18–20 and Acts 2:33.

## HOUSEHOLD CODE

Scholars use the term "household code" to refer to lists of duties within the context of household relationships. Such lists are common in Hellenistic literature. Household codes take various forms but usually govern reciprocal relations between husbands and wives, fathers and children, and masters and slaves. The New Testament contains a number of household codes (Eph. 5:21–6:9; Col. 3:18–4:1; 1 Tim. 2:8–15; Titus 2:1–10; 1 Pet. 2:13–3:7). Each has been "Christianized" and has its own distinctive emphases (e.g., Colossians has more to say to slaves while Ephesians expands upon marital relations). The hierarchical character of the codes offends the sensibilities of many modern readers. Some scholars have noted that New Testament household codes occupy a middle ground on the spectrum between patriarchy and egalitarianism.

## JOSEPHUS

One of the most prolific Jewish writers in antiquity, the writings of Josephus (ca. 37–100 CE) include a brief autobiography, a sweeping paraphrase of the Hebrew Bible and survey of post-biblical Jewish history (*The Antiquities of the Jews*), and a detailed account of Jewish political and military affairs in the first century (*The Jewish War*). For a time he served as a general in the revolt against Rome but, after his capture, spent the remainder of his life under the patronage of the Flavian emperors. He is an invaluable source for understanding the politics and society of first-century Palestine, especially the intra-Jewish conflicts in which he was a participant. His retellings of biblical narratives provide a vivid example of how a Jewish contemporary of the New Testament authors reads the Bible and strives to explain and defend Judaism before a Greco-Roman audience. His writings are also noteworthy for including what may be the only explicit references to the beginnings of Christianity in a non-Christian source written in the first century, with brief reports mentioning John the Baptist, Jesus, and James.

## JUSTIFICATION

Justification (Gr. *dikaiōsis*) is the putting or declaring a person to be in a right relation to God. "Righteousness" (*dikaiosynē*) is the state that results from the process of justification. It is traditionally understood as the heart of Paul's teachings. Justification by faith in Jesus rather than on account of obedience to Jewish law as manifested in good works is the heart of the gospel, a view, according to Martin Luther, that is expressed most fully by Paul (Rom. 3:22; 4:25; 5:18; 2 Cor. 5:21; Gal. 2:15–16). It is disputed by many scholars whether Paul's formulation is an accurate representation of Jewish belief in the first century. Others believe that Paul does not set faith and "works" in opposition and thus fits within mainstream Jewish teaching, but that his writings (and hence his understanding of Jesus in relation to Judaism) have been misinterpreted by later thinkers such as Augustine and Luther.

## KERYGMA

Kerygma is the transliteration of a Greek word that denotes the proclamation of good news. In Greek it usually refers to the act of preaching, and among biblical scholars it refers to the basic content of early Christian preaching, with its focus on the saving events of Jesus' life, death, resurrection, and ascension.

## KINGDOM OF GOD/HEAVEN

God's reign on earth was hoped for by Jews in the Second Temple period, and its nature was a major subject of eschatological speculation. It was a major motif in the preaching of Jesus in the Synoptic Gospels (Matt. 4:17; Mark 1:14–15; 9:1; Luke 8:1; 21:31). "Kingdom of God" and "kingdom of heaven" are used interchangeably though preferred by different authors. It is often said to be "at hand," which may mean that it is already present or still to come in the near future. Whether its arrival is presented in the New Testament as coming about mainly as a result of a cosmic transformation wrought by God or through the efforts of humanity striving to establish a more just social order, is a matter of interpretive dispute.

## LAW

In ancient Judaism, *Torah* was the first of the three subdivisions of the canon (Law, Prophets, Writings). When used in this sense, it is synonymous with the Pentateuch. Torah is more generally translated as "instruction" and it can thus refer to any of the Pentateuch's contents and not just the legal material contained in the Decalogue and the Covenant Code (Exodus 20–23). In the first century, the Pharisees took a special interest in the interpretation of the law, as did Jesus and Paul. This shared concern and the disputes it generated over time were a major factor in the eventual distinction between Judaism and Christianity as separate religions.

## LORD

English translations of the Hebrew Bible use "Lord" for various divine titles (*Yahweh, Adonai, El Shaddai*). New Testament writers use *kyrios* in a similar sense. Since *kyrios* can also be used in Greek as a term of honor, much like "sir" and "master" in English, its application to Jesus can be ambiguous. Although it has been suggested that the view of Jesus as divine only arises among Gentile converts for whom *kyrios* was a common term for their former objects of worship, Aramaic sources (e.g., in 1 Cor. 16:22 and in the Dead Sea Scrolls) indicate that Jews could also speak of God in such terms.

## MESSIAH

In the Hebrew Bible, *messiah* means "anointed one," and the title is usually applied to a king or priest who acts as a special agent of God on behalf of Israel. Over time it becomes associated with an heir of David who will enact the promises made by God to establish a dynasty that will last forever. Different types of messianic expectation are attested in the Second Temple period, with some texts envisioning a military conqueror and others (e.g., the Dead Sea Scrolls) mentioning multiple messiahs. *Christos* is the Greek equivalent used in the Septuagint and the New Testament. This designation is applied to Jesus hundreds of times in the New Testament. None of the messianic profiles current in first-century Judaism corresponds perfectly to the biblical portrayals of Jesus, who essentially redefines the title in the eyes of his followers.

## MIDRASH

Midrash is a creative Jewish method of interpretation that may focus on scriptural narrative (haggadic midrash) or legal material (halakhic midrash). The term also applies to the genre of literature that features the results of the method, found most prominently in the Mishnah. It often takes the form of verse-by-verse commentary and homiletical application for the purposes of edification and guidance in daily affairs. Many scholars label various New Testament treatments of scriptural texts (e.g., Matt. 2:1–12; 1 Cor. 10:1–13) as examples of midrash.

## MIRACLE

In the Bible, miracles are special interventions by God in the world of nature or human affairs, either directly or through a human or angelic agent. Healings, resuscitations, exorcisms, and feedings are among the miracles described in the New Testament. Such wondrous deeds are usually called "signs" in the Fourth Gospel. Although Jesus was not unique in the first-century Mediterranean in being acclaimed as a wonder-worker, his miracles were regarded by his followers as special tokens of God's salvation to be fully realized in the establishment of the kingdom.

## MISHNAH

The Mishnah is a compilation of Jewish legal commentary based on rabbinic interpretations of the Torah, codified in second century CE by Rabbi Judah ha-Nasi, but circulating earlier in oral form. Much of it arises in the effort to adapt for a new setting laws that had been formulated when the sacrificial system was still operative prior to the destruction of the Jerusalem temple. It is later incorporated in the Talmud, wherein it becomes the subject of further commentary.

## MYTH

In popular usage, "myth" simply means an untrue story. Its specialized meaning among scholars can denote any story that conveys a profound "truth," often without any necessary implication as to the historical accuracy of accounts that include supernatural agents or forces acting in the world. Rudolf Bultmann popularized the concept of myth in the study of the New Testament. According to Bultmann, modern readers embrace a scientific worldview that renders language and stories about intervention by transcendent powers unbelievable. In this view, mythological language does not constitute the "kernel" of Christian faith, which addresses unconscious hopes and fears common to humanity and involves an authentic existential response regarding one's own self-understanding, but the "husk," which must be interpreted through a process of "demythologization."

## ORAL TRADITION

When New Testament scholars refer to oral tradition, they are usually speaking of the period between the life of Jesus (ca. 30 CE) and the writing of the first gospels (ca. 70 CE), when Jesus' followers are circulating his teachings and retelling stories about his ministry, death, and resurrection.

## PARABLE

A parable is a short story designed to convey a moral or spiritual lesson, typically drawn from the sphere of everyday life. Famous examples include the Good Samaritan (Luke 10:30–35), the Prodigal Son (Luke 15:11–32), and the Ten Bridesmaids (Matt. 25:1–12). According to Jesus in his explanation of the Sower (Mark 4:3–8, 10–12), however, the result or even the purpose of speaking in parables can be to confound outsiders. A number of questions about the nature of the parables and their interpretation divide scholars: Are they meant to function as allegories? Do they illuminate timeless truths or insights into specific situations? Do they speak to the way the world operates now or to a new vision of how it might or ought to be (e.g., in the kingdom of God)? Must one know about daily life in first-century Judea to understand any point intended by Jesus? And is it possible to sort through any "editing" carried out by the early church to arrive at the version(s) delivered by Jesus himself?

## PARAENESIS

Paraenesis is a style of moral exhortation found in Greek and Roman rhetoric as well as in the New Testament letters. Rather than introduce original teaching, it reminds the audience of what the author believes the audience should already know and cites concrete examples to follow in choosing the proper course of action.

## PAROUSIA

Literally, "presence" or "arrival" in Greek, *parousia* usually refers to the "Second Coming" of Jesus in the end-times to judge the world and redeem the faithful (Matt. 24:3; 1 Cor. 15:23; 2 Thess. 2:1; Jas. 5:8; 2 Pet. 3:3–9), though the concept often appears even where the vocabulary is absent. Precisely what the earliest Christians thought about the nature and timing of the Parousia—Is it imminent or further in the future? Has it in some sense already arrived? Will it be a "public" or "private" occurrence? To what extent is Christian ethical teaching contingent on a literal understanding of Jesus' words on the matter?—remains one of the thorniest questions faced by New Testament scholars, many of whom believe that the so-called "delay of the Parousia" is the most consequential (non-)event of the first century. (See also Eschatology.)

## PASSION

"Passion" refers generally to the suffering and death of Jesus. Biblical scholars normally use it in reference to the canonical accounts of the events leading up to his crucifixion, including his arrest and trial (Matt. 26–27; Mark 14; Luke 22–23; John 18–19). Although each document has its own distinctive emphases, the level of agreement among the four gospels is much higher here than in other sections. Many scholars believe that the passion narratives were the first accounts of Jesus' life set down in writing. So central is this aspect of the early Jesus tradition that "gospel" has been defined, in the phrase of Martin Kähler, as a "passion narrative with an extended introduction."

## PATRISTICS

Patristics is the study of the Greek and Latin writings produced by "Church Fathers" such as Irenaeus, Tertullian, Origen, Cyprian, Eusebius, Augustine, and many others in the centuries following the close of the "apostolic era." The patristic period witnesses the growth and expansion of Christianity and the gradual emergence of the New Testament canon. Many patristic authors are deeply involved in theological controversies that influence the shape the canon eventually takes. Their accounts of these controversies give evidence of the diverse understandings of Jesus to be found in this period. Their writings also include extensive scriptural commentary and early church traditions about various biblical figures. As such, they are valuable witnesses to the transmission of the biblical text as well as the ways in which ancient readers could understand that text.

## PERICOPE

A pericope is a short, self-contained unit of text that has literary integrity even when it is isolated from the larger text for the purpose of analysis by commentators. (The term derives from the Greek verb meaning "to cut around.") Because the original authors did not formally mark the ending of one passage and the beginning of the next, the delineation of a given pericope's boundaries is sometimes a matter of dispute.

## PHARISEES

The Pharisees were one of the main Jewish sects in first-century Palestine. They were above all concerned with interpretation and application of the Mosaic law. They held that Moses had received the Oral Torah at Sinai along with the Written Torah. According to Acts and to his own letters, Paul was a Pharisee, as were the prominent first-century rabbis

Hillel, Shammai, and Gamaliel. Whether or not Jesus was formally of their number, his manner of disputation was frequently very similar to that of the Pharisees. The attention devoted to Jesus' clashes with the Pharisees, seen in such texts as Matthew 23, may in part reflect the heightened rivalry between the early church and this Jewish sect that had gained ascendancy after the destruction of the temple in 70 CE.

## PHILO OF ALEXANDRIA

Philo (ca. 20 BCE–50 CE) was one of the most prolific Jewish writers of the first century. His writings attempt to reconcile Jewish religious traditions with Greek (especially Platonic) philosophy. He is frequently cited to illustrate the diversity of Hellenistic Judaism in the New Testament world as well as the Jewish exegetical strategies that may lie behind the interpretation of Scripture in such books as Hebrews. His use of allegory deeply influenced later Christian writers, above all his fellow Alexandrians, Clement and Origen.

## PROPHECY

Prophets in the Bible act as messengers who speak for God. In the Hebrew Bible, their oracles are both public and private, deal with both religious and political affairs, and offer both comfort for and critique of God's people. They provide commentary on events of Israel's past, present, and future. In the New Testament, Jesus is frequently depicted as a prophet and, even more frequently, as the fulfillment of prophecies contained in the Scriptures. Prophecy is mentioned as one of the gifts of the Holy Spirit (1 Cor. 12:28–29; 14:26–32). The phenomenon was sufficiently widespread that one finds several warnings about false prophets (Matt. 24:24; 2 Pet. 2:1; 1 John 4:1). Prophecy appears to have been a regular feature of communal worship that differed from speaking in tongues in that the former took the form of intelligible speech.

## PSEUDEPIGRAPHA

Scholars refer to several dozen non-canonical Jewish writings produced between roughly the third century BCE and the third century CE as "Old Testament pseudepigrapha." They are usually written under the name of a revered figure from the Jewish Scriptures, such as Adam, Abraham, Joseph, Solomon, and Elijah. Different genres are represented, e.g., psalms, apocalypses, historical narratives, and wisdom literature. Many are expansions of narratives contained in biblical books. Although they emerge from the same cultural context and are often very similar in character, the pseudepigrapha are distinguished from the books included in the Apocrypha as they were not a part of the Greek version of the Hebrew Bible (Septuagint). These works are valuable in reconstructing the history of the so-called "intertestamental" period and the diverse Jewish milieu out of which Christianity emerged. A few are quoted or alluded to in the New Testament (*1 Enoch*, *Assumption of Moses*).

## PSEUDONYMITY

The practice of writing under a false name was widespread in Jewish and Greco-Roman antiquity. How widespread and how readily accepted as a transparent fiction is somewhat less clear. Pseudonymity usually invokes the name of a revered figure of the past— e.g., Abraham, Solomon, Elijah, Socrates—to whom the unnamed author seeks to pay homage and whose legacy is thereby perpetuated for a new time and place. In some cases, however, it appears that pseudonymity may be a mechanism for exercising authority over an audience that might not otherwise concede it and is thus deceptive in intent. Whether the New Testament books are pseudonymous and, if so, where they fall on this spectrum is one of the perennial questions addressed in critical biblical scholarship. If the title appearing at the head of a document has not been put there by its author, as is widely thought to be true for many New Testament books, the author may not have intended to present himself as the named author. In this scenario, it may be more accurate to speak of anonymity than of pseudonymity.

## Q

Q (from the German *Quelle*, "source") refers to a hypothetical collection of Jesus' sayings that predates the canonical gospels. It "survives" in the form of approximately 230 verses shared by Matthew and Luke, but not Mark. As a compendium of sayings, it is thought to lack any narrative about Jesus' birth, death, resurrection, and miracle-working, leading many scholars to conclude that it attaches little significance to these aspects of the Jesus tradition. What, if anything, can be said about its original form, proximity to the historical Jesus, use by the gospel writers, or the theological orientation of its author or readership remains a matter of intense debate.

## REDACTION CRITICISM

Redaction criticism focuses on the gospel writers' selection and editing of source material in the course of composing their gospels. The method is routinely practiced with Matthew and Luke, since most scholars are confident in identifying at least one major source with which they are working, namely, the Gospel of Mark. Close attention to the additions, deletions, differences in emphasis, and other alterations made by Matthew and Luke to their Markan source reveal their special concerns and perspectives, including their particular understanding of the significance of Jesus.

## RESURRECTION

Belief in the rising of Jesus from the dead is perhaps the most fundamental belief of the early Christians. Each of the gospels includes resurrections stories, and it is a central teaching of Paul (cf. 1 Cor. 15). A number of individuals are resuscitated in the Old and New Testaments, though the resurrection of Jesus as described by Christian writers is qualitatively different in that he does not merely resume his previous life in an identical body but, rather, in a transformed body. His return from the dead, moreover, is an event that affects all other humans at the most basic level. Thus, while some Jewish groups (e.g., the Pharisees) believed in the bodily resurrection of the faithful at the end of the ages, the nature, timing, and implications of Jesus' resurrection as described in the New Testament are distinctive.

## SADDUCEES

The Sadducees were one of the main Jewish sects in first-century Palestine. They were members of a conservative aristocracy associated with the high priesthood that oversaw the sacrificial cult centered at the temple in Jerusalem. They rejected the Oral Law prized in Pharisaic tradition as well as beliefs they believed were not found in the Written Law, such as resurrection and the immortality of the soul. They were seen by many Jews as collaborators with the Romans. They lose all influence in Jewish affairs after 70 CE.

## SALVATION

Whereas salvation in the Hebrew Bible usually involves rescue by God from imminent this-worldly peril, New Testament writers tend to emphasize its spiritual or eschatological aspects. Salvation (Grk. *sōtēria*) has both an individual dimension, as when believers are offered forgiveness of sins, as well as a corporate dimension, when the believer becomes a part of the body of Christ. Various writers can speak of salvation as having already taken place, as an ongoing process in the present, and as a future event (Luke 19:9; 1 Cor. 1:18; 5:5; 2 Cor. 2:15; Eph. 2:8–9). Both God and Jesus are called "savior" (John 4:42; 1 Tim. 4:10), yet their initiative in the process does not preclude a role for the individual (Phil. 2:12–13).

## SEPTUAGINT

The Septuagint is the Greek translation of the Hebrew Bible carried out in Alexandria beginning in the third century BCE. It is often referred to by the abbreviation LXX, the Roman numeral for the number seventy, in connection with a Jewish legend contained in the *Letter of Aristeas* about its miraculous production by seventy (or seventy-two) translators. It is critical for understanding the state of the text read and quoted by the New Testament authors. Works found in the Septuagint but not in the Hebrew version of the Old Testament, such as 1–2 Maccabees and Tobit, are included in the Apocrypha. It is thought that the Christian reliance on the Septuagint may have motivated rabbis meeting at Jamnia to bring formal closure to the canonization process for Judaism late in the first century.

## SIN

Sin (Grk. *hamartia*) in the New Testament is opposition to the divine will, described variously as immoral human behavior that "misses the mark" or as a cosmic "power" that holds humans in bondage. Thus it can be described in the singular (1 Cor. 15:56; Gal. 3:22) or the plural (Acts 2:38; Heb. 7:27). There are sins of omission (Matt. 25:31–46) and of commission (1 Cor. 6:18). Some are forgivable but some are not (Matt. 12:31). Although the New Testament does not explicitly articulate a doctrine of "original sin," the problem of sin is one that affects all humans (Rom. 3:23; 5:12; 1 John 1:8–10). Jesus is an exception to this rule (Heb. 4:15), and his death is seen by New Testament writers as providing a solution to the problem of sin that the Levitical system sought to address through sacrifice.

## *SITZ IM LEBEN*

In form criticism, interpreters seek to identify the "setting in life" (Ger. *Sitz im Leben*) in the ministry of Jesus or the context of the early church in which particular miracle reports, parables, sayings, controversy stories, prophecies, and the like took literary shape.

## SON OF MAN

In Hebrew and Aramaic, this phrase can mean, simply, "a certain human," but it is also used in Daniel (7:13–14) of an eschatological figure who "comes with the clouds of heaven" to bring about judgment and salvation on behalf of God. Jesus repeatedly speaks of himself as the Son of Man in the gospels, especially in Mark but also in other texts (Matt. 16:27; Mark 8:38; 14:62; Luke 12:40; John 5:27). The degree to which Jesus' use of this title in reference to himself is (1) historically accurate, (2) distinctive within the world of Second Temple Judaism, and (3) reflective of a messianic self-consciousness, remains a matter of vigorous debate.

## SOURCE CRITICISM

Source criticism is the analysis of biblical texts in order to determine the sources, whether oral or written, that have been used in their composition. The identification of passages in which an author appears to be using a source depends in part on a prior understanding of what constitutes that author's customary literary style. Solving the "Synoptic Problem" by demonstrating that Mark was most likely the first gospel written and then used by Matthew and Luke in composing their own gospels has been the most noteworthy achievement of New Testament source critics. Literary analysis indicates that Paul may have occasionally incorporated primitive Christian creeds or hymns in his letters (e.g., Rom. 3:25; Phil. 2:6–11). Redaction criticism builds on the findings of source critics by studying the manner in which writers adapt sources for their own literary or theological purposes.

## SYNAGOGUE

In the Gospels and Acts, Jesus and his followers frequently visit synagogues, places of Jewish study and prayer (e.g., Luke 4:16; Acts 6:9). Synagogues, as distinct from the temple where sacrifices were offered, arose as houses of worship and Torah study in the aftermath of the destruction of Jerusalem in 586 BCE, though the earliest archaeological evidence dates to the third century BCE. In many ways, the structure of and communal activities performed at synagogues influence the development of Christian churches (Grk. *ekklēsia*, "assembly").

## SYNCRETISM

This term refers to the practice—often unconscious—of combining variegated religious beliefs and practices into a single system. In ancient Greece, Rome, and Israel, this often takes the form of attributing the characteristics of one deity to another. In the New Testament, syncretistic tendencies are sometimes explicit, as when Paul and Barnabas are taken to be Hermes and Zeus in Acts 14. Some scholars have further suggested that rituals such as baptism and the Lord's Supper should be understood on the analogy of contemporary pagan practices, or that the designation of Jesus as "son of God" is meant to evoke or challenge the honors accorded to the heroes of Greek myth or Roman emperors.

## SYNOPTIC

This adjective refers to the first three canonical gospels (Matthew, Mark, and Luke). Due to their structural similarities, it is possible to print them in parallel columns such that their similarities as well as their differences can be "seen" (-optic) "together" or at the same time (syn-). The first modern Gospel synopsis was published by J. J. Griesbach (1774–1776). John is not usually included in published synopses. The analysis made possible by a synopsis includes the Two-Source Hypothesis, the most commonly accepted solution to the Synoptic Problem, which addresses the question of how the first three gospels are interrelated. Most scholars believe that Mark was written first and later used by Matthew and Luke in composing their narratives.

## TALMUD

The Talmud, divided into the Jerusalem Talmud and the Babylonian Talmud, is a vast body of authoritative commentary on the Mishnah, a Jewish legal code compiled ca. 200 CE. Written mostly in Aramaic, it also includes early rabbinic interpretations of Scripture and other Jewish lore. Alongside the Torah, the Babylonian Talmud forms the basis for orthodox Jewish belief and practice. The Talmuds were completed by the middle of the sixth century CE, and despite the time that separates them, many scholars believe that the controversies discussed in this literature may shed light on debates about the law taking place when the New Testament was being written.

## TARGUM

Targums are Aramaic translations, paraphrases, and interpretations of the Hebrew Bible first produced in and for synagogues after the Babylonian Exile and written down beginning in the third century CE. These documents aid scholars in understanding the form in which the biblical texts were transmitted over several centuries. Because Jesus and his followers likely spoke Aramaic as their first or only language, it may also be the case that the Targums provide a glimpse of how they and other first-century Jews understood certain biblical passages (as has been suggested for the interpretation of Isa. 6:9–10 in Mark 4:11–12). (See also Midrash.)

## TEXTUAL CRITICISM

Textual criticism is the systematic process by which scholars sort through the evidence provided by thousands of ancient and medieval manuscripts in an attempt to determine the original wording of the biblical text. The majority of the differences seen in these manuscripts (called textual variants) are minor and easily explained by the logistics of scribal activity (e.g., dictation errors, repetition or deletion of words or letters, marginal glosses mistakenly incorporated into the text). Others are intentional. For example, scribes sometimes revise the author's spelling or grammar or make some other alteration in order to "correct" readings deemed theologically problematic. While no major Christian doctrine is based solely on a disputed New Testament text, a number of well-known passages still appearing in many Bibles— e.g., the "longer ending" of Mark (16:9–20), the woman caught in adultery (John 7:53–8:11), Paul's instructions on women's speaking in the assembly (1 Cor. 14:33–36), the trinitarian language of 1 John (5:7)—are widely thought to be later additions.

## VULGATE

The Latin translation of the entire Bible produced by Jerome late in the fourth century at the request of Pope Damasus I was called the *editio vulgata* because it was written in the common language of the time. While he was not the first to translate the Scriptures into Latin, Jerome's text becomes the authoritative version of the Scriptures for Western Christianity for the next millennium. He translated from the Hebrew version of the Old Testament (rather than relying on the Septuagint) and the Greek version of the New Testament, but also included the Deuterocanonical works. Because Jerome diligently compared various manuscripts in different languages in producing his own translations, the Vulgate is an important witness to the state of the New Testament text in late antiquity.

## SUGGESTIONS FOR FURTHER READING

Non-technical definitions of the terms included here and many others are found in A. G. Patzia and A. J. Petrotta, *Pocket Dictionary of Biblical Studies* (Downers Grove, IL: InterVarsity, 2002); and W. R. Tate, *Interpreting the Bible: A Handbook of Terms and Methods* (Peabody, MA: Hendrickson, 2006). Much more exhaustive and more detailed is D. N. Freedman, ed., *The Anchor Bible Dictionary* (6 vols.; New York: Doubleday, 1992).

# 6

## GENERAL ISSUES

This chapter discusses a baker's dozen of "frequently asked questions" that arise when reading the New Testament and attempting to make sense of the myriad interpretations of its contents. The questions addressed include:

*What do we know about the life of Jesus?*
*What language did Jesus speak?*
*How do we know what Jesus really said?*
*How should the miracles in the New Testament be understood?*
*Did Jesus found a new religion?*
*Is the New Testament anti-Semitic?*
*Who wrote the New Testament?*
*How do we know when the books of the New Testament were written?*
*Why does the New Testament contain (only) twenty-seven books?*
*How should one read the non-canonical writings?*
*How are the Dead Sea Scrolls related to the New Testament?*
*Should the New Testament be read "literally"?*
*What special methods do scholars use to interpret the New Testament?*

While the brief essays in the following pages do not contain exhaustive answers to these questions, they provide a sense of where scholars have reached consensus, the grounds on which that consensus rests, and the areas in which debate is not settled.

\* \* \*

## WHAT DO WE KNOW ABOUT THE LIFE OF JESUS?

To observe that the Gospel writers were not historians or biographers in the modern sense is a truism that happens to be true. It was not their objective to provide a comprehensive account of the life of Jesus but, rather, to help their readers come to or continue in faith that Jesus is the Messiah (John 20:31). They were not as interested in his life as in his death and in his indestructible life after that horrific death. The passion narratives (Matt. 26–27; Mark 14; Luke 22–23; John 18–19) were most likely the earliest accounts of Jesus' life set down in writing. Although Jesus is not unique among ancient figures in this respect, it is a source of frustration to modern historians that no contemporary written sources from his lifetime exist. The gospels are written decades later. Luke and John indicate that they have had contact with eyewitnesses, though they include no footnotes identifying which portions of the narrative may be based on early sources. Paul, who writes even earlier, either takes the details of the earthly life of Jesus for granted or is relatively disinterested in them, at least when he is writing letters. (Unlike Jesus, Paul left behind firsthand information. Because he was writing letters and not a memoir, however, these valuable primary sources present separate challenges for scholars attempting to piece together the story of Paul's life.)

If the aim of the authors is to elicit faith in Jesus and to explicate his meaning and significance within God's unfolding plan for Israel and the rest of the world, then they see their task as theological rather than as strictly historical in nature. Early Christian writers recognized this, as when Clement of Alexandria described John as having composed "a spiritual Gospel" (Eusebius, *Hist. eccl.* 6.14.7). Clement is often quoted in support of the notion that the evangelists had purely theological interests. In context, however, he is saying that John wrote his "spiritual Gospel" only after being satisfied that the "bodily facts had [already] been made plain." History and theology were not deemed to be mutually exclusive, however complicated it might prove to disentangle them when viewing historical events in retrospect through a generation or two of theological reflection. Another claim that is sometimes heard is that the evangelists had no interest in conveying historically accurate accounts because ancient writers had no sense of objective history. Yet it is one thing to fail in achieving objectivity or to subordinate it to other aims, and quite another to fail to grasp the idea or eschew it entirely. Plutarch, writing at roughly the same time as the evangelists, takes Herodotus to task for his errors as well as for his prejudices—a criticism that makes little sense unless the critic has some appreciation for the value of objective reporting. Although it is difficult to extract facts about Jesus that are not shaped by theological conviction, to assume that the evangelists intend their works to function as extended metaphors or parables or as pious fictions is to overcorrect for their bias.

That the authors had some interest in history is evident. Discerning their accuracy as historians is another matter. One may divide scholars who study the life of Jesus into three groups—minimalists, maximalists, and those who fall somewhere in between these stances at either end of the spectrum. However much they lean in one direction or the other, most belong to the third group. Maximalists are confident that the gospels are reliable sources with which it is possible to write a robust account of Jesus' ministry. Minimalists believe very little at all can be known with any certainty; any authentic nuggets mined from the gospels are so thoroughly tainted by mythical, propagandistic, and theological residues as to render them useless for writing a biography. (The ultimate minimalist position is the "mythicist" theory, according to which Jesus never actually existed. Few scholars take this theory seriously.)

At a minimum, the consensus of current scholarly opinion is that we can trust in the historicity of at least a few basic facts reported in the gospels: Jesus was born ca. 4 BCE. He was descended from David and raised as an observant Jew in Nazareth. He was baptized by John. He embarked on the career of itinerant preacher in Galilee during the reign of Tiberius and attracted disciples, whose number included women. His preaching was devoted to announcing the arrival of

God's kingdom. He was regarded as a wonder worker. He came into conflict with Jewish leaders and was crucified in Jerusalem under Pontius Pilate, the Roman prefect of Judea, at Passover around 30 CE after being betrayed by one of his followers. The canonical sources are largely in agreement on these points, and extrabiblical texts from Jewish and Roman writers provide independent attestation of certain facts. Many of these details are unlikely to have been fabricated because they would have had great potential to cause embarrassment to the church. Beyond this, when any two scholars are asked to weigh in on a given question, one is likely to hear at least three different answers.

Maximalists recognize that the gospels are incomplete. The Fourth Gospel says as much (21:25). They also concede that the gospels contain material that appears incredible (because they involve supernatural interventions and other miraculous occurrences) and inconsistent (because episodes featured by more than one evangelist include elements that do not line up when placed side by side). What if the evangelists have made crucial omissions, not concerning trivial matters but on questions of greater consequence such as whether he had siblings or a wife, rose from the dead, designated Peter as "successor," or thought he was divine? The desire to fill out the picture of Jesus found in the New Testament as completely as possible—not easily dismissed as idle curiosity—coupled with the rationalistic and iconoclastic tendencies of the Enlightenment gave birth to the "Quest for the Historical Jesus." The quest takes its name from the title of Albert Schweitzer's 1906 classic, *The Quest of the Historical Jesus.*

Schweitzer reviews the various attempts to reconstruct the life of Jesus from the eighteenth century down to his own day, incisively revealing the strengths and weaknesses of each successive attempt at writing a biography. Common to all these works is that they are, to a greater or lesser extent, exercises in projection. Marxists find a Marxist Jesus. Evangelicals find an Evangelical Jesus. Minimalists, who believe that Christian claims to maintain fidelity to Jesus' enduring message are without warrant, tend to find a "lowest common denominator" Jesus who cannot even be assumed to have taught what most Jewish teachers of the first century taught. Schweitzer's final judgment was that the quest revealed as much about the questers as it did about Jesus: "There is no historical task which so reveals a man's true self as the writing of a Life of Jesus" (1968: 4). Minimalists (who skew toward skepticism) and maximalists (who tend to arrive at traditionalist conclusions) would both do well to write this maxim on their doorposts.

## WHAT LANGUAGE DID JESUS SPEAK?

Aramaic was the first language of most residents of the Galilee in which Jesus was raised. It is therefore remarkable that almost nothing written by Christians in that language has survived from the first century. Traces of the Aramaic spoken by Jesus and his earliest disciples can be found in the New Testament (Mark 5:41; 7:34; 15:22), most notably in his use of "*abba*" in addressing God and in the exclamation from the cross "*Eli, Eli, lema sabachtnaï*" (Matt. 27:46: "My God, my God, why have you forsaken me?"). As it was the language of Scripture and of legal and theological debate, it is also possible that he was competent in Hebrew. Outside of the aristocracy and temple bureaucracy in Jerusalem, Hebrew was spoken by very few Jews in this period.

Since the New Testament is written in Greek, it is natural to wonder if Jesus could speak that language. (Few scholars believe it was originally written in Aramaic and only later translated into Greek.) Any Greek phrases going back to Jesus himself would not stand out in the biblical text in the same way Aramaic phrases do. His hometown, Nazareth, was just a few miles from Sepphoris, a bustling Roman city where Greek was widely spoken as it was in many other parts of Palestine where the effects of Hellenization were still on display. It is not at all inconceivable that carpenters and other locals might be proficient in the language of those with whom they were engaged in business affairs. In the gospels, Jesus is depicted as interacting with crowds in regions where Greek was spoken and with Diaspora Jews and other individuals who were unlikely to know any Aramaic (Matt. 4:25; 8:5–13; John 12:20–21). Paul's letters exhibit the fluency of a native Greek speaker, though Acts also depicts him speaking in Aramaic (21:40; 22:2).

## HOW DO WE KNOW WHAT JESUS REALLY SAID?

In part because Jesus spoke Aramaic, it is difficult to determine whether the New Testament, which is written in Greek, preserves the words he actually spoke. If he ever wrote anything, it has long since been whisked away like his scribbles in the sand mentioned in John (8:6–8). Given the widespread use of pseudepigraphy, it is surprising that hardly anyone uses "Jesus" as a pen name. Only the third-century "Letter of Christ to Abgar" even claims to be written by Jesus. His teachings were delivered orally and passed down in oral form before their inclusion in the canonical gospels a few decades later. They may have been put down in writing a little earlier in a collection of sayings referred to by scholars as Q (from the German *Quelle*, "source"), a hypothetical document that, if it existed, has been lost and is no longer available for analysis. Those interested in knowing what Jesus said must sift the material preserved by his followers. On this score, they face the same situation as those interested in Socrates who must distill the philosopher's ideas from those of his students, Plato and Xenophon.

That only a portion of Jesus' teachings have been preserved is not disputed. Upon reading the gospels, two questions arise. First, did he or did he not say the things he is depicted as saying? And second, if he did say the things he is depicted as saying, do the gospels preserve his very words or have they edited them? A cursory examination of a Gospel Synopsis, in which the texts of Matthew, Mark, and Luke (and sometimes John) are arranged side by side in parallel columns, reveals that each Gospel portrays Jesus saying things he says nowhere else, omits sayings uttered by Jesus in the other gospels, and quotes in different forms sayings that are included in multiple sources. For example, only in Luke does he pray from the cross, "Father, forgive them; for they do not know what they are doing" (Luke 23:34). Luke also omits the cry "My God, my God, why have you forsaken me" while both Matthew and Mark include it (Matt. 27:46; Mark 15:34). And whereas Matthew, in the Sermon on the Mount, has Jesus say, "Blessed are the poor in spirit" and "Blessed are those who hunger and thirst for righteousness," Luke has Jesus say, more concisely, "Blessed are you who are poor" and "Blessed are you who are hungry now" (Matt. 5:3, 6; Luke 6:20–21). In addition, it has been wondered whether Jesus ever referred to himself as "messiah" or "son of God" or "Son of Man," predicted his death or the destruction of the temple, or tended to speak of "the kingdom of heaven" or "the kingdom of God."

The differences among the gospels are greater in some cases than in others. To separate the proverbial wheat from the chaff, scholars have generated a list of criteria that they apply to the words attributed to Jesus (Allison 1998: 1–77). Sayings found in only one source are deemed less reliable than those found in more than one Gospel (*multiple attestation*). By this criterion, very few statements in John are given the benefit of the doubt. Not only are Jesus' many "I am" sayings distinctive to John, but they are also attached to lengthy discourses, in violation of the criterion of *brevity*, according to which the accuracy of a quotation is considered to be inversely proportional to its length. If a saying is in too close conformity with the teachings of first-century Judaism or with the teachings of the post-Easter church, it is also judged less reliable on the grounds that early scribes may have "re-Judaized" Jesus or put words in his mouth that affirm early Christian doctrine and practice. Stated differently, this criterion (*dissimilarity*) holds that a saying accurately preserves an authentic teaching when it is distinct from the teachings of contemporary Judaism as well as from those of early Christianity. A related criterion is *embarrassment*. It is unlikely that the early church would fabricate a saying that would potentially embarrass it, as with Jesus' apparently mistaken prediction about the timing of the second coming in Matt. 10:23. Finally, it is more probable that a saying is authentic if it is consistent with and does not contradict other authentic sayings of Jesus (*coherence*).

These criteria have a certain prima facie plausibility and operate according to a logic that seeks to avoid subjective judgments. By no means are they foolproof, and their application is sometimes more like art than science. It makes perfect sense, for example, that an authentic saying will cohere with and not contradict other authentic sayings, but this obviously depends on a prior determination of which sayings are authentic and which ones are not. Furthermore, while "embarrassing" sayings have a higher degree of reliability, it is unlikely that Jesus spoke exclusively in ways that might prove awkward for the early church. Likewise, it seems obtuse to assume that the Jewish Jesus never reiterated commonplace Jewish teachings and never taught anything that those who proclaimed him as the Messiah could manage to quote accurately. The criterion of dissimilarity may thus yield positive determinations about what Jesus said, but it is more suspect when it is used to determine that he could not have said something he is reported to have said. Otherwise, one must assume that Jesus was utterly unique each and every time he spoke—a tall order, even for (someone who may or may not have claimed to be) God's son.

So, how do we know what Jesus really said? In short, we cannot know with absolute certainty. Simply deferring to the experts does not solve the problem, since the experts do not agree. Are his teachings those of an apocalyptic prophet? A Greco-Roman sage with little interest in eschatology? A pious Jew concerned above all to uphold the Torah? A political subversive? An illiterate peasant? A rabbi skilled in the style of debate practiced by the Pharisees? Support for each of these portrayals can be found among scholars. Minimalists assume that any saying is inauthentic until proven authentic by means of the aforementioned criteria, which results in a very taciturn Jesus about whose teachings little can be said. Members of the "Jesus Seminar" usually fall into this camp. Practitioners of form criticism assume that the gospels give access only to the ideas of their authors or of the early church, which may on occasion have coincided with those of the historical Jesus. Toward the other end of the spectrum are those who believe the gospels contain the *ipsissima vox* ("the very voice") if not the *ipsissima verba* ("the very words")—not a word-for-word transcript, to be sure, but a trustworthy summary of Jesus' teaching—and that the burden of proof is on those who see the early church and its oral tradition as thoroughly tendentious or overzealous in its editorial activity.

## HOW SHOULD THE MIRACLES IN THE NEW TESTAMENT BE UNDERSTOOD?

The New Testament is replete with depictions of and references to astonishing events that go against the normal order of things, usually called "deeds of power" (*dynameis*) or "signs" (*sēmeia*). It is natural for readers to wonder about such wondrous occurrences: Did they really take place? At one level, this is a philosophical question which is, moreover, unanswerable in a way that will satisfy most people who ask it. Those who believe Jesus was born of a virgin or healed the blind and those who are skeptical of such reports usually disagree about the fundamental terms of the debate. Skeptics say, "By the physical laws of nature, things *do* not happen that way; therefore, it *could* not have happened that way." Believers respond, "It was a miracle, contravening the regular laws of nature, and thus you are simply begging the question since one of the things we are arguing about is precisely whether the laws of nature can be or ever have been broken." While believers do not necessarily give credence to every miracle report they encounter, they hold open the possibility that events may have transpired more or less as described. Skeptics tend to see this approach as credulous and incompatible with sober historiography.

Fortunately, there are many viable ways to read the New Testament and much to be learned even when there is no agreed-upon answer to the philosophical question. It is not enough to say, as many would, that the miracles are included because they happened, since John states that Jesus performed many others that were not included (20:30–31). Neither will it usually do to reduce the accounts to naïve misunderstandings, say, by conjecturing that Jesus was actually treading on an unseen sandbar rather than on the water or that he "fed" the five thousand by setting an example of generosity that the crowds emulated or by some other naturalistic or psychological explanation. Furthermore, according to ancient sources, Jesus was not alone in possessing the ability to work wonders. Jewish holy men such as Hanina ben Dosa and Honi the Circle Drawer and pagans such as Pythagoras and Apollonius of Tyana reportedly performed similar miracles. Hellenistic authors often composed aretologies that recite the great deeds of gods, heroes, or "divine men" for a variety of propagandistic purposes, and the gospels certainly serve aretological functions (Kee 1973). The healings, exorcisms, and resuscitations in the gospels are meant to announce the dawning of God's kingdom by demonstrating Jesus' power over disease, demons, and death, and thereby to elicit the reader's faith.

The formulaic manner in which they are often narrated highlights this connection between the divine authority manifested in Jesus and the response of those who witness it. And yet it may miss the mark to conclude that the authors simply intend to employ mythical language and imagery in conveying a purely spiritual lesson. To be sure, ancient authors did not conceive of the universe as a Newtonian system closed off to incursions from some transcendent realm, and their readers did not possess scientific knowledge of the sort produced by means of the experimental method and widely disseminated after the

Enlightenment. But it is quite another thing to assert that "belief in Mary's physical virginity is based on the need to translate the mystery of the Incarnation into terms intelligible to unsophisticated people" (Louis Evely, quoted in Brown 1973: 25). These "unsophisticated people" were not totally ignorant of the way the natural world normally operates and were not incapable of distinguishing metaphors and symbols from literal statements.

A contemporary analogy may put into perspective the exceeding difficulty of understanding how early Christian authors and readers may have understood miracle reports. According to an official biography written before his death in 2011, Kim Jong Il was not only an outstanding leader but also an accomplished golfer. The "Dear Leader" of North Korea allegedly made eleven holes-in-one in his first outing. At first blush, it seems that anyone telling a story about a golfer who scores eleven aces in a single round is clearly signaling that they are writing fiction or fable or humor since no one would ever believe anything so far-fetched. Perhaps this "biography" should be read as Communist hagiography, designed to send the message that Kim is capable of great deeds like leading the nation through difficult times, but certainly not as a literal account of his prowess on the golf course (or in film-making, horticulture, literary criticism, military strategy, or several other fields to which he purportedly made seminal contributions). But the cult of personality that dominates North Korean society makes one pause. Whether out of fear or out of the ignorance resulting from extensive censorship, it is difficult to imagine an ordinary citizen (or even the author) saying, "That is a symbolic story, nothing more." If authorial intent and audience reception can be so opaque when dealing with contemporary claims, how much more difficult can it be to fathom the mindset of writers and readers living nearly 2,000 years ago in a culture far removed from that of the industrialized West?

Efforts at understanding early Christian claims about the greatest miracle of all—the resurrection—are subject to the same caveats. People who die normally remain dead. This was no less true in antiquity than it is today. Does this mean that those who heard the news that God had raised Jesus from the dead would have understood it in literal terms and either accepted or dismissed it? Would they have reflexively understood it in figurative terms, say, as a declaration of Jesus' holiness, a sign of God's conquest over the power of death, or a symbol of hope and rebirth? Would the zombie-like image of a revivified corpse have physically and intellectually repulsed them?

Paul doubtless believes that the significance of the resurrection extends well beyond the reanimation of a particular corpse. To reduce the resurrection to the status of an exception, however marvelous, to the general rules governing the physical universe is to misrepresent the convictions of Paul and other early Christians. To reduce it to the dawning of new possibilities for authentic existence, as does Rudolf Bultmann (1960), without anything "objective" having occurred to bring about this new existence is to misrepresent them in a different way. Whatever the explanation for it, early Christians claimed to have witnessed Jesus in bodily form after his death. Had someone claimed that the body of Jesus were still moldering in the grave, Paul would not have reacted with indifference or replied, "Well, yes, but when we proclaim that Lord Jesus has risen, we are simply saying that God has wrought a change in the heart of the believer." To the contrary, he believes that belief in the bodily resurrection of Jesus is non-negotiable for Christians, declaring that "if Christ has not been raised, then our proclamation has been in vain and your faith has been in vain" (1 Cor. 15:14; cf. Rom. 10:9). There is surely a difference between events that are truly "historic" and those that are merely "historical," but it makes little sense to describe any event as "historic" that was not first, mini-mally, "historical" in the plain sense of having actually occurred (Neill 1964: 233–34). That Paul and other early Christians believed Jesus rose bodily from the dead seems indisputable on historical grounds, even if the precise grounding for that belief eludes modern interpreters.

## DID JESUS FOUND A NEW RELIGION?

Few of the figures traditionally regarded as founders of religions— e.g., Muhammad, Confucius, the Buddha—consciously set out to start something new. Conversely, most people who do intend to found a new religion quickly fade from memory. Jesus is more like the former than the latter. He never claims to be "founding" a new "religion." Matthew has Jesus say that he will build his "church" (*ekklēsia*) on Peter, but this does not appear to indicate a new belief system distinct from Judaism insofar as he came "not to abolish but to fulfill" the law of Moses (5:17; 16:18).

What becomes Christianity begins in the first century as a sect within Judaism. Jesus was Jewish, his earliest followers were all Jewish, and the set of convictions that comes to be labeled Christianity is expressed primarily in categories derived from Jewish tradition. Today, Judaism and Christianity are regarded as separate religions. At some point in between, then, these two roads diverge. Where, when, and why they diverge; how sharply they diverge; whether the decision to part ways is mutual; what consequences follow from this parting—answers to these questions inform any discussion of the sense(s) in which Jesus should be identified as the founder of Christianity. Intentionally or not, Jesus acts as the catalyst for its founding. Soon after his death, Jesus' followers spread the good news that he has been raised from the dead and that those who have faith in him can gain salvation (Matt. 28:18–20; John 20:31; Heb. 5:8–9). These and other bold claims about Jesus distinguish early Christianity from other sects within Judaism. Try as they might to demonstrate that their good news aligns with the divine plan as revealed long ago in the Scriptures of Israel, his followers do not deny the novelty of what they claim takes place in the person of Jesus. The accompanying disagreements with other Jewish sects ultimately prove too large to overcome, and the effective result is the birth of a new religion. Is this an organic outgrowth of the movement started by Jesus? If this is not what Jesus anticipated, should he be considered the "accidental" founder of Christianity?

If it was not Jesus who was responsible, many historians conclude that it was instead Paul. The claim is usually intended as a backhanded compliment and implies that Paul distorted the message preached by Jesus, either out of ignorance or as part of a well-intended yet ill-conceived strategy of outreach to non-Jews. While Paul certainly left an indelible stamp on the movement, this view overlooks the contributions of (largely unnamed) individuals from whom he says he learned the Gospel and who preceded him in sharing it with Gentiles. It also glosses too quickly over the complicated question of determining the authentic teachings of Jesus and the nature of his self-consciousness (see above). Precisely who Jesus thought he was and what he thought he was doing remain a mystery. No writings survive that bring later readers into closer proximity to this mystery than the New Testament, yet they do not quite solve it.

## IS THE NEW TESTAMENT ANTI-SEMITIC?

Whether and to what extent one may think of Jesus or Paul founding a new religion remains a contested question (see above). Less controversial is the observation that Judaism and the movement that becomes Christianity do eventually part ways, at different times in different places. Because this parting coincided with heightened hostility toward Jews and Judaism, it has been asked whether Christianity should be considered anti-Semitic. A point about terminology is in order before answering this question. "Anti-Semitism" is a term of nineteenth-century coinage with racial connotations that make it anachronistic when applied to antiquity (Cohen 2006: 39–40). In the New Testament, there is little in the way of hatred of Jews as an ethnic or racial group like one sees in the modern world. It is more accurate to refer to texts that denigrate Jews or Judaism as a religion as "anti-Jewish."

Despite the anachronism of labeling the New Testament anti-Semitic, there is little question that it has often inspired hatred of Jews as Jews (Eckhardt 1967). Jews have been branded "Christ-killers" for the part they played in Jesus' death as narrated in the gospels. The so-called "blood curse" of Matt. 27:25 ("His blood be on us and on our children!") has been cited as the Jews' willing acceptance of this perfidious role. Even more useful to anti-Semites over the centuries is the statement of Jesus in the Gospel of John that "the Jews" are of the Devil (8:44). Paul has been invoked as well. His descriptions of the Jews as "blind" and "hardened" in a way that believers in Christ are not (2 Cor. 3:14–16) and "under a curse" because of their reliance on the Torah (Gal. 3:10) have figured prominently in assertions that there is an intrinsic defect in Jewishness as such and that God has rejected the Jews, past and present, as a people.

Were these and other texts intended to express anti-Semitic sentiments? Probably not, since Jesus was a Jew who came to uphold rather than abolish the law (Matt. 5:17) and taught his disciples the *Shema* ("Hear O Israel"; cf. Mark 12:29); his earliest followers were Jews who understood him through the lens of Jewish tradition and professed their devotion to him at the temple and in the synagogue and, even in the Gospel of John, observe Jewish holidays (4:45; 7:2; 10:22; 13:1); and many of the New Testament authors were Jewish, though how many is unclear since not all of their identities are known. Can Jews be anti-Semitic? Normally one would answer no. Can Jews be anti-Jewish? If "Jew" can denote a member of an ethnic group and "Jewish" can denote a religious community or sensibility, then yes, it is possible for a Jew to be anti-Jewish in a certain sense. Here again, it is critical to read the harsh statements in the New Testament in literary and historical context. Yes, most of the implacable enemies of Jesus in these writings are Jews, but so are most of his friends. The arguments about Jesus and his significance for how one ought to think and act are for the most part intramural in nature. In other words, when reading the New Testament, one is usually eavesdropping on debates between Jews—some who believe that Jesus is the Messiah and others who do not, or who disagree as to the appropriate response to his messianic status—about what constitutes authentic Jewishness.

It is thus anachronistic to choose one side in these debates and declare the other "anti-Jewish," even if that is how it appears in retrospect (Evans and Hagner 1993: 9–15). Otherwise, one might label Amos and Hosea anti-Jewish on account of their prophetic critiques that equal in harshness any of the calumnies hurled at Israel by its ancient enemies. Neither should Jesus be deemed "anti-Jewish" because of the caustic language he directs at the Pharisees in Matt. 23 when he is simply employing standard polemical strategies found among rival schools in the Greco-Roman world, including those used by the Pharisees against their opponents. The dynamic changes dramatically, however, as more and more Gentiles join the messianic movement, beginning before the ministry of Paul and continuing without pause during the following decades and centuries when one sees unambiguously anti-Jewish sentiments on display in such works as the *Epistle of Barnabas*, in many Gnostic sects that reject the Hebrew Bible and vilify the God of Israel as an evil demiurge, and in the writings of many church fathers. These non-Jewish Christians hear this bitter rhetoric not as part of the "insider" back and forth between one Jewish sect and another about the propriety of this or that Jewish belief or custom. Rather, they generalize the criticism and are all too happy to apply it to all Jews, with whom they have increasingly infrequent contact. This represents a different sort of anachronism that has all too often led to pain and suffering for Jews caused by citizens of the Christian societies among whom they have been dispersed. Since the Holocaust, Jews and Christians have become sensitive to this danger. But relations were different in antiquity. Whereas Christians have been in the majority and Jews in the minority almost everywhere for the last 1,700 years, the Jews who acclaimed Jesus as the Messiah were far outnumbered by "mainstream" Jews perhaps until the reign of Constantine. What one often hears in the New Testament is thus the outcry of an aggrieved minority that sees itself as vulnerable and marginalized. By no means does this excuse the invidious uses to which the New Testament has been put. Reading it responsibly, however, entails attending to the shifting relationship between the original context and the interpretive traditions that have fostered antipathy toward Jews and Judaism.

## WHO WROTE THE NEW TESTAMENT?

The New Testament is the product of many hands. How many hands is uncertain. Just as ancient texts lack copyright dates, they often lack the names of their authors and formal titles as well. The gospels may belong in this category. None contains a normal claim of authorship, and only the authors of Luke and John speak even occasionally in the first person (Luke 1:1–4; John 21:24–25). The titles they now bear were likely added in the early- to mid-second century when they were collected together. "According to Matthew" and "According to Mark" are often thought to constitute attributions of authorship, though it is not clear that they were intended to function this way when they were first appended to the manuscripts containing them. Given the heavy emphasis placed on apostolic connections by the early church, it may be that the gospels of Mark and Luke—neither of whom were among the twelve apostles—are more likely to bear the name of their actual authors than Matthew and John. If the "titles" have not been put there by their authors, it is more accurate to speak of anonymity than of pseudonymity (see below).

At one end of the spectrum, one finds the view that all of the traditional attributions of authorship are accurate. Matthew wrote Matthew, Peter wrote 1–2 Peter, Jude wrote Jude, and so forth. At the other end of the spectrum, one finds the view that hardly any of these traditional attributions can be trusted except for seven of Paul's letters and possibly Revelation. This is the most widely held position among critical scholars. (One of the most influential scholars of the nineteenth century, F. C. Baur, thought that Paul wrote only four of the letters in the canon. Bruno Bauer and the Dutch Radicals were even more skeptical, arguing that Paul wrote none of the letters.) Modern critics, however, are not alone in expressing reservations. Doubts about Pauline authorship of the Letter to the Hebrews are voiced as soon as his name is attached to it. Dionysius, the third-century bishop of Alexandria, believed that the author of Revelation was not John the Apostle but someone else named John—a very common name among ancient Christians, as it turns out.

Whoever they were, all of the New Testament authors were proficient in the Koine dialect of Greek and held an abiding conviction that Jesus' death and resurrection marked a pivotal development in God's dealings with humanity. On the hypothesis that they are not who the documents suggest they are, one might add one more fact: that they prefer to write under a pen name. This pertains to the letters more so than to the gospels. Some readers find the suggestion that the New Testament may contain texts written under a false name scandalous in that it would in some sense delegitimize them. Others consider the notion unproblematic on the grounds that what the texts say matters more than who says it. The practice of writing under a false name was widespread in Jewish and Greco-Roman antiquity. How widespread and how readily accepted as a transparent fiction is somewhat less clear. Pseudonymity usually invokes the name of a revered figure of the past, e.g., Abraham, Solomon, Elijah, Socrates—to whom the unnamed author seeks to pay homage and whose legacy is thereby perpetuated for a new time and place. In some cases, it appears that pseudonymity may also be a mechanism for exercising authority over an audience that might not otherwise concede it and thus is deceptive in intent.

There is no one-size-fits-all approach when it comes to determining when and whether the original audiences would have seen pseudonymous authorship as improper. Much of it would have depended on the tacit understanding of the relationship between the author and the reader. Moreover, the case for pseudonymity is stronger for some New Testament books than others. It may be too clever by half to believe that not a single Christian in the first century except for Paul ever saw fit to write anything in his or her name, and perhaps what Origen writes in the second century about the authorship of Hebrews goes for the rest of the canonical books: "God knows."

## HOW DO WE KNOW WHEN THE BOOKS OF THE NEW TESTAMENT WERE WRITTEN?

Ancient writings do not come with copyright dates, and even documents like letters often do not indicate their date of composition. New Testament scholars have an easier task than their Old Testament counterparts in that the Hebrew Bible was written over the course of several hundred years while the New Testament authors started and finished their work in less than one century. Within this shorter timeframe, it nonetheless remains quite difficult to date the texts with any precision or certainty.

Although there is great disagreement, most scholars would probably name Paul's letters as the earliest (1 Thessalonians or perhaps Galatians or 1 Corinthians, around 49 or 50 CE). The last to be written—depending on the authority one consults—may be 2 Peter or the Pastoral Epistles, perhaps around the end of the first century or as late as the first few decades of the second century. These determinations are in turn based partly on contested claims of pseudonymous authorship in the case of several writings. While few would agree with J. A. T. Robinson's attempt to date the entire New Testament prior to 70 CE, that he can marshal such plausible arguments for his theories is a reminder that the conclusions of even the most conscientious attempts to settle the chronology should remain tentative (Robinson 1976).

With so few fixed points, scholars must be content with approximate ranges and datings of the texts relative to one another. External attestation is the most important criterion at work in this process. If one text appears to quote or allude to another, then it is possible to date one later and the other earlier. On this basis, most scholars date Matthew and Luke a little later than Mark. But how much later? A few months? A few decades? There is no sure way to tell. This is all the more true when the question of literary dependence cannot be definitively answered, as is the case with the relationship between the Synoptic Gospels and the Fourth Gospel and between Paul and James.

Other approaches focus on Christology. If a book evinces a "high" view of Jesus as divine or quasi-divine, this is often thought to correlate with a later dating on the assumption that such a Christology would have emerged only after a considerable amount of theological reflection. A "low" Christology emphasizing Jesus' humanity is thought to correlate with an earlier dating. Yet Paul's letters already reflect a "high" Christology, and Hebrews simultaneously suggests that Jesus was "the exact imprint of God's very being" yet "like his brothers and sisters in every respect" (1:3; 2:17). And where should one fit James, who mentions Jesus only twice (1:1; 2:1)? Concern about hierarchy and organization within the church is also thought to be evidence for a later dating, with the attention paid to "church order" in 1 Timothy and Titus cited as the most prominent example. How one should assess this criterion in light of Paul's "early" references to bishops and deacons (Rom. 16:1; Phil. 1:1) and his inclusion of "forms of leadership" (1 Cor. 12:28) among the spiritual gifts is unclear.

One of the few events that can be dated with precision, amply documented by non-biblical sources, is the Roman destruction of the Jerusalem temple in 70 CE as a response to the Jewish revolt that had begun four years earlier. It is all the more frustrating, not to mention surprising, that nowhere in the New Testament is it unambiguously mentioned as having already occurred. Many scholars contend that Jesus's predictions of the temple's demise are post hoc fabrications of his followers and thus evidence of a post-70 composition for the gospels that record them. Others focus on the aftermath of the Roman conquest, taking 70 CE as a pivotal point in charting increasingly hostile relations between Judaism and the messianic sect that would eventually break away and set up shop as a separate religion. The Jewish Eighteen Benedictions, usually dated to ca. 85 CE, contains the *Birkhat ha-minim* "blessing" on heretics usually taken as a sign of a decisive break between church and synagogue. The perceived "fit" of the theological perspectives reflected in a given book within this reconstructed trajectory is then used to generate a possible date of composition. But the parting of the ways between Judaism and Christianity likely took place at different times in different locales since neither had a central authority strong enough to issue binding pronouncements on such matters. The surviving documentation of Jewish–Christian relations is simply too sparse to permit decisive conclusions, especially when even a margin of error as small as five years can radically alter any provisional timeline constructed on such grounds.

## WHY DOES THE NEW TESTAMENT CONTAIN (ONLY) TWENTY-SEVEN BOOKS?

Twenty-seven seems like a suspiciously biblical number. Is it simply a coincidence that the number of books included in the New Testament is equal to three to the third power? Yes, it probably is. It is not until late in the fourth century, in the Thirty-ninth Festal Letter of Bishop Athanasius of Alexandria, that the current "table of contents" of the New Testament canon first appears. But this is best understood as an ecclesiastical recognition of the results of a process that unfolded over time rather than as a dictate from on high, as it were. Earlier lists can be found, beginning with the so-called "Muratorian fragment" late in the second century, yet the process goes back even further than this.

"Scripture," for Jesus and his earliest followers, meant the Hebrew Bible, whether in its original language or in the Greek translation of the Septuagint. When Paul and others begin writing the texts that are later canonized, they are not under the impression that they are composing "additions" to the Bible. Within a few decades, however, they are being read alongside the law and the prophets in the worship gatherings of the Christians. This is a sign of the authority they are beginning to acquire, as is the fact that groups of Christians in various locales are copying these writings and sharing them with like-minded readers around the Mediterranean. Their relevance was not seen as limited to the original audiences and circumstances addressed by their authors.

As this process was not coordinated from the outset, different communities possessed different collections of writings that were accorded varying levels of authority. A collection of Paul's letters is mentioned in 2 Pet. 3:15–16, and a saying of Jesus that is recorded in Luke 10:7 and nowhere else ("The laborer deserves to be paid") is quoted as "Scripture" alongside Deuteronomy in 1 Tim. 5:18. The second century was a period of especially vigorous debate about which books belonged in the canon. There were advocates of expansion, who valued works like the *Apocalypse of Peter*, gospels attributed to Peter and Thomas, and other works such as the *Protevangelium of*

*James* and the *Acts of Paul and Thecla*. There were also advocates of contraction such as Tatian, who wanted to consolidate the four gospels into a single narrative in his *Diatesseron*, and Marcion of Pontus, who accepted only Luke and ten of Paul's letters. It is sometimes claimed that the popularity of Marcion was the primary impetus for the promulgation of an "orthodox" canon intended to check the spread of "heresy" by rejecting suspect works. The Muratorian fragment, for example, states that nothing from Arsinoes, Valentinus, or Metiades should be recognized by the church. While Marcion and others had a significant following, it should be remembered that the collection process had already started and that Marcion was capable of generating heterodox teachings purely on the basis of creative readings of texts that were otherwise deemed "safe."

A few criteria appear to have guided the decision-making process of the church. An apostolic provenance, whether direct or indirect, was usually deemed necessary for acceptance. Matthew and John were thought to have been written by apostles, while Mark and Luke were associated with Peter and Paul though they were not apostles themselves. But apostolicity was not sufficient, as several documents attributed to apostles but written well after the end of the first century were not able to achieve the broader consensus to be had for most of the books that made their way into the canon. This may imply a desire for historically reliable narratives relating to the life of Jesus. Catholicity—the broad acceptance of a book throughout the church rather than only in limited areas—was also valued, though it is difficult on this basis alone to make sense of the eventual status of works like Philemon, 2–3 John, and Jude. Orthodoxy was likewise crucial, if not sufficient by itself to merit inclusion. Many works, such as the late-first-century church manual known as the *Didache*, raised no doctrinal objections whatsoever, yet were not included. It is only natural that a religious movement would invest with authority only those documents that affirm, or at least do not violate, its fundamental convictions. In this connection, it is important to remember that the church preceded the New Testament and even the composition of its individual books, thus the New Testament is properly speaking a product of the church. As such, decisions about its contents were theological (and in some sense, political) in nature, as is any discontent about those decisions and what might have been had other books made the cut. Insofar as widespread, longstanding use in the church is one of the criteria for canonization (re-affirmed in 1546 at the Council of Trent), it is unlikely that the *Gospel of Mary* or the *Acts of Peter* will ever be admitted into a re-opened canon. By this criterion, even if it could be determined, for example, that *3 Corinthians* or the *Letter to the Laodiceans* were truly written by Paul, they would not be treated as holy writ.

## HOW SHOULD ONE READ THE NON-CANONICAL WRITINGS?

Virtually everything written by Christians in antiquity technically falls under the heading "non-canonical," since only a tiny fraction of the literary output of the ancient church was canonized. "Non-canonical," however, typically applies to writings often referred to as "New Testament apocrypha." Books in this category run the literary gamut from gospels and letters to "acts" and apocalypses and beyond. They are frequently attributed to an apostle and modeled, sometimes only very loosely, after their analogues in the canon. Much of this literature was nothing more than pious entertainment in the form of imaginative retellings of the lives of Jesus and his disciples and aimed at a general readership. Certain documents were accorded authoritative status in certain communities (occasionally intended only for the eyes of "insiders"). Some of the theological speculation they contain was considered heretical by church authorities, but much of it posed no doctrinal problems.

"Just like any other book" is perhaps the simplest answer to this question, paying close attention to historical context, literary genre, authorial intent, and the like. Even if texts like the *Teachings of Silvanus* and the *Apocryphon of James* are not accorded scriptural status, they are worth reading if only as a vivid reminder that the New Testament could have looked quite different, both in terms of form and content. Reading them makes it possible to locate the New Testament on a continuum with respect to their attitudes about such issues as gender, social ethics, sin, eschatology, cosmology, and the relationship between Judaism and Christianity.

For understanding the New Testament (the focus of this volume), the value of the non-canonical writings is not primarily historical.

The possibility that they yield any reliable information about the life of Jesus not already found in the canonical gospels is quite small. With the possible exception of the Coptic *Gospel of Thomas*, few scholars would argue that the non-canonical gospels contain any hitherto unknown authentic sayings of Jesus. Their value lies chiefly in their preservation of some of the earliest interpretations of the New Testament. They illustrate the diverse ways in which Christians in the second century and later understood Jesus, often by "filling in the gaps" in the Gospel narratives or pursuing theological trajectories hinted at in the letters. For example, the *Protevangelium of James* provides an early clue as to what the claim that Jesus was virginally conceived was thought to imply about Mary. The *Gospel of Judas* airs a theory aimed at explaining why and how the apostles misunderstood and abandoned Jesus. The *Acts of Paul* sheds light on early thinking about martyrdom. And the *Infancy Gospel of Thomas* explores the mystery of the incarnation by spinning a yarn about a five-year-old Jesus who knows he is divine.

## HOW ARE THE DEAD SEA SCROLLS RELATED TO THE NEW TESTAMENT?

If the non-canonical Christian writings testify to the "afterlife" of the New Testament books by shedding light on the ways they were received by ancient readers, non-canonical Jewish writings are valuable for what they reveal about the "gestation" of Christianity in that they demonstrate the literary and theological diversity of the Jewish milieu from which the movement sprang. Discovered in 1947, the Dead Sea Scrolls are a part of this vast body of literature. The scrolls are widely thought to have constituted the library of the Essene sect living in semi-isolation at Qumran. Many of the scrolls contained manuscripts of biblical books that enable scholars to determine the form taken by Jewish Scriptures in the period when Jesus gained a following. Other scrolls contain original writings marked by ascetic and apocalyptic motifs that parallel some strands of early Christian thought. The more fantastic claims sometimes made, e.g., that John the Baptist lived at Qumran or that the scrolls contain coded references to Jesus and Paul, have no basis. Their discovery nonetheless enables scholars to compare and contrast the shape and intensity of messianic expectation found in certain Jewish sects and the early church, as well as different forms of community organization and ritual practice.

## SHOULD THE NEW TESTAMENT BE READ "LITERALLY"?

Too often, this question is asked—and answers to it asserted—with inadequate attention to what it actually means. It is not simply a matter of contrasting the approaches of traditionalists and skeptics. When it is asked, the question may mean at least three different things. Take, for example, this brief excerpt from the Decalogue in Exod. 20:13 (KJV): "Thou shalt not kill." On one level, to ask if this should be read literally is to ask if the author's intended meaning is directly conveyed by the plain meaning of the words he uses. In this sense, it is clear that everyone is and should be a literalist, at least on occasions like this. To read the text in a non-literal way—as if it contains a prohibition of "figurative" killing, whatever that might mean—would be obtuse. No one believes that the Gospel writers mean to say that Jesus was figuratively or symbolically baptized by John or crucified by Roman soldiers. Asking if "Thou shalt not kill" should be read literally might instead be an inquiry about historical accuracy: Did Moses really and truly receive the Ten Commandments at Sinai on tablets of stone "written with the finger of God" (Exod 31:18)? This is quite a different question, about which reasonable people may disagree. Further still, reading the Bible "literally" may refer to the appropriate response to or application of a text made by an individual or community: Should I obey this text "literally"? Again, this is a different question about which reasonable people disagree, and not always in predictable patterns. There are many people who do not believe the text literally but nevertheless think that literally all killing should be avoided, and many others who believe that Moses literally received this law from God but think that some killing (e.g., in war or for self-defense) is morally permissible. Characterizing various readings simply as "literalist" or "non-literalist" all too often confuses these discrete issues.

Just as there are many instances in the New Testament where the only sensible reading is a literal reading, there are others where no one would venture a literal interpretation. When Jesus tells the parable of the ten bridesmaids, no one wonders what their names were, neither do his disciples protest, "We thought you were a carpenter!"

when he says, "I am the good shepherd" (Matt. 25:1–13; John 10:11). There is likewise a broad consensus that the Book of Revelation is not intended by its author as a literal account, whether of events in the past, the present, or the future. Beyond such easy cases, there are numerous instances in which it is far from clear whether the authors expected to be understood in a literal rather than a figurative or metaphorical fashion. Does Jesus really mean that his followers have to eat his flesh and drink his blood? Those who hear him say it in John 6 are themselves not sure. Does the author of Acts offer his narrative as an objective historical account of the spread of Christianity, or does he anticipate that his audience will see it as an idealized telling that communicates a more general truth about God's providential guidance of "salvation history?" Should Christians meet on the first day of the week, baptize by immersion, and handle serpents (Mark 16:18; John 3:23; 1 Cor. 16:2)? Discerning whether the author's intentions are to convey literal truths is a precursor to, but distinct from, deciding whether to accept as true any literal claims the text may make or to follow any precedents or directives they contain as normative.

## WHAT SPECIAL METHODS DO SCHOLARS USE TO INTERPRET THE NEW TESTAMENT?

Ancient readers of the Bible interpreted it "literally" (see above) but they also interpreted it in other ways. They occasionally adapted rabbinic methods such as Hillel's seven *middoth* ("rules" of inference), including *qal wahomer* (whatever is true in a "light" case also applies in a "heavier" case, and vice versa), *gezerah shavah* (whatever is true of comparable words or expressions may be applied interchangeably to two separate passages), and *davar hilamed me'inyano* (the meaning of a text may be established by its context). During the Middle Ages, interpreters attended to the "fourfold sense of Scripture." In addition to the literal sense expressed directly by the human authors, readers explored the *allegorical*, *tropological*, and *anagogic* senses of a biblical text. These three terms denoted, respectively: (1) hidden meanings wherein apparent contradictions could be reconciled or the Hebrew Bible could be shown to anticipate later realities in the life of Jesus and the church; (2) moral lessons imparted by the text; and (3) truths about the ultimate fate of the individual, the church, and the world.

Since the Reformation, scholars have focused more of their energies on recovering the literal sense of the text. The questions they ask in their efforts to understand the context of the original authors and the specific messages they sought to convey differ from those of earlier interpreters at many points, as do the methods they deem to be suitable for answering those questions. It is often said that modern interpreters aim above all to read the Bible "like any other book." This is not untrue, though in reality they subject the text to a far greater variety of modes of analysis than Homer, Shakespeare, or most other texts—in part, no doubt, due to its immense cultural and historical influence that is a function of the widespread view that it is not quite "like any other book."

Many of these methods seek to understand the historical processes by which the text itself came to its present form (Hayes and Holladay 2007). Textual criticism is the process of sorting through thousands of ancient and medieval manuscripts to determine the original wording of the biblical text. Form criticism examines the individual literary units of which the gospels are composed toward the goal of reconstructing the form in which they were circulated as oral tradition and the function they served in the ministry of Jesus or the context of the early church. Source criticism is the analysis of biblical texts with the aim of identifying the sources, whether oral or written, which have been used in their composition. Redaction criticism builds on the findings of source critics by studying the manner in which writers edit and adapt sources for their own literary or theological purposes.

Other methods seek to elucidate the relationship between the form of the text and its meaning and function in its original context. Genre analysis assumes that a classification of a text according to its literary type will clarify the significance of individual elements it contains. Rhetorical criticism attends to the strategies by which an author—in the New Testament, in the letters as well as in the speeches found in the Gospels and Acts—attempts to persuade an audience to adopt a certain point of view or pursue a course of action. Narrative criticism similarly concerns itself with the ways in which authors of stories interact with their audiences by focusing on plot, character, setting, and the like. Ancient literary genres, modes of argumentation, and plot devices do not always operate exactly like their modern counterparts, thus to ignore Jewish and Greco-Roman conventions in these areas is to risk anachronistic interpretations of the New Testament.

In the last several decades, other methods have emerged that take as their focus the many and varied readers "in front of the text" rather than the world of the author and the original audience (McKenzie and Kaltner 2013). Practitioners of feminist, Afrocentric, Latino/a, queer, postcolonial, and Asian American criticism embrace a range of theoretical assumptions and methodological approaches that highlight the advantages of reading the text consciously and consistently from the perspective of marginalized identities or sensibilities. Such perspectival readings may uncover aspects of a text that have gone largely ignored or overlooked by more conventional interpreters, but just as importantly they seek ways to make the text speak to the concerns modern readers bring to the table. Ecological, theological, and psychological approaches likewise look to the biblical text as a resource for answering questions that may not have occurred to the original authors. As with every other method, different tools produce different results. Whether the meaning of a text depends on the author or the reader would appear to depend on what the meaning of "meaning" is. This is properly asking a philosophical rather than a historical question. Hermeneutics is the formal term for the field of study that attempts to answer it.

## SUGGESTIONS FOR FURTHER READING

Single-volume surveys of the New Testament typically cover most of the questions discussed here. Reliable guides include R. E. Brown, *An Introduction to the New Testament* (New York: Doubleday, 1997); D. C. Duling and N. Perrin, *The New Testament: Proclamation and Parenesis, Myth and History* (3rd ed.; New York: Harcourt Brace Jovanovich, 1993); C. R. Holladay, *A Critical Introduction to the New Testament: Interpreting the Message and Meaning of Jesus Christ* (Nashville, TN: Abingdon, 2005); L. T. Johnson, *The Writings of the New Testament: An Interpretation* (3rd ed.; Minneapolis, MN: Fortress, 2010); and M. A. Powell, *Introducing the New Testament: A Historical, Literary, and Theological Survey* (Grand Rapids, MI: Baker Academic, 2009). Attuned to specific dimensions of the various books and more concise in their treatment are G. R. O'Day and D. L. Petersen, eds., *Theological Bible Commentary* (Louisville, KY: Westminster John Knox, 2009); and C. A. Newsom and S. H. Ringe, eds., *Women's Bible Commentary* (Louisville, KY: Westminster John Knox, 1998).

# 7

## FOR FURTHER STUDY

This chapter contains questions formulated with the aim of facilitating close reading and engagement with major exegetical, theological, and historical issues raised by the New Testament texts.

### THE CONTEXT OF EARLY CHRISTIANITY AND THE NEW TESTAMENT

What impact did Alexander the Great have on the world in which Christianity was born? How were the New Testament authors affected by the omnipresent reality of Roman rule?

During the Hellenistic and Roman periods, are "religion" and "philosophy" two species of the same genus, or are they fundamentally different types of pursuits?

To what extent is it appropriate to think of the New Testament writings as a form of first-century Jewish literature? In what sense, if any, do early Christian writers regard the Hebrew Bible as a repository of prophecies about Jesus?

What were the consequences of the Jewish revolt that led to the destruction of the temple in Jerusalem by the Romans in 70 CE?

What factors led to the eventual "parting of the ways" between Judaism and Christianity as separate religions?

What impression did the early Christians make on "outsiders"?

## THE GOSPELS AND THE ACTS OF THE APOSTLES

What is implied in the claim that the gospels are "passion narratives with extended introductions"?

Most scholars believe that the Synoptic Gospels predate John but are divided on the question of literary dependence. What aspects of the Fourth Gospel suggest that its author is dependent on or independent of the other three? Apart from the question of dependence, does John present more explicitly particular aspects of the Synoptic Gospels that are present but only implicit or under the surface?

If a first-century community were totally reliant on Matthew (or Mark or Luke or John) for its information about Jesus, what would it not know? Conversely, if a first-century community were ignorant of Matthew (or Mark or Luke or John), what would it not know?

*Matthew*: How does Matthew's genealogy of Jesus differ from Luke's in terms of content, placement, and literary and theological function?

Most scholars believe that Matthew and Luke are using Mark as a source but are independent of one another. On this hypothesis, what may be inferred from the ways in which each author presents the virginal conception of Jesus? The temptation in the desert? The transfiguration? The Last Supper?

The Sermon on the Mount (Matthew 5–7) has been read in many different ways: as guidelines akin to "counsels of perfection" applying mainly to clergy; as an "interim ethic" to follow while awaiting the imminent arrival of God's reign; as a series of impossible demands intended to drive us from the law to grace; and as a literal guide to cultivating a just social order, among others. What texts offer the strongest support for these differing views?

What does Jesus mean when he says that he has come to fulfill rather than to abolish the law, and that his followers should be "perfect" like their heavenly father (Matt. 5:17, 48)?

If Matthew is "the Jewish Gospel," as many interpreters have remarked, how does its view of Jesus' message fit within the Jewish context of the first century? Is the call to go "into all the nations" in the Great Commission (Matt. 28:18–20) consistent with this characterization of Matthew?

Are the five major discourses (chapters 5–7; 10; 13; 18; 24–25) distinguished in terms of theme, tone, and subject matter, or is there substantial overlap in the concerns they address?

When Matthew quotes or alludes to the Hebrew Bible, does he seem cognizant of the broader literary and historical context of the passage he is citing?

*Mark*: What is the effect of the abrupt beginning, with no "preface," no birth stories, and no formal introduction of Jesus?

Why does Jesus continually tell the individuals he heals not to tell anyone about it? Why do they routinely ignore his instructions?

According to Mark 4:10–12, why does Jesus speak in parables? Why do the disciples regularly misunderstand or resist his teachings, despite their privileged access to his explanations? Is Peter's confession that Jesus is the Messiah (8:27–33) an exception to this pattern?

Most scholars believe that Mark's gospel originally ended without any appearance of the risen Jesus (after 16:8). Does the account of the women at the tomb nevertheless anticipate the "longer ending" of 16:9–20? Do the particular elements in the longer ending recapitulate earlier motifs or do they introduce ideas that are alien to Mark's literary and theological aims pursued elsewhere in the gospel?

*Luke*: Luke states at the outset that he aims at providing "assurance" for his readers (1:1–4). About what does he suspect that they may have doubts?

What common themes are found in the birth and resurrection narratives that Luke has added to his primary source (Mark)?

What does the rejection at Nazareth (Luke 4:14–30) suggest about the prophetic nature of Jesus' ministry?

Which parables are found only in Luke and what do any recurring motifs they contain suggest about his thinking about Christian discipleship?

Luke features more female characters than the other gospels. Does their function in the story yield any consistent insight into the author's message, or is their gender incidental to the roles they play?

Was Luke's gospel originally intended as a stand-alone work, or does it appear to have been written with a "sequel"—Acts—in view?

*John*: Are the images of Jesus as "the Word become flesh" (1:14) and "the lamb of God who takes away the sins of the world" (1:29) unique to John, or are they similar to the Christological images and concepts found in the other gospels?

What do the minor characters that appear only in John (e.g., Nicodemus, Nathanael, the woman at the well) add to his narrative that are missing from the Synoptic Gospels?

Why could both the second-century Gnostics as well as their "orthodox" critics embrace John as expressive of their own convictions?

The original phrasing of John 20:31 is uncertain: Does the author write "so that you may believe" or "so that you may continue to believe"? Does the rest of the narrative suggest that he has Christians in view or, rather, those who are not yet in the fold? Of all the many miracles the author says he could have included, he chooses only seven. How do these seven "signs" contribute to his stated purpose?

*Acts*: If we did not have the Acts of the Apostles, what would we know about life in the early church and how would we know it? What are the major "turning points" in the plot of Acts, that is, crucial moments at which the story—and thus the history of the early church—changes course in a fundamental way?

Many of the characters in Acts deliver speeches that take the form of summaries of Israelite history. Which events receive special emphasis? Which are conspicuously absent? Does Luke portray Christianity and Judaism as separate religions?

How does the Holy Spirit as described in Luke-Acts compare with the "comforter" or "advocate" promised by Jesus in the Fourth Gospel (14:16, 26; 15:26; 16:7)?

How does Paul's relationship with other disciples of Jesus in Acts compare with the impression one receives from his letters?

Paul's fate is unresolved at the end of Acts. How might the reaction of a reader who knows of his ultimate fate differ from that of a reader who does not? Or is Paul's fate of little significance to the larger story?

## THE LETTERS

### PAUL'S LETTERS

*Romans*: To what extent should divine impartiality be considered the central theme of Romans? If one translates *pistis Christou* (Rom. 3:22, 26) as "the faith of Christ" rather than "faith in Christ," how, if at all, would it affect one's reading of the rest of Romans? Should chapters 9–11 be read as a digression or as the centerpiece of Paul's argument? How are the moral exhortations in the latter part of the letter related to the theological exposition in the earlier sections?

*1 Corinthians*: Is there any common thread that connects Paul's replies to the various questions posed to him by the Corinthians? Of all the issues he addresses, which trouble him the most? How many different "factions" are there in the Corinthian church, based on the different controversies it is experiencing?

*2 Corinthians*: How might one's view of the literary integrity of 2 Corinthians—in its present form, is it one intact letter or a composite document stitched together from multiple letters?—influence one's construal of the various arguments he makes? Based on his self-defense, which of the many implied criticisms stings Paul the most?

*Galatians*: How does Paul's use of Abraham as an example in Galatians (3:6–9) differ from his use of Abraham in Romans (4:1–25)? Does his use of Sarah develop his argument about the role of faith or does it function in support of a different point? Why does he adopt such an acerbic tone in this letter?

*Ephesians*: On the assumption that the author of Ephesians draws on Colossians as a source, what can be surmised from the "added" material about the situation that prompted its composition? What distinctive emphases can be detected in the overlapping material (e.g., the household codes in Col. 3:18–4:1 and Eph. 5:21–6:9)? Are the ways in which the church is described here and in other Pauline letters consistent, contradictory, or complementary?

*Philippians*: Is the Christology of Philippians, especially the characterization found in the "Christ hymn" in Phil. 2:6–11, peculiar to that letter, or is it similar to the Christological images and concepts found in his other letters? Are the concepts present in the Christ hymn integrated with the rest of Philippians, or does it feel out of place?

*Colossians*: If Col. 1:15–20 is from an early Christian hymn, do its claims about Jesus fit well with the rest of the letter? Does it present Jesus as divine? What are the implications of the author's instructions in Col. 4:16 that the Colossians and Laodiceans should exchange and read the letters he has written to each group?

*1 Thessalonians*: How do the virtues of faith, hope, and love function in Paul's letter of encouragement to the Thessalonians? How do Paul's comments on the Parousia in chapters 4–5 compare with Jesus' eschatological teaching in the Synoptic Gospels (e.g., Matthew 24–25; Mark 13)?

*2 Thessalonians*: What if scholars have it backwards in their reading of 2 Thess. 2:1–2? That is, what if 2 Thessalonians is unquestionably written by Paul and 1 Thessalonians is suspicious? How does Paul address the audience's experience of persecution?

*1 Timothy*: Which arguments for the pseudonymous authorship of the Pastoral Epistles are the strongest? Which are the weakest? If Paul is not the real author, what purpose(s) might be served by the use of the pseudonym? Compared with the gospels, is it more or less important to know the identity of the authors?

*2 Timothy*: What qualities are most important for exercising leadership in the church, according to 2 Timothy? In tone and content, which of the other Pauline letters does 2 Timothy most closely resemble?

*Titus*: What might account for the subtle differences in the lists of qualifications for leadership positions included in 1 Timothy, 2 Timothy, and Titus? Do the Pastoral Epistles read as if they are addressed to individuals rather than groups?

*Philemon*: If Paul wants Philemon to free Onesiumus from slavery, why does he not say so more clearly? Alternatively, does he think it possible for masters and slaves to be "brothers and sisters in Christ" while remaining master and slave? Why doesn't Paul say so explicitly if he finds the institution of slavery morally objectionable?

## HEBREWS AND THE GENERAL EPISTLES

*Hebrews*: Does the argument about the tabernacle and the Levitical system of sacrifice make sense within a pre-70 context or a post-70 context in which the Jerusalem temple has been destroyed? What interpretive assumptions does the author make in his discussion of Melchizedek and the high priesthood of Jesus? Faith "in" or "of" Jesus Christ—if Hebrews 11 were factored into the *pistis Christou* debate, which understanding of faith would it support? How might one respond to the charge that Hebrews is anti-Jewish?

*James*: In declaring that "a man is justified by works and not by faith alone" and that "faith without works is dead" (2:24–26), is James contradicting Paul when he says that God "justifies him who has faith in Jesus" (Rom. 3:26; cf. Gal. 2:16)? Why does the author mention Jesus only twice (1:1; 2:1)?

*1 Peter*: How does the implied persona of the author fit with other descriptions of Peter in the New Testament (e.g., Matt. 16; John 21)? Which passages support the theory that 1 Peter was composed to serve as a baptismal homily?

*2 Peter*: Which aspects of Paul's letters might have been "twisted" or misunderstood (2 Pet. 3:15–16), on the basis of the argument made by the author of 2 Peter? On the assumption that the author draws on Jude as a source, what can be surmised from the "added" material about the situation that prompted its composition?

*1–2–3 John*: What themes and perspectives does the author of the Johannine Letters share with the Fourth Gospel? According to the author of 1–2 John, who is the antichrist?

*Jude*: How does the author use non-canonical sources in his polemical response to his opponents? How does he situate himself and his readers in relation to the apostles?

## REVELATION

How well does Revelation conform to the standard description of the apocalyptic literary genre? Do the author's beliefs about Jesus affect his apocalyptic outlook, or does his apocalyptic outlook influence his beliefs about Jesus?

Revelation has been read as a book of prophecies or predictions about the future as well as a commentary on first-century events taking place when the author is writing. What aspects of the text might be cited in support of these divergent readings? Do proponents of one approach miss anything important by rejecting the other approach?

Is it possible to speak of Revelation as having a plot? If so, where do the major turning points occur? If not, how else might one summarize its contents?

# REFERENCES

Allison, Dale C. *Jesus of Nazareth: Millenarian Prophet*. Minneapolis, MN: Fortress, 1998.

Ambrozic, Aloysius M. "Mark's Concept of the Parable: Mark 4,11f. in the Context of the Second Gospel." *Catholic Biblical Quarterly* (29) 1967: 220–27.

Ascough, Richard S. "The Thessalonian Christian Community as a Professional Voluntary Association." *Journal of Biblical Literature* 119 (2000): 311–28.

Aune, David E. *The New Testament in its Literary Environment*. Philadelphia, PA: Westminster, 1987.

Barclay, John M. G. "Paul, Philemon and the Dilemma of Christian Slave-Ownership." *New Testament Studies* 37 (1991): 161–86.

Bartlett, Joseph M. "Bourgeois Right and the Limits of First Phase Communism in the Rhetoric of 2 Thessalonians 3:6–15." *The Bible and Critical Theory* 8.2 (2012): 36–56.

Bassler, Jouette M. "The Widows' Tale: A Fresh Look at 1 Tim 5:3–16." *Journal of Biblical Literature* 103 (1984): 23–41.

Bateman IV, Herbert W., ed. *Four Views on the Warning Passages in Hebrews*. Grand Rapids, MI: Kregel, 2007.

Bauckham, Richard, ed. *The Gospels for All Christians: Rethinking Gospel Audiences*. Grand Rapids, MI: Eerdmans, 1998.

Becker Adam H., and Annette Y. Reed, eds. *The Ways that Never Parted: Jews and Christians in Late Antiquity and the Early Middle Ages*. Texts and Studies in Ancient Judaism 95. Tübingen, Germany: Mohr Siebeck, 2003.

Beker, J. Christian. *Heirs of Paul: Their Legacy in the New Testament and the Church Today*. Minneapolis, MN: Augsburg Fortress, 1991.

Bond, Helen K., and Larry W. Hurtado, eds. *Peter in Early Christianity*. Grand Rapids, MI: Eerdmans, 2015.

Brown, Raymond E. *The Gospel According to John.* Anchor Bible 29–29A. Garden City, NY: Doubleday, 1966.

———. *The Virginal Conception & Bodily Resurrection of Jesus.* New York: Paulist, 1973.

———. *The Birth of the Messiah: A Commentary on the Infancy Narratives in the Gospels of Matthew and Luke.* Garden City, NY: Doubleday, 1977.

———, and John P. Meier, *Antioch and Rome: New Testament Cradles of Catholic Christianity.* New York: Paulist, 1983.

Bultmann, Rudolf. "Jesus and Paul." *Existence and Faith: Shorter Writings of Rudolf Bultmann.* Trans. S. M. Ogden. New York: Meridian, 1960, pp. 183–201.

Burkert, Walter. *Greek Religion.* Trans. J. Raffan. Cambridge, MA: Harvard University Press, 1985.

Callahan, Allen Dwight. "'Brother Saul': An Ambivalent Witness to Freedom." *Semeia* 83/84 (2004): 235–50.

Cargal, Timothy B. "'His Blood Be Upon Us and Upon Our Children': A Matthean Double Entendre?" *New Testament Studies* 37 (1991): 101–12.

Chilton, Bruce D. "(The) Son of (the) Man, and Jesus." *Authenticating the Words of Jesus.* Ed. Bruce D. Chilton and Craig A. Evans. Leiden, The Netherlands: Brill, 1999, pp. 259–87.

Cohen, Shaye J. D. *From the Maccabees to the Mishnah.* 2nd ed. Louisville, KY: Westminster John Knox, 2006.

Collins, Adela Yarbro. "The Apocalyptic Rhetoric of Mark 13 in Historical Context." *Biblical Research* 41 (1996): 5–36.

Collins, John J. "Introduction: Towards the Morphology of a Genre." *Semeia* 14 (1979): 1–20.

Crook, John. "Patria Potestas." *Classical Quarterly* 17 (1967):113–22.

Crossan, John D. *Who Killed Jesus? Exposing the Roots of Anti-Semitism in the Gospel Story of the Death of Jesus.* San Francisco, CA: HarperSanFrancisco, 1995.

Cullmann, Oscar. *Christ and Time: The Primitive Christian Conception of Time and History.* 3rd ed. Trans F. V. Filson. London: SCM, 1964.

Culpepper, R. Alan *Anatomy of the Fourth Gospel: A Study in Literary Design.* Philadelphia, PA: Fortress, 1983.

Dahl, Nils A. "The Crucified Messiah." *The Crucified Messiah and Other Essays.* Minneapolis, MN: Augsburg, 1974, pp. 10–36.

———. *Jesus in the Memory of the Early Church.* Minneapolis, MN: Augsburg, 1976.

Dawes, Gregory W. "The Danger of Idolatry: First Corinthians 8:7–13." *Catholic Biblical Quarterly* 58 (1996): 82–109.

Dibelius, Martin. "The Apostolic Council." *Studies in the Acts of the Apostles.* Trans. M. Ling. London: SCM, 1956, pp. 93–101.

Dodd, Charles H. *The Interpretation of the Fourth Gospel.* Cambridge, UK: Cambridge University Press, 1953.

Dunn, James D. G. "The New Perspective on Paul." *Bulletin of the John Rylands Library* 65 (1983): 95–122.

Eckhardt, A. Roy *Elder and Younger Brothers: The Encounter of Jews and Christians.* New York: Schocken, 1967.

Elliott, John H. *1 Peter*. Anchor Bible 37A. New York: Doubleday, 2000.

Evans, Craig A., and Donald A. Hagner, eds. *Anti-Semitism and Early Christianity: Issues of Polemic and Faith*. Minneapolis, MN: Fortress, 1993.

Feldman, Louis H. *Jew and Gentile in the Ancient World*. Princeton, NJ: Princeton University Press, 1993.

Fitzgerald, John T. "Philippians in the Light of Some Ancient Discussions of Friendship." *Friendship, Flattery and Frankness of Speech: Studies on Friendship in the New Testament World*. Ed. John T. Fitzgerald. Novum Testamentum Supplements 82. Leiden, The Netherlands: Brill, 1996, pp. 141–60.

Foster, Robert J. *The Significance of Exemplars for the Interpretation of the Letter of James*. Wissenschaftliche Untersuchungen zum Neuen Testament 376. Tübingen, Germany: Mohr Siebeck, 2014.

Francis, Fred. O., and Wayne A. Meeks, eds. *Conflict at Colossae: A Problem in the Interpretation of Early Christianity Illustrated by Selected Modern Studies*. 2nd ed. Missoula, MT: Scholars Press, 1975.

Goodacre, Mark. "Scripturalization in Mark's Crucifixion Narrative." *The Trial and Death of Jesus: Essays on the Passion Narrative in Mark*. Eds. Geert Van Oyen and Tom Shepherd. Leuven, Belgium: Peeters, 2006, pp. 33–47.

Greenman, Jeffrey P., Timothy Larson, and Stephen R. Spencer, eds. *The Sermon on the Mount through the Centuries: From the Early Church to John Paul II*. Grand Rapids, MI: Brazos, 2007.

Greer, Rowan A. *The Captain of Our Salvation: A Study in the Patristic Exegesis of Hebrews*. Beiträge zur Geschichte der Biblischen Exegese 15. Tübingen, Germany: J.C.B. Mohr, 1973.

Hayes, John H., and Carl R. Holladay. *Biblical Exegesis: A Beginner's Handbook*. 3rd ed. Louisville, KY: Westminster John Knox, 2007.

Hays, Richard B. "ΠΙΣΤΙΣ and Pauline Christology: What is at Stake?" *Pauline Theology, Vol. 4: Looking Back, Pressing On*. Eds. E. Elizabeth Johnson and David M. Hay. Atlanta, GA: Scholars Press, 1997, pp. 35–60.

——. *Reading Backwards: Figural Christology and the Fourfold Gospel Witness*. Waco, TX: Baylor University Press, 2014.

Hemer, Colin J. "The Letters to the Seven Churches of Asia in Their Local Setting." Journal for the Study of the New Testament Supplement Series 11. Sheffield: Sheffield Academic Press, 1986.

Hengel, Martin. *Judaism and Hellenism*. Tran. J. Bowden. 2 vols. Philadelphia, PA: Fortress, 1974.

Heschel, Susannah. *The Aryan Jesus: Christian Theologians and the Bible in Nazi Germany*. Princeton, NJ: Princeton University Press, 2008.

Hooker, Morna D. *Not Ashamed of the Gospel: New Testament Interpretations of the Death of Christ*. Carlisle, UK: Paternoster, 1994.

Horton, Jr., Fred L. *The Melchizedek Tradition: A Critical Examination of the Sources to the Fifth Century A.D. and in the Epistle to the Hebrews*. London: Cambridge University Press, 1976.

Humphreys, Colin J. *The Mystery of the Last Supper: Reconstructing the Final Days of Jesus*. Cambridge, UK: Cambridge University Press, 2011.

Jacobs, Alan. *Original Sin: A Cultural History*. San Francisco, CA: HarperOne, 2008.

Johnson, Luke T. *The Literary Function of Possessions in Luke-Acts*. Society of Biblical Literature Dissertation Series 39. Missoula, MT: Society of Biblical Literature, 1977.

——. "The New Testament's Anti-Jewish Slander and the Conventions of Ancient Polemic." *Journal of Biblical Literature* 108 (1989): 419–41.

——. *The Writings of the New Testament*. Rev. ed. Minneapolis, MN: Fortress, 1999.

——. *The First and Second Letters to Timothy*. Anchor Bible 35A. New York: Doubleday, 2001.

Kähler, Martin. *The So-Called Historical Jesus and the Historic Biblical Christ*. Trans. C. E. Braaten. Philadelphia, PA: Fortress, 1964.

Käsemann, Ernst. "An Apologia for Primitive Christian Eschatology." *Essays on New Themes*. Trans. W. J. Montague. London: SCM, 1964, pp. 169–95.

Kee, Howard C. "Aretalogy and Gospel." *Journal of Biblical Literature* 93 (1973): 402–22.

Kim, Lloyd. *Polemic in the Book of Hebrews: Anti-Judaism, Anti-Semitism, Supersessionism?* Eugene, OR: Wipf & Stock, 2006.

Kissinger, Warren S. "Parables of Jesus." *Dictionary of Biblical Interpretation*, Vol. 2. Ed. John H. Hayes. Nashville, TN: Abingdon, 1999, pp. 235–39.

Kysar, Robert. "Anti-Semitism and the Gospel of John." *Anti-Semitism and Early Christianity: Issues of Polemic and Faith*. Ed. Craig A. Evans and Donald A. Hagner. Minneapolis, MN: Fortress, 1993, pp. 113–27.

Lentz, John C., Jr. *Luke's Portrait of Paul*. Society for New Testament Studies Monograph Series 77. Cambridge, UK: Cambridge University Press, 1993.

Lincoln, Andrew T. "The Promise and the Failure: Mark 16:7, 8." *Journal of Biblical Literature* 108 (1989): 283–300.

Longenecker, Bruce. "On Israel's God and God's Israel: Assessing Supersessionism in Paul." *Journal of Theological Studies* 58 (2007): 26–44.

MacDonald, Margaret Y. *The Pauline Churches: A Socio-Historical Study of Institutionalization in the Pauline and Deutero-Pauline Writings*. Society for New Testament Studies Monograph Series 60. Cambridge, UK: Cambridge University Press, 1988.

Malherbe, Abraham J. "Ancient Epistolary Theorists." *Ohio Journal of Religious Studies* 5(2) (1977): 1–77.

——. *Paul and the Thessalonians: The Philosophic Tradition of Pastoral Care*. Philadelphia, PA: Fortress, 1987

Martin, Ralph P. "An Early Christian Hymn (Col. 1: 15–20)." *Evangelical Quarterly* 36 (1964): 195–205.

——, and Brian J. Dodd, eds. *Where Christology Began: Essays on Philippians 2*. Louisville, KY: Westminster John Knox, 1998.

Matera, Frank J. *Passion Narratives and Gospel Theologies: Interpreting the Synoptics Through Their Passion Stories*. Eugene, OR: Wipf and Stock, 2001.

McKenzie, Steven L., and John Kaltner, eds. *New Meanings for Ancient Texts: Recent Approaches to Biblical Criticisms and Their Applications*. Louisville, KY: Westminster John Knox, 2013.

McKnight, Scot "James 2:18a: The Unidentifiable Interlocutor." *Westminster Theological Journal* 52 (1990): 355–64.

Meeks, Wayne A., and John T. Fitzgerald, eds. *The Writings of St. Paul.* 2nd ed. New York: Norton, 2007.

Moessner, David P. *Lord of the Banquet: The Literary and Theological Significance of the Lukan Travel Narrative.* Minneapolis, MN: Fortress, 1989.

Moxnes, Halvor. *A Short History of the New Testament.* London: I. B. Tauris, 2014.

Moyise, Steven. *The Later New Testament Writings and Scripture: The Old Testament in Acts, Hebrews, the Catholic Epistles and Revelation.* Grand Rapids, MI: Baker Academic, 2012.

Muddiman, John. *A Commentary on the Epistle to the Ephesians.* London: Continuum, 2001.

Murphy-O'Connor, Jerome. *St. Paul's Corinth: Texts and Archaeology.* 3rd ed. Collegeville, MN: Liturgical Press, 2002.

Neill, Stephen *The Interpretation of the New Testament, 1861–1961.* London: Oxford University Press, 1964.

Nock, Arthur Darby. *Conversion: The Old and the New in Religion from Alexander the Great to Augustine of Hippo.* Oxford, UK: Clarendon, 1933.

Orlando, Robert. *Apostle Paul: A Polite Bribe.* Cambridge, UK: James Clarke, 2015.

Porter, Stanley E. *The Paul of Acts: Essays in Literary Criticism, Rhetoric, and Theology.* Wissenschaftliche Untersuchungen zum Neuen Testament 115. Tübingen, Germany: Mohr Siebeck, 1999.

Ricoeur, Paul. *Hermeneutics and the Human Sciences.* Cambridge, UK: Cambridge University Press, 1981.

Robinson, John A. T. *Redating the New Testament.* London: SCM, 1976.

Rowe, C. Kavin. *Early Narrative Christology: The Lord in the Gospel of Luke.* Beihefte zur Zeitschrift für neutestamentliche Wissenschaft 139. Berlin: de Gruyter, 2006.

Schnackenburg, Rudolf. *Jesus in the Gospels: A Biblical Christology.* Trans. O. C. Dean, Jr. Louisville, KY: Westminster John Knox, 1995.

Schweitzer, Albert. *The Quest of the Historical Jesus: A Critical Study of Its Progress from Reimarus to Wrede.* Trans. W. Montgomery. New York: Macmillan, 1968.

Shauf, Scott "Locating the Eunuch: Characterization and Narrative Context in Acts 8:26–40." *Catholic Biblical Quarterly* 71 (2009): 762–75.

Smith, D. Moody "John and the Synoptics: Some Dimensions of the Problem." *New Testament Studies* 26 (1980): 425–44.

Smith, Jonathan Z. "Dying and Rising Gods." *The Encyclopedia of Religion,* Vol. IV. Ed. Mircea Eliade. New York: Macmillan, 1987, pp. 521–27.

Soares-Prabhu, George M. *The Formula Quotations in the Infancy Narrative of Matthew: An Enquiry into the Tradition History of Matthew 1–2.* Analecta Biblica 63. Rome: Pontifical Biblical Institute, 1976.

Stegman, Thomas D. *The Character of Jesus: The Linchpin to Paul's Argument in 2 Corinthians.* Analecta Biblica 158. Rome: Pontifical Biblical Institute, 2005.

Sterling, Gregory E. *Historiography & Self-Definition: Josephos, Luke-Acts, and Apologetic Historiography.* Supplements to Novum Testamentum 64. Leiden, The Netherlands: Brill, 1992.

Stockhausen, Carol K. *Moses' Veil and the Glory of the New Covenant: The Exegetical Substructure of II Cor. 3,1–4,6.* Analecta Biblica 116. Rome: Pontifical Biblical Institute, 1989.

Stowers, Stanley K. "Romans 7.7–25 as a Speech-in-Character *(prosōpopoiia).*" *Paul in His Hellenistic Context.* Ed. Troels Engberg-Pedersen. Minneapolis, MN: Fortress, 1994, pp. 180–202.

Sumney, Jerry L. "'Servants of Satan', 'False Brothers', and Other Opponents of Paul." Journal for the Study of the New Testament Supplement 188. Sheffield, UK: Sheffield Academic Press, 1999.

Talbert, Charles H. "II Peter and the Delay of the Parousia." *Vigiliae Christianae* 20 (1966): 137–45.

Theissen, Gerd. *The Social Setting of Pauline Christianity.* Trans. J. H. Schutz. Philadelphia, PA: Fortress, 1982.

Thiselton, Anthony C. "Realized Eschatology at Corinth." *New Testament Studies* 24 (1978): 510–26.

Trebilco, Paul. *The Early Christians in Ephesus from Paul to Ignatius.* Wissenschaftliche Untersuchungen zum Neuen Testament 166. Tübingen, Germany: Mohr Siebeck, 2004.

Tuckett, Christopher, ed. *The Messianic Secret.* London: SPCK, 1983.

Wilken, Robert L. *The Christians as the Romans Saw Them.* New Haven, CT: Yale University Press, 1984.

Winn, Adam. *The Purpose of Mark's Gospel: An Early Christian Response to Roman Imperial Propaganda.* Wissenschaftliche Untersuchungen zum Neuen Testament 245. Tübingen, Germany: Mohr Siebeck, 2008.

# INDEX